SEASONS OF WORSHIP

Table of Contents

Songtitle	Sheet Music

SEASONS OF WORSHIP

Table of Contents

SEASONS OF WORSHIP

Table of Contents

INLCUDES

Index of Songs by Theme

Index of Songs by Key

Index of Songs by Tempo

Theme Index

Theme Index

Page	Songtitle	Primary Theme	Celebration	Christmas	Communion	Easter	Memorial
166	How Majestic Is Your Name	Celebration	●				
170	I Could Sing Of Your Love Forever	Celebration	●				
176	I Still Believe	Memorial					●
174	I Will Exalt Your Name	Celebration	●				
183	In Christ Alone	Memorial					●
188	In The Cross Alone I Glory	Easter			●	●	
192	In The Presence of Jehovah	Memorial					●
198	Indescribable	Celebration	●			●	
202	Jesus Lover Of My Soul	Memorial					●
205	Jesus You Are Worthy	Easter			●	●	
210	Kindness	Communion			●		
216	King Of Glory	Easter				●	
219	Lamb Of God	Easter				●	
238	Let Everything That Has Breath	Celebration	●				
222	Let My Words Be Few	Memorial			●		●
226	Like The Angels	Memorial	●				●
230	Lord You Have My Heart	Communion			●		●
232	Lord, Let Your Glory Fall	Celebration	●			●	
243	Lost In Wonder	Communion			●		
246	Majesty	Easter			●	●	
252	Marvelous Light	Easter	●			●	
258	Mighty Is The Power Of The Cross	Easter	●		●	●	●
261	My Drink	Communion			●		
264	My Glorious	Celebration	●				
268	My Tribute	Celebration	●			●	●
276	Name Above All Names	Celebration	●				●
281	No One Like You	Celebration	●				
286	Not To Us	Easter	●			●	
292	Nothing But The Blood	Easter	●			●	
296	O Come Be Born Again	Christmas		●			
299	O Come Let Us Adore Him	Christmas	●	●			
300	O Lord You're Beautiful	Communion			●		●
304	O Praise Him	Celebration	●			●	
307	O Worship The King	Celebration	●	●		●	
312	On The Third Day	Easter	●			●	
316	Once Again	Easter				●	
318	Our Comforter	Memorial					●

Theme Index

Page	Songtitle	Primary Theme	Celebration	Christmas	Communion	Easter	Memorial
324	Our Love Is Loud	Celebration	●				
328	Overflow	Communion	●		●		
334	People Need The Lord	Memorial					●
321	Praise The Name Of Jesus	Celebration	●				
338	Redeeming King	Celebration	●				
346	Sing To The King	Celebration	●				
342	Soon and Very Soon	Memorial	●				●
349	Take My Life	Communion	●		●		●
352	Thank You For The Blood	Easter			●	●	
358	The Father's Song	Easter				●	
362	The Happy Song	Celebration	●				
355	The Heart Of Worship	Memorial			●		●
366	The Power Of The Cross	Easter				●	
369	The Wonderful Cross	Easter				●	●
372	There Is A Redeemer	Memorial				●	●
374	Unchanging	Celebration	●				
386	Undignified	Celebration	●				
378	Unfailing Love	Memorial			●		●
380	We Fall Down	Communion			●		●
382	When The Tears Fall	Memorial	●				●
389	Whole World In His Hands	Celebration	●		●		●
392	Wonderful Maker	Communion			●	●	
396	Worth It All	Memorial					●
408	Yesterday, Today and Forever	Celebration	●				
400	You Alone	Memorial	●		●		●
404	You Are My King	Easter	●			●	●

Index of Songs by Key

Index of Songs by Key

Index of Songs by Key

Index of Songs by Tempo

All Heaven Declares

Words and Music by
NOEL and TRICIA RICHARDS

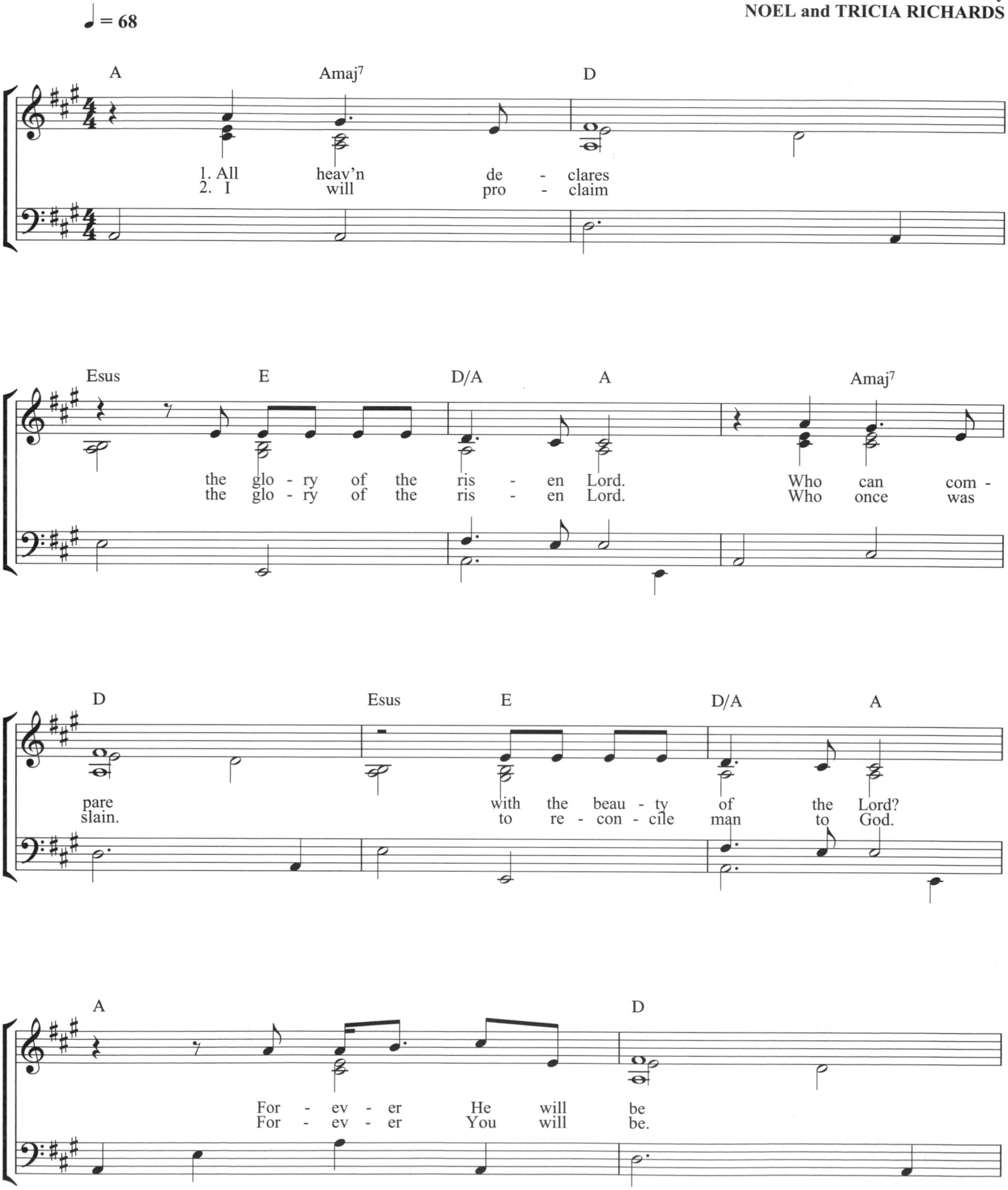
♩ = 68
A Amaj7 D
1. All heav'n de - clares
2. I will pro - claim
Esus E D/A A Amaj7
the glo - ry of the ris - en Lord. Who can com -
the glo - ry of the ris - en Lord. Who once was
D Esus E D/A A
pare with the beau - ty of the Lord?
slain. to re - con - cile man to God.
A D
For - ev - er He will be
For - ev - er You will be.

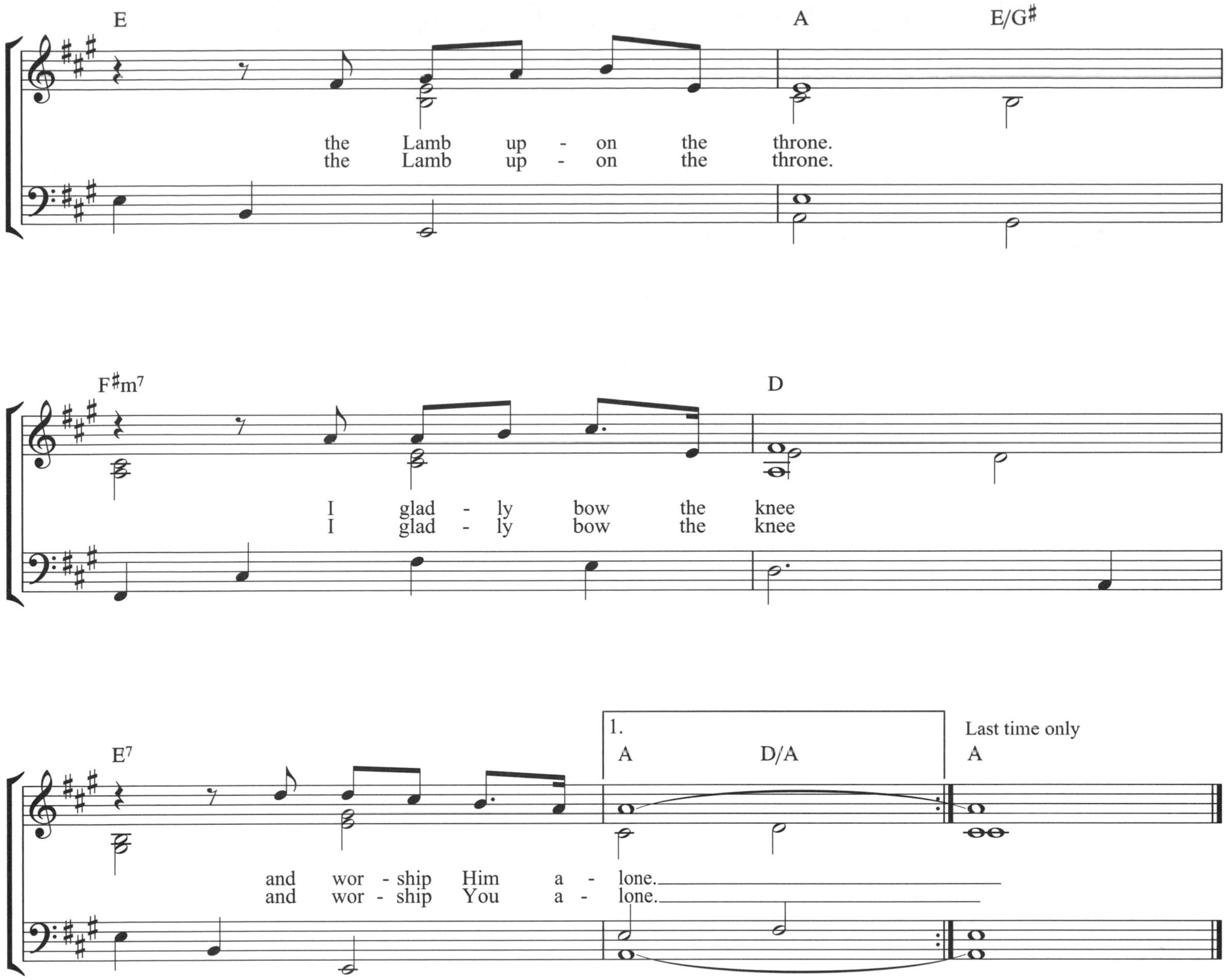
E
A
E/G#
the Lamb up - on the throne.
the Lamb up - on the throne.
F#m7
D
I glad - ly bow the knee
I glad - ly bow the knee
E7
1.
A
D/A
Last time only
A
and wor - ship Him a - lone.
and wor - ship You a - lone.

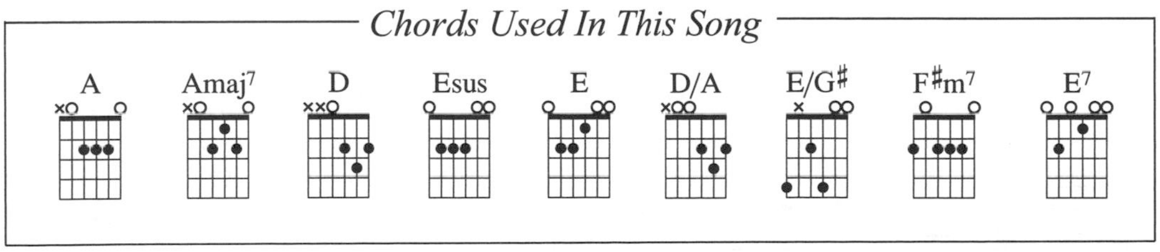
Chords Used In This Song
A
Amaj7
D
Esus
E
D/A
E/G#
F#m7
E7

All Creatures Of Our God And King

Words and Music by
ST FRANCIS OF ASSISI
Arrangement and additional Chorus
by David Crowder

With praise ♩ = 69

1. All crea - tures of our God and King,
2. Thou rush - ing wind that art so strong,
3. Let all things their Cre - at - or bless,

lift up your voice and with us sing, O_____
ye clouds that sail in Heav'n a - long, O_____
and wor - ship Him in hum - ble - ness. O_____

praise_____ Him, Al - le - lu - ia!
praise_____ Him, Al - le - lu - ia!
praise_____ Him, Al - le - lu - ia!

Thou burn - ing sun with gold - en beam,
Thou ris - ing moon, in praise re - joice,
Praise, praise the Fa - ther, praise the Son,

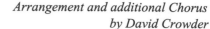

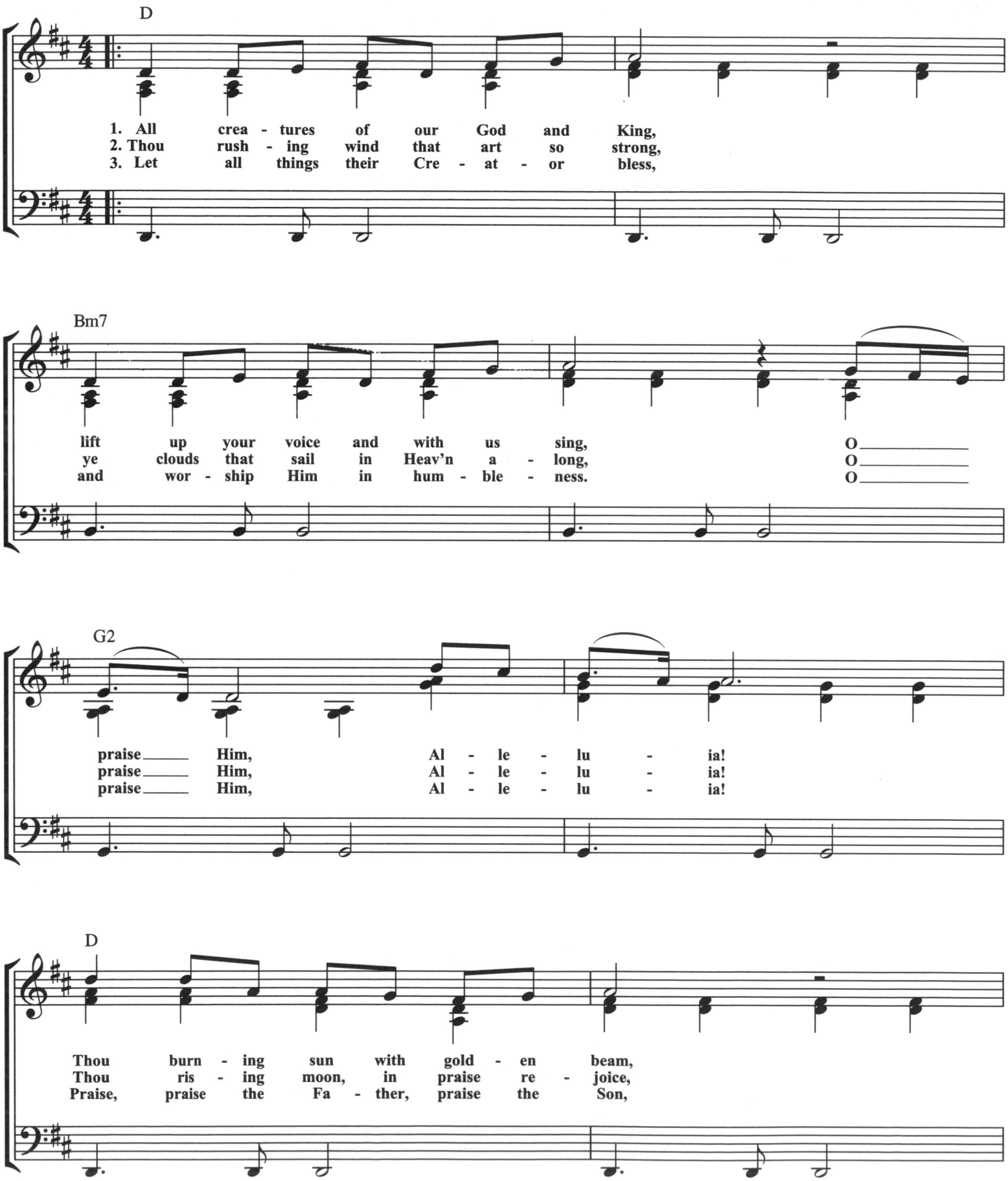

Bm7
thou sil - ver moon with soft - er gleam; O
ye lights of eve - ning, find a voice,
and praise the Spir - it, three in One.
G2
D/F♯
praise Him, O praise Him, Al - le -
G2
D/F♯
lu - ia! Al - le - lu - ia! Al - le -
1. 2.
Asus
D
lu - ia!
3.
Asus
G
A
lu - ia!

Chords Used in This Song

Angels From The Realms Of Glory

Traditional Words
Music by STEVEN CURTIS CHAPMAN

♩= 110
E5
E/D♯
C♯m
An - gels from the realms of glo - ry, wing your flight o - ver
A2
C♯m9
E2/G♯
all the earth. Ye who sang cre - a - tion's sto - ry,
F♯m
E/G♯
Bsus
E5
now pro - claim Mes - si - ah's birth.
E/D♯
Shep - herds, in the fields a - bid - ing,
Sin - ners, wrung with true re - pen - tance,

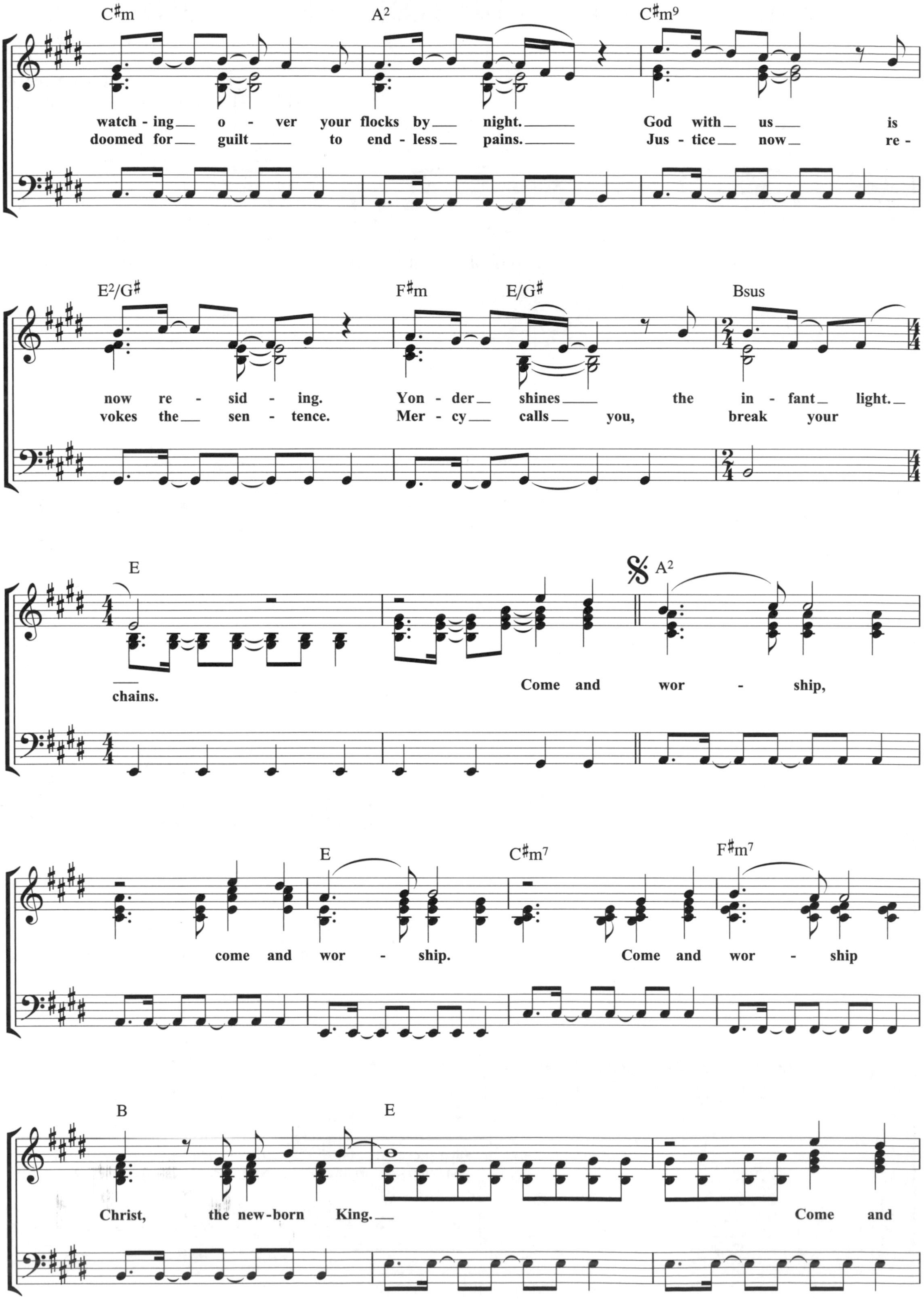
C#m
A2
C#m9
watch - ing o - ver your flocks by night.
God with us is
doomed for guilt to end - less pains.
Jus - tice now re -
E2/G#
F#m
E/G#
Bsus
now re - sid - ing.
Yon - der shines the in - fant light.
vokes the sen - tence.
Mer - cy calls you, break your
E
A2
chains.
Come and wor - ship,
E
C#m7
F#m7
come and wor - ship.
Come and wor - ship
B
E
Christ, the new-born King.
Come and

A2
C#m7
wor - ship, come and wor - ship. Come and
F#m7
B
3rd time to CODA
1.
E
wor - ship Christ the new - born King.
Ooo,
ooh.
A2
2.
E
King.
Dmaj7
A2
Though an In - fant now we view Him,
Dmaj7
A2
G#m
He shall fill His Fath - er's throne. Gath - er all the

C#m
F#m
E/G#
A2
nations to Him. Ev - 'ry knee shall then bow
B
E
down. All cre - a - tion,
E/D#
C#m
A2
join in prais - ing God the Fa - ther, Spi - rit, Son.
C#m
E2/G#
F#m
E/G#
Ev - er - more your voic - es rais - ing to the e - ter - nal
D.S. al CODA
B
E
Three in One. Come and

CODA
C#m
F#m7
King.
Come and wor - ship
B
E
Christ, the new - born
King.
E
Repeat & fade
Ooo,
ooh.

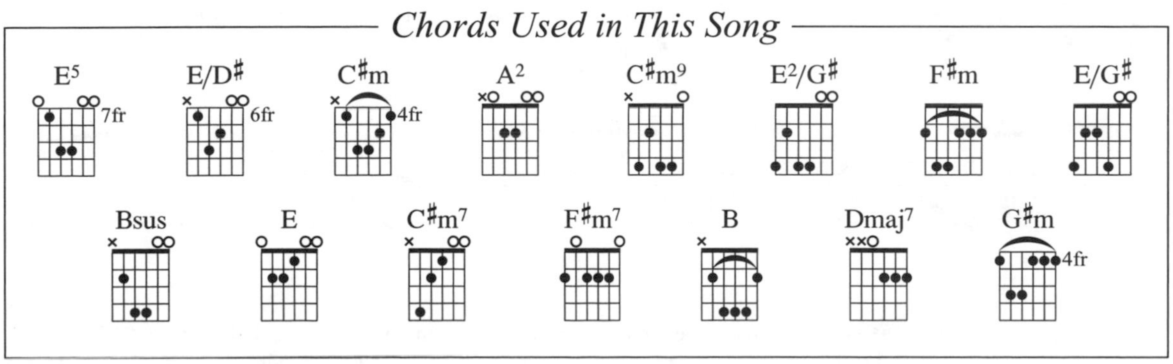
Chords Used in This Song
E5
7fr
E/D#
6fr
C#m
4fr
A2
C#m9
E2/G#
F#m
E/G#
Bsus
E
C#m7
F#m7
B
Dmaj7
G#m
4fr

Be Glorified

Words and Music by
CHRIS TOMLIN, LOUIE GIGLIO
and JESSE REEVES

♩ = 120

G C2 F2 C2/E G C2
Your love has cap - tured me, Your grace has
D G C2 F2 C2/E
set me free; Your life, the air I breathe.
Am7 D G C2
Be glo - ri - fied in me.
F2 C2/E G C2 F2 C2/E

C2
G
You set my feet to danc - ing, You set my heart on fire. In the
C2
G
pres - ence of a thou - sand kings, You are my one de - sire.
C2
Em
D
And I stand be - fore You now with trem - bling hands lift - ed high.
C2
3rd time to CODA
Be glo - ri - fied.
1.
G
C2
F2
C2/E
G
C2
F2
C2/E

2. G G/B C D
Be glo - ri - fied in me,
G/B C D G/B C
be glo - ri - fied in me, be glo - ri - fied
D G/B C
in me, be glo - ri - fied.
1. G/B C 2. D.S. al CODA
Be glo - ri - fied
CODA
G C2 F2 C2/E

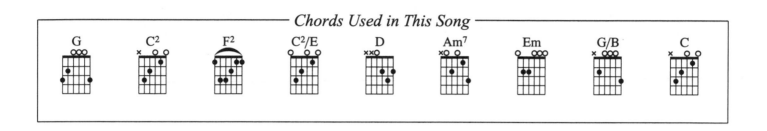

Chords Used in This Song

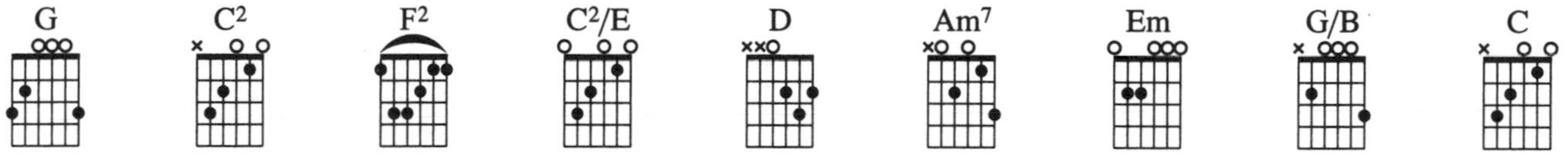

Beautiful One

Words and Music by
TIM HUGHES

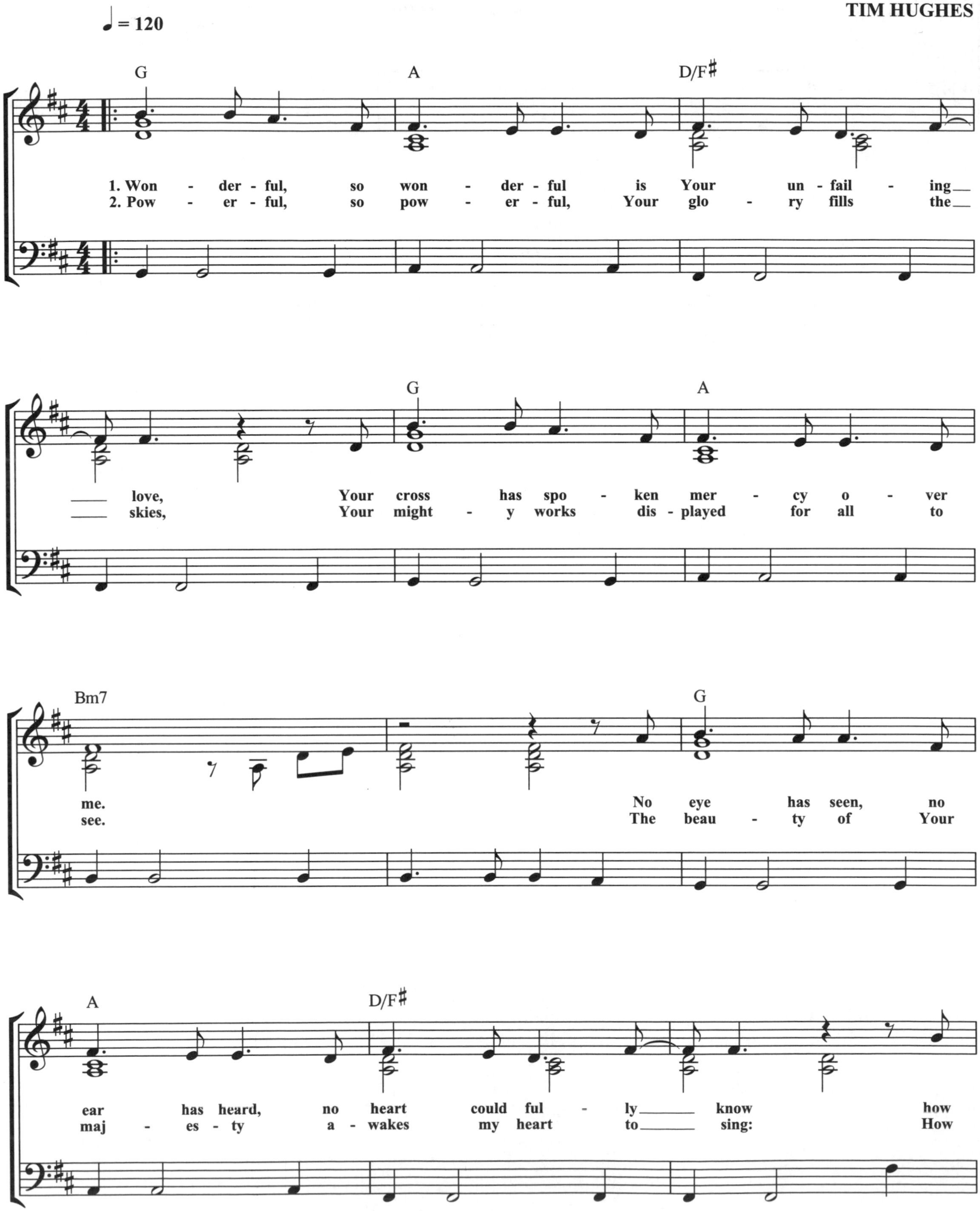
♩ = 120
G A D/F♯
1. Won - der - ful, so won - der - ful is Your un - fail - ing
2. Pow - er - ful, so pow - er - ful, Your glo - ry fills the
G A
love, Your cross has spo - ken mer - cy o - ver
skies, Your might - y works dis - played for all to
Bm7 G
me. No eye has seen, no
see. The beau - ty of Your
A D/F♯
ear has heard, no heart could ful - ly know how
maj - es - ty a - wakes my heart to sing: How

G
A
D
glo - ri - ous, how beau - ti - ful You are.
mar - vel - ous, how won - der - ful You are.
3
G
Beau - ti - ful One I
A
3
G
love, beau - ti - ful One I a -
A
3
G
A
dore, beau - ti - ful One my soul must
D
4th time to CODA
1.
FINE
2.
3
D.S.
sing.
Beau - ti - ful

3.
G
You o - pened my eyes to Your won -
A
G
- ders a - new, You cap - tured my heart with this
A
1.
G
A
love 'cause noth - ing on earth is as beau - ti - ful as You.
D
2.
G
You o - - thing on earth is as beau-
D.S. al CODA
A
D
3
- ti - ful as You.
Beau - ti - ful

CODA

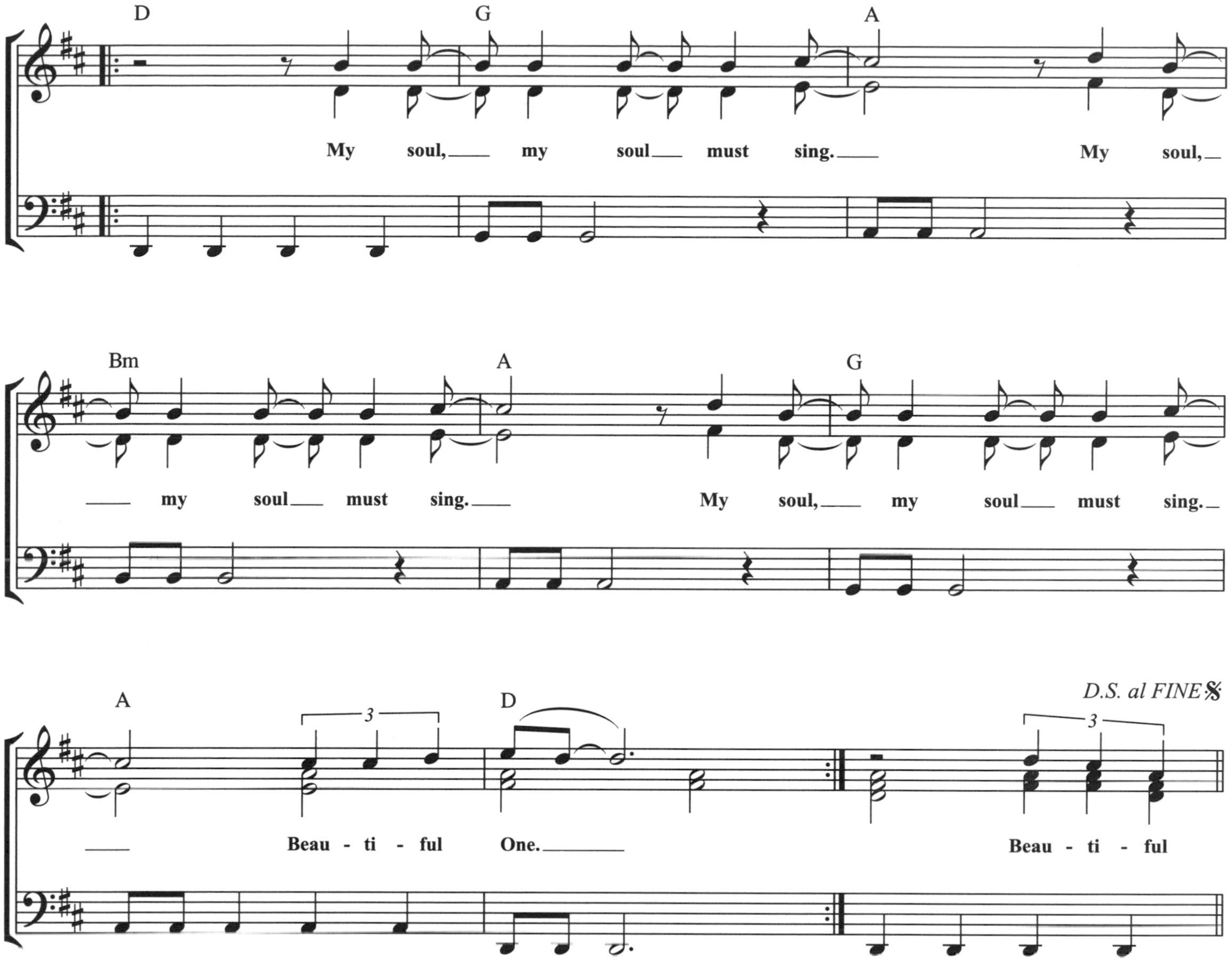
D
G
A
My soul, my soul must sing. My soul,
Bm
A
G
my soul must sing. My soul, my soul must sing.
A
D
D.S. al FINE
3
Beau - ti - ful One.
Beau - ti - ful

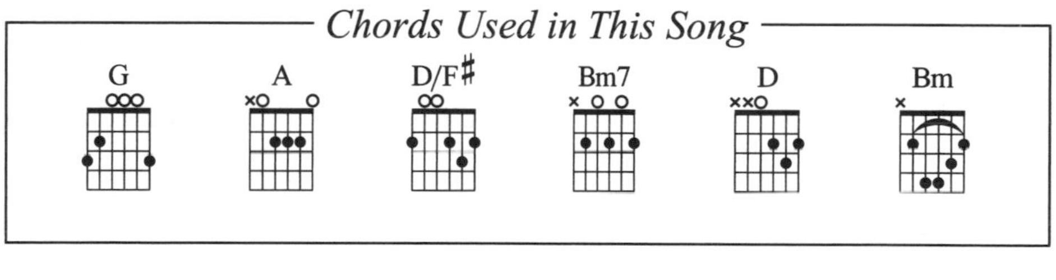
Chords Used in This Song
G
A
D/F♯
Bm7
D
Bm

Be Near

Words and Music by
SHANE BARNARD

♩ = 60
Bm7 G2 Bm7
1. You are all, big and small, beau - ti - ful.
G2 Bm7
And won - der - ful
G2 3 Bm7
to trust in grace through faith. But I'm ask - ing to
G2 Em7
taste. For dark is light to you.
D2/F♯ G2
Depths are height to you. Far is near but

Asus A D2 D/C♯
Lord I need to hear from You. Be near, O God. Be near,
Bm7 D2/A G2 D2/F♯
O God of us. Your near - ness is to us our
Asus A D D2/C♯ Bm7 D2/A
good. Be near, O God. Be near, O God of us. Your near-
G2 D2/F♯ Asus A
- ness is to us our good, our
Bm7 A Bm7 A
good.

G2
D2/F#
G2
Bm7
2. Your full - ness is mine
G2
Bm7
G2
rev-e-la - tion di- vine.
Bm7
G2
3
But oh to taste, to know much more than a page,
Bm7
G2
to feel Your em - brace.
Em7
D2/F#
For dark is light to You.
The depths are height to You.

G2 Asus A
Far is near, but Lord I need to hear from You. Be
D2 D/C♯ Bm7 D2/A
near, O God. Be near, O God of us. Your near-
G2 D2/F♯ Asus A
ness is to us our good. Be near,
D D2/C♯ Bm7 D2/A
O God. Be near, O God of us. Your near
G2 D2/F♯
1.
Asus A
- ness is to us our good Be

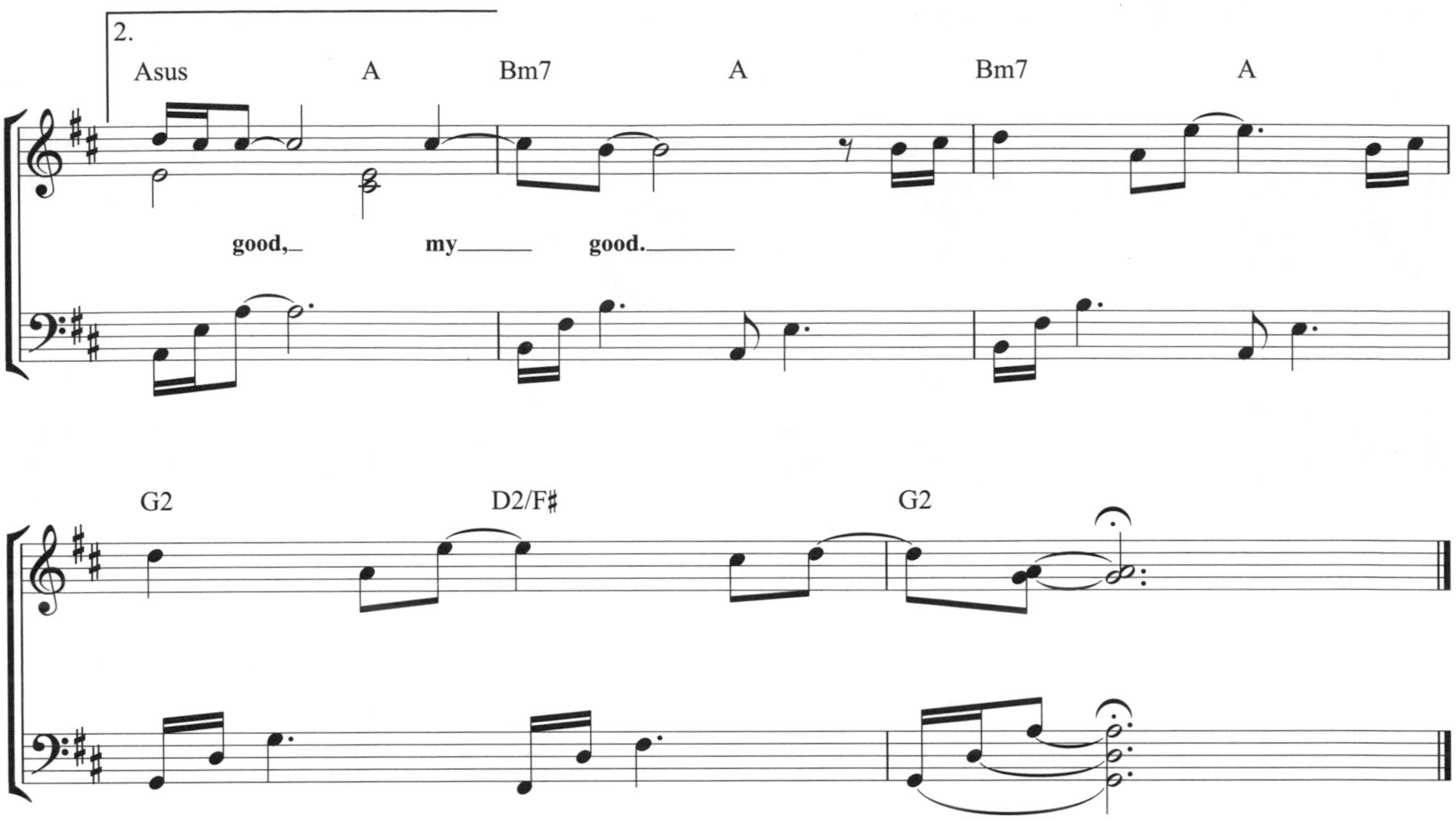
2.
Asus
A
Bm7
A
Bm7
A
good,
my
good.
G2
D2/F♯
G2

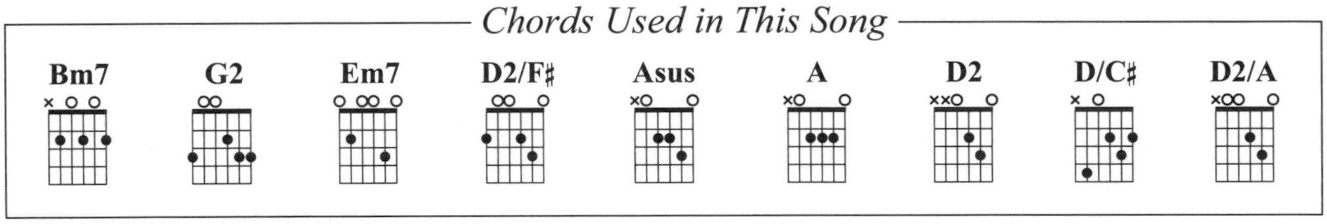
Chords Used in This Song
Bm7
G2
Em7
D2/F♯
Asus
A
D2
D/C♯
D2/A

Beautiful Savoir

(All My Days)

Words and Music by
STUART TOWNEND

Capo 3 (D) ♩. = 50

Keyboard
(Guitar)
Dm7 (Bm7) Eb2 (C2) F (D) Bb/D (G/B)
Eb (C) Bb (G) Dm7 (Bm7) Eb2 (C2)
F (D) Bb/D (G/B) Eb (C) Cm7 (Am7) Ebmaj7 (Cmaj7)
F (D) Eb (C) Bb/D (G/B) F (D)
1. All my days I will sing this song of gladness, give my praise to the Fountain of delights; for in my helplessness You heard my cry, and
2. I will trust in the cross of my Redeemer, I will sing to the blood that never fails, of sins forgiven, of conscience cleansed, of
(3.) long to be where the praise is never-ending, yearn to dwell where the glory never fades, where countless worshippers will share one song, and

Cm7 (Am7) E♭maj7 (Cmaj7) Dm7 (Bm7)
waves of mer - cy poured down on my
death de - feat - ed and life with - out
cries of "wor - thy" will hon - or the
G/B (E/G♯)
1. C (A)
2.,3. C (A) C/B♭ (A/G)
life.
end.
Lamb!
Beau - ti - ful
F/A (D/F♯) B♭ (G) C (A) C/E (A/C♯)
Sav - ior, won - der - ful Coun - sel -
F (D) Gm (Em) Gm/F (Em/D)
or, clothed in maj - es - ty, Lord of his - to - ry, You're the
C/E (A/C♯) Cm7 (Am7) C (A) C/B♭ (A/G) F/A (D/F♯)
Way the Truth, the Life. Star of the Morn - ing,

B♭ (G) C (A) C/E (A/C♯) F (D)
glo - rious in ho - li - ness, You're the
Gm (Em) Gm/F (Em/D) C/E (A/C♯) Dm7 (Bm7)
Ris - en One, heav - en's Cham - pi - on, and You reign, You
C (A) Dm7 (Bm7) E♭2 (C2)
reign o - ver all!
F (D)
1. D.C.
2.
3. I

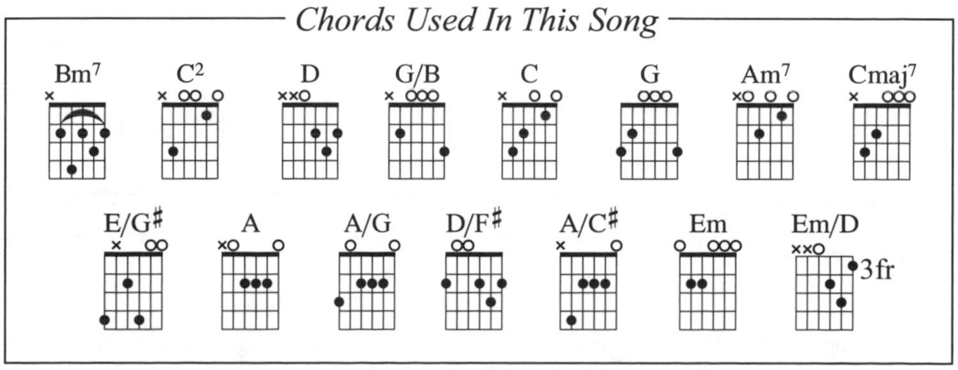
Chords Used In This Song
Bm7 C2 D G/B C G Am7 Cmaj7
E/G♯ A A/G D/F♯ A/C♯ Em Em/D
3fr

Better Is One Day

Words and Music by
MATT REDMAN

♩ = 50
E (no3)
1. How love - ly is Your dwell - ing place,
(2.) thing I ask and I would seek:
A2
Bsus
E (no3)
O Lord al - might - y. For my soul longs and
to see Your beau - ty, to find You in the
Bsus
e - ven faints for You. For
place Your glo - ry dwells. One
E (no3)
A2
here my heart is sat - is - fied with - in Your pres -
thing I ask and I would seek: to see Your beau -
Bsus
E (no3)
- ence. I sing be - neath the shad - ow of Your
- ty, to find You in the place Your glo - ry

Bsus
A2
wings.
dwells.
Bet - ter is one day in Your courts, bet - ter is
Bsus
A2
A/C♯
one day in Your house, bet - ter is one day in Your courts than thou - sands
Bsus
E/G♯
A2
else - where.
Bet - ter is one day in Your courts, bet - ter is
3rd time to CODA
Bsus
A2
A/C♯
one day in Your house, bet - ter is one day in Your courts than thou - sands
1.
Bsus
E (no3)
else - where, than thou - sands else - where.
2. One

2.
Bsus
else - where.
C♯m7
B
A2
Bsus
My heart and flesh cry out for You, the liv - ing God.
C♯m7
B
A2
Bsus
Your Spir - it's wa - ter to my soul.
C♯m7
B
A2
I've tast - ed and I've seen. Come once a - gain to me.
E/G♯
F♯m7
I will draw near to You, I will draw near to You,

Bsus
A2
to You.
Bsus
A2
Bsus
Bet - ter is
A2
Bsus
E/G♯
one day, bet - ter is one day, bet - ter is
A2
A/C♯
Bsus
one day than thou - sands else - where. Bet - ter is
A2
Bsus
one day, bet - ter is one day, bet - ter is

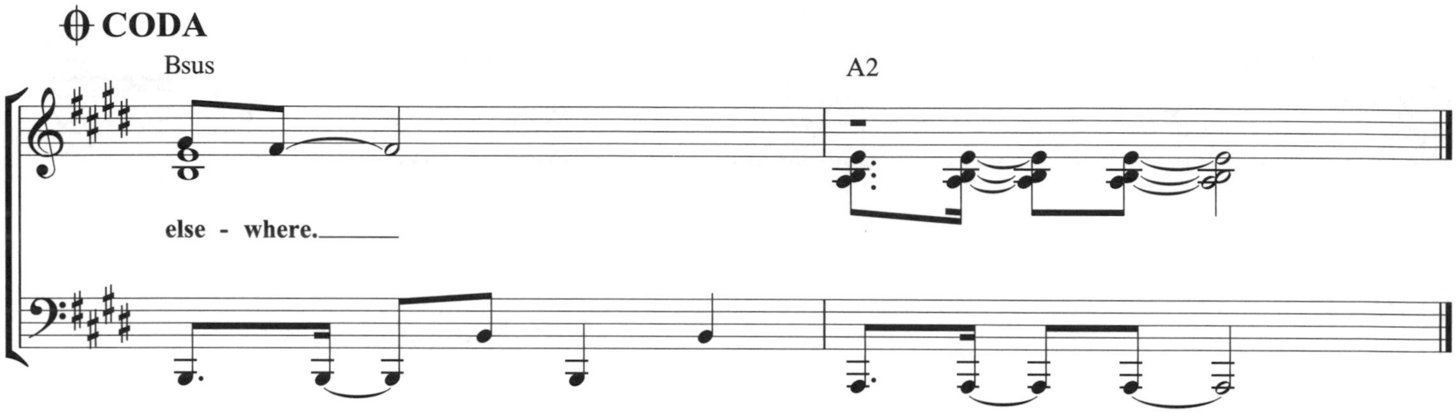

Chords Used in This Song

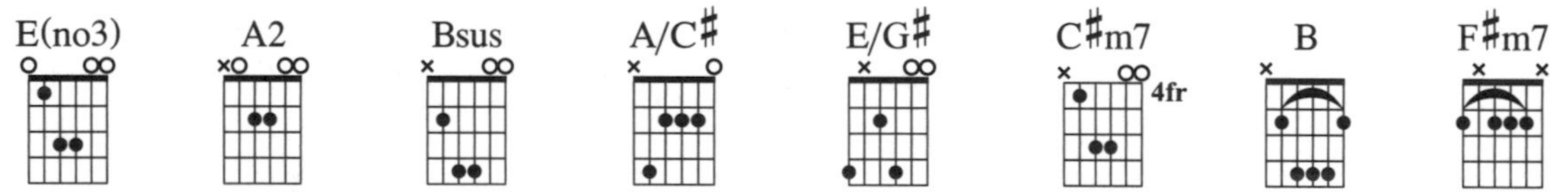

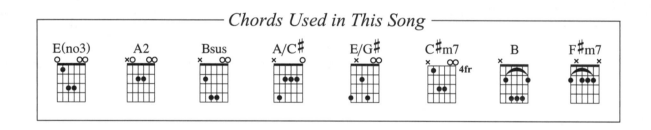

Bless the Lord

Words and Music by
JEFF DEYO

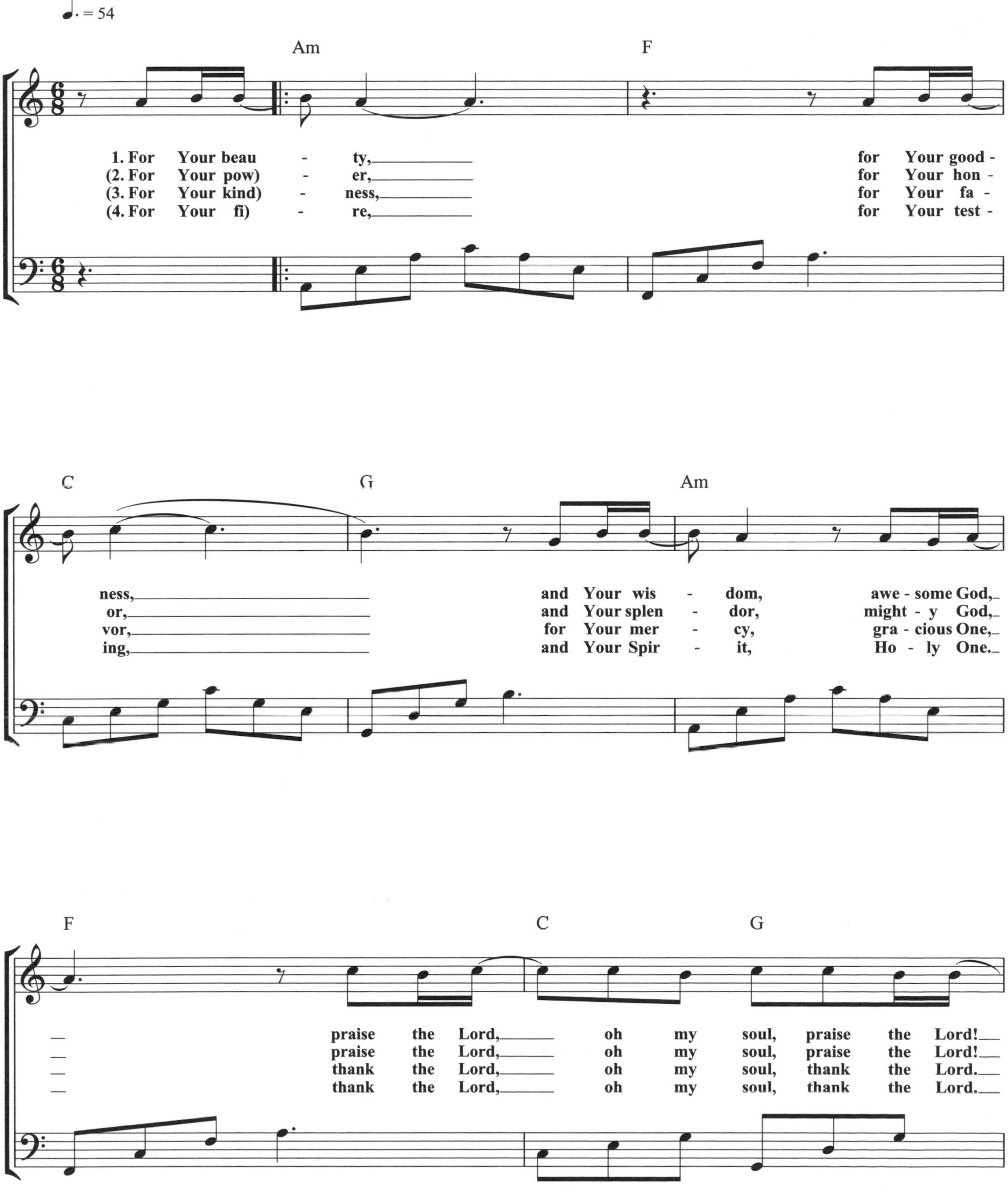
♩. = 54
Am
F
1. For Your beau - ty,
(2. For Your pow) - er,
(3. For Your kind) - ness,
(4. For Your fi) - re,
for Your good -
for Your hon -
for Your fa -
for Your test -
C
G
Am
ness, and Your wis - dom, awe - some God,
or, and Your splen - dor, might - y God,
vor, for Your mer - cy, gra - cious One,
ing, and Your Spir - it, Ho - ly One.
F
C
G
praise the Lord, oh my soul, praise the Lord!
praise the Lord, oh my soul, praise the Lord!
thank the Lord, oh my soul, thank the Lord.
thank the Lord, oh my soul, thank the Lord.

1.3.
F
2.4.
F
2. For Your pow
4. For Your fi
Praise the Lord,
Thank the Lord,
C G F
oh my soul, praise the Lord!
oh my soul, thank the Lord.
And I will
C Dm C
wor - ship You; I will bless Your name for -
Gm7 C Dm
ev - er. I will wor - ship You. Bless the Lord,
C G F
oh my soul, bless the Lord. Bless the Lord,

3rd time to CODA
1.
2.
C G F F
oh my soul, bless the Lord.
3. For Your kind
For Your suf -
Am Fmaj7 C
f'ring,
for You're an - guish,
G/B Am Fmaj7
and Your sor - row, hum - ble King, bless the Lord,
C G F
oh my soul, bless the Lord! Bless the Lord,
C G F
oh my soul, bless the Lord! For Your

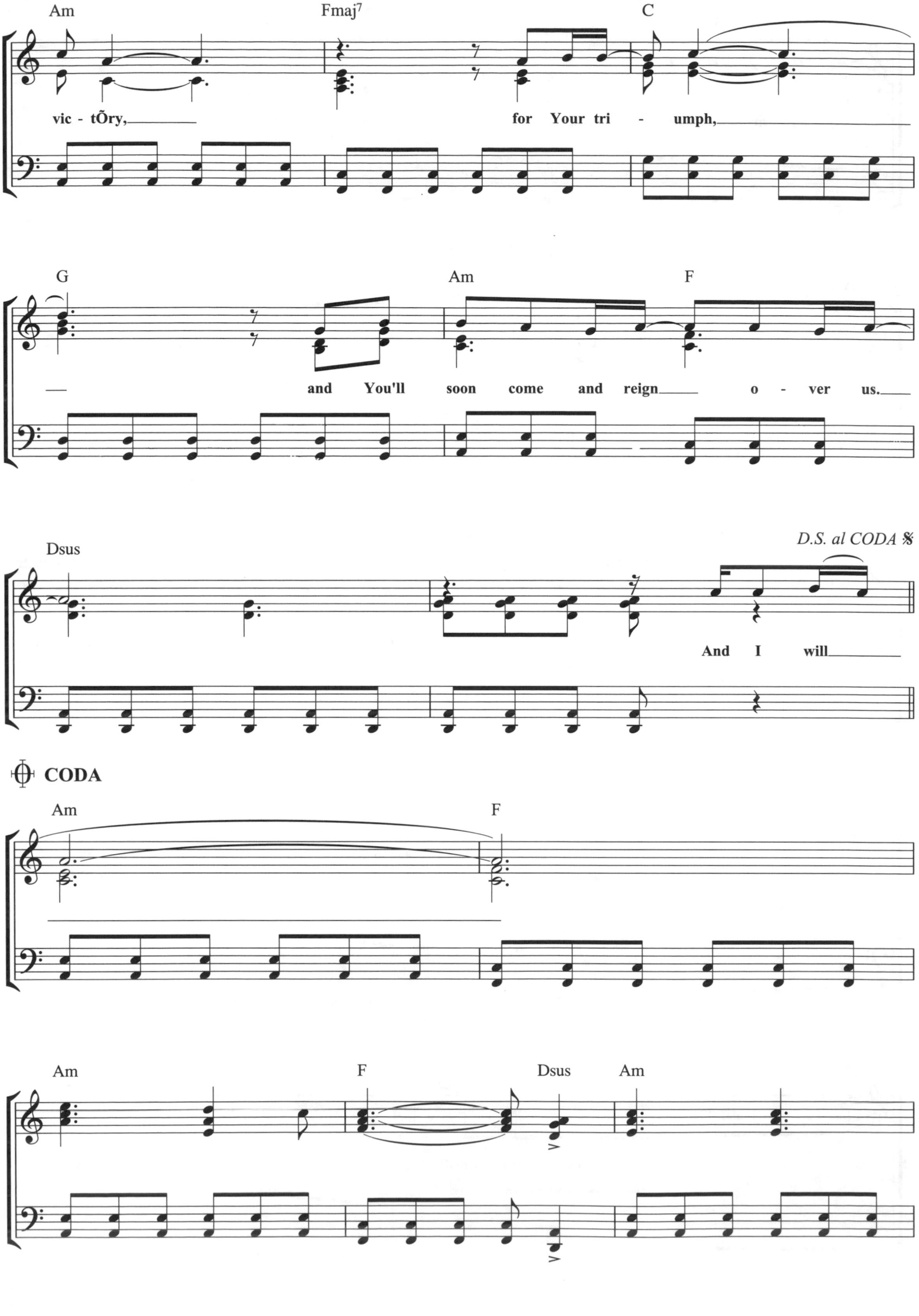
Am
Fmaj7
C
vic - tÕry,
for Your tri - umph,
G
Am
F
and You'll soon come and reign o - ver us.
Dsus
D.S. al CODA 𝄋
And I will
CODA
Am
F
Am
F
Dsus
Am

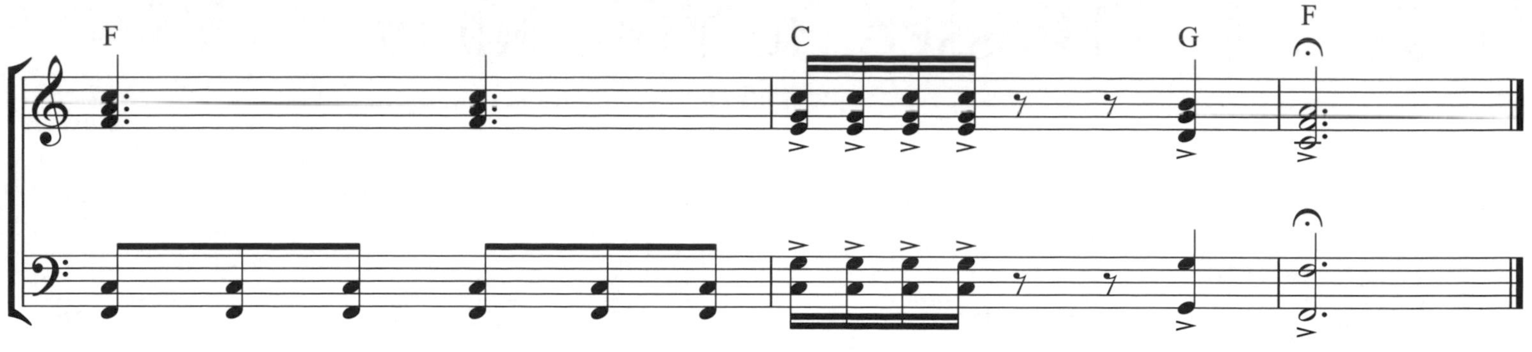

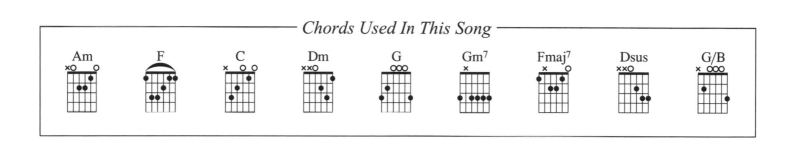

Chords Used In This Song

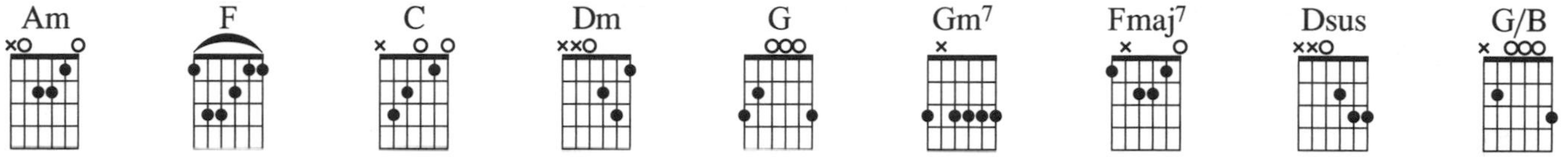

Blessed Be Your Name

Words and Music by
MATT and BETH REDMAN

Capo 2 (A)

♩ = 116
Keyboard
(Guitar)
B
(A)
F♯
(E)
1. Bless - ed be Your name in the
2. Bless - ed be Your name when I'm
3. Bless - ed be Your name when the
4. Bless - ed be Your name on the
G♯m7
(F♯m7)
E
(D)
land that is plen - ti - ful, where Your
found in the des - ert place, though I
sun's shin - ing down on me, when the
road marked with suf - fer - ing, though there's
B
(A)
F♯
(E)
streams of a - bun - dance flow,
walk through the wil - der - ness,
world's "all as it should be."
pain in the of - fer - ing,
bless - ed
E
(D)
1. 3.
2. 4.
be Your name.

B (A)
F♯ (E)
Ev - ’ry bless - ing You pour out I’ll
G♯m7 (F♯m7)
E (D)
turn back to praise.
B (A)
F♯ (E)
When the dark - ness clos - es in, Lord,
G♯m7 (F♯m7)
E (D)
still I will say, “Bless - ed be the
B (A)
F♯ (E)
name of the Lord, bless - ed be Your

G♯m7
(F♯m7)
E
(D)
name.
Bless - ed be the
B
(A)
F♯
(E)
name of the Lord,
bless - ed be Your
G♯m7
(F♯m7)
F♯
(E)
E
(D)
Last time to CODA
1.
D.C.
glo - ri - ous name."
2.
B
(A)
You give and take a -
F♯
(E)
G♯m7
(F♯m7)
way, You give and take a -

E
(D)
B
(A)
way. My heart will choose to
F♯
(E)
G♯m7
(F♯m7)
say, "Lord, Bless - ed be Your
1.
E
(D)
2.
E
(D)
D.S. al CODA
name."_ You name."_ Bless - ed be the
CODA
E
(D)
B
(A)

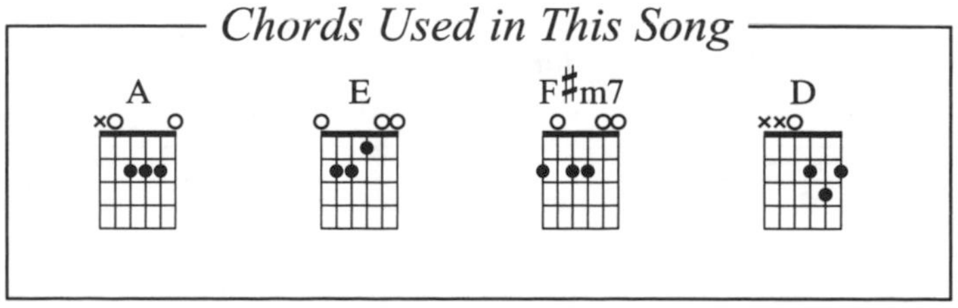
Chords Used in This Song
A
E
F♯m7
D

Captivated

Words and Music by
VICKY BEECHING

♩ = 72
A2
B7sus
C♯m
1. Your laugh - ter it ech - oes like a joy - ous thun - der,
2. Be - hold - ing is be - com - ing, so as You fill my gaze,
A2
C♯m
B7sus
Your whis - per it warms me like a sum - mer breeze.
I be - come more like you and my heart is changed.
A2
B7sus
C♯m7
Your an - ger is fierc - er than the sun in its splen - dor,
Be - hold - ing is be - com - ing, so as You fill my view,
A2
C♯m7
B
You're close and yet full of mys - ter - y.
trans - form me in - to the like - ness of You.
And ev - er since the
This is what I

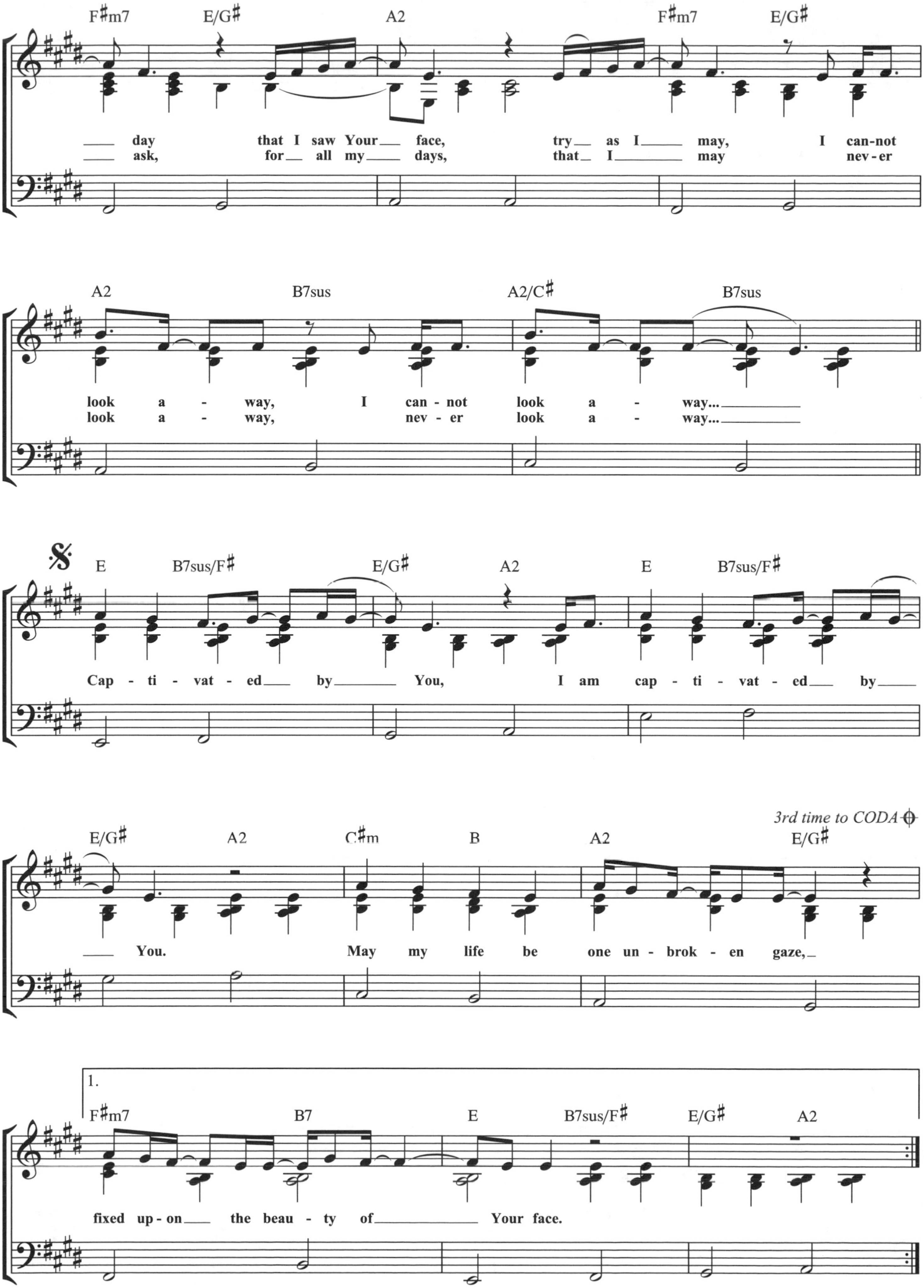
F♯m7 E/G♯ A2 F♯m7 E/G♯
day that I saw Your face, try as I may, I can-not
ask, for all my days, that I may nev-er
A2 B7sus A2/C♯ B7sus
look a - way, I can - not look a - way...
look a - way, nev - er look a - way...
E B7sus/F♯ E/G♯ A2 E B7sus/F♯
Cap - ti - vat - ed by You, I am cap - ti - vat - ed by
3rd time to CODA
E/G♯ A2 C♯m B A2 E/G♯
You. May my life be one un - brok - en gaze,
1.
F♯m7 B7 E B7sus/F♯ E/G♯ A2
fixed up - on the beau - ty of Your face.

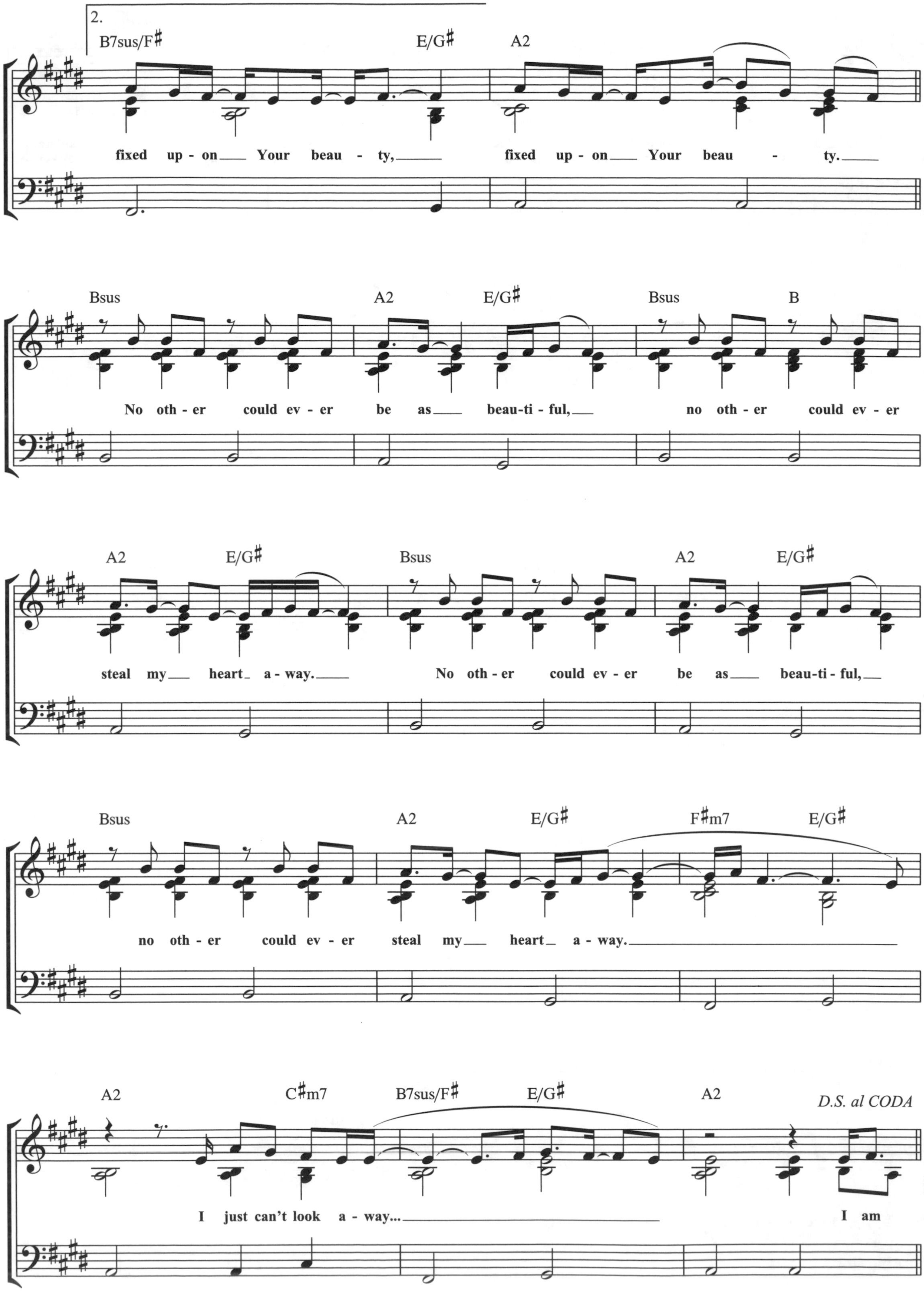
2.
B7sus/F♯ E/G♯ A2
fixed up - on Your beau - ty, fixed up - on Your beau - ty.
Bsus A2 E/G♯ Bsus B
No oth - er could ev - er be as beau-ti - ful, no oth - er could ev - er
A2 E/G♯ Bsus A2 E/G♯
steal my heart a - way. No oth - er could ev - er be as beau-ti - ful,
Bsus A2 E/G♯ F♯m7 E/G♯
no oth - er could ev - er steal my heart a - way.
A2 C♯m7 B7sus/F♯ E/G♯ A2
D.S. al CODA
I just can't look a - way... I am

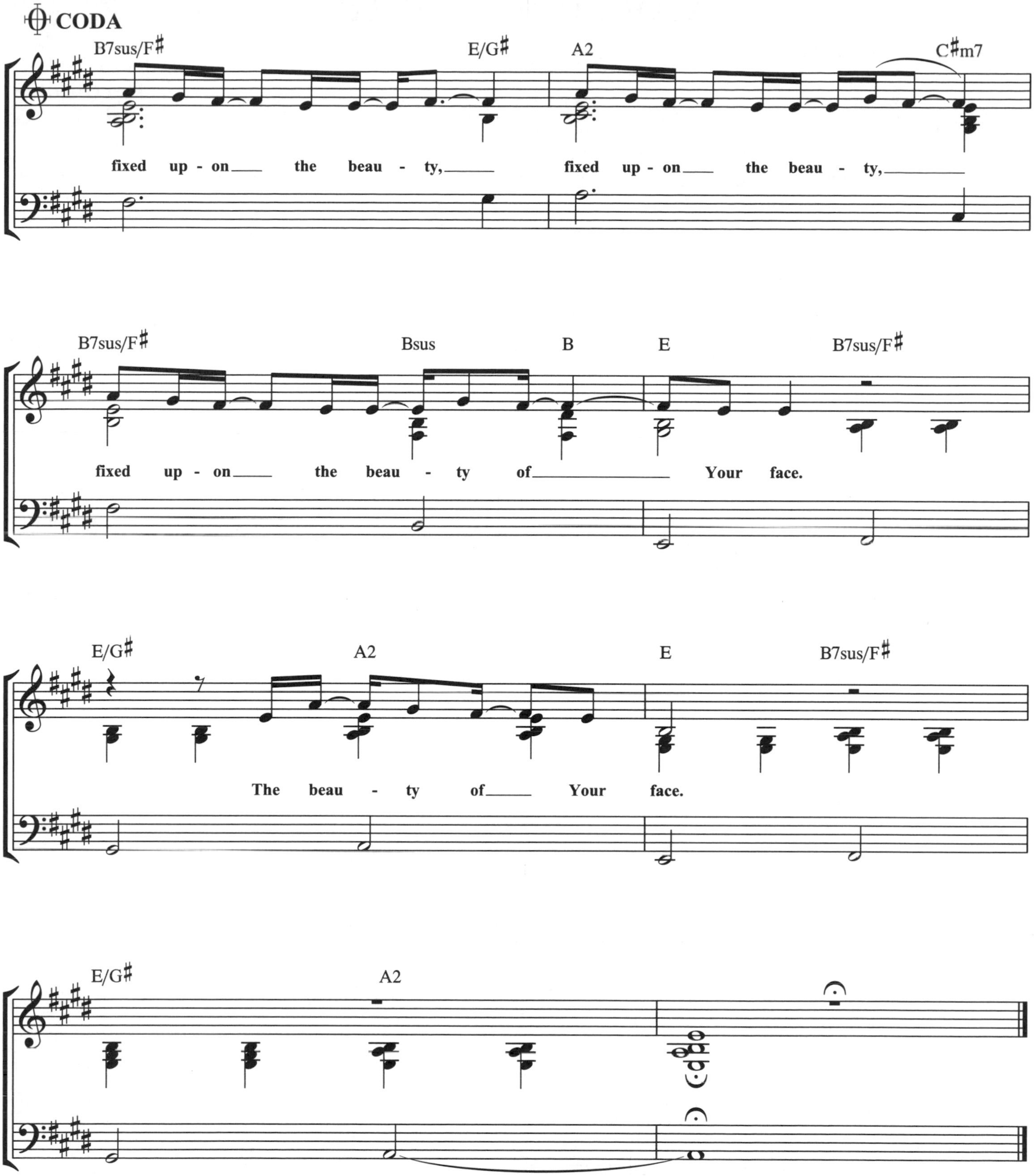
CODA
B7sus/F♯
E/G♯
A2
C♯m7
fixed up - on the beau - ty, fixed up - on the beau - ty,
B7sus/F♯
Bsus
B
E
B7sus/F♯
fixed up - on the beau - ty of Your face.
E/G♯
A2
E
B7sus/F♯
The beau - ty of Your face.
E/G♯
A2

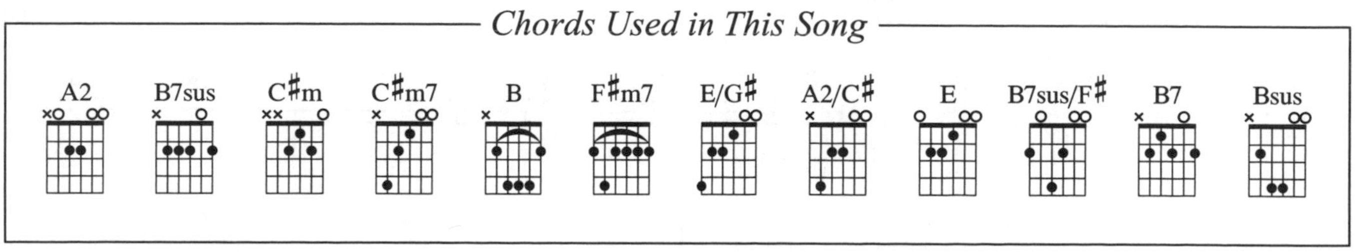
Chords Used in This Song
A2
B7sus
C♯m
C♯m7
B
F♯m7
E/G♯
A2/C♯
E
B7sus/F♯
B7
Bsus

Consuming Fire

Words and Music by
TIM HUGHES

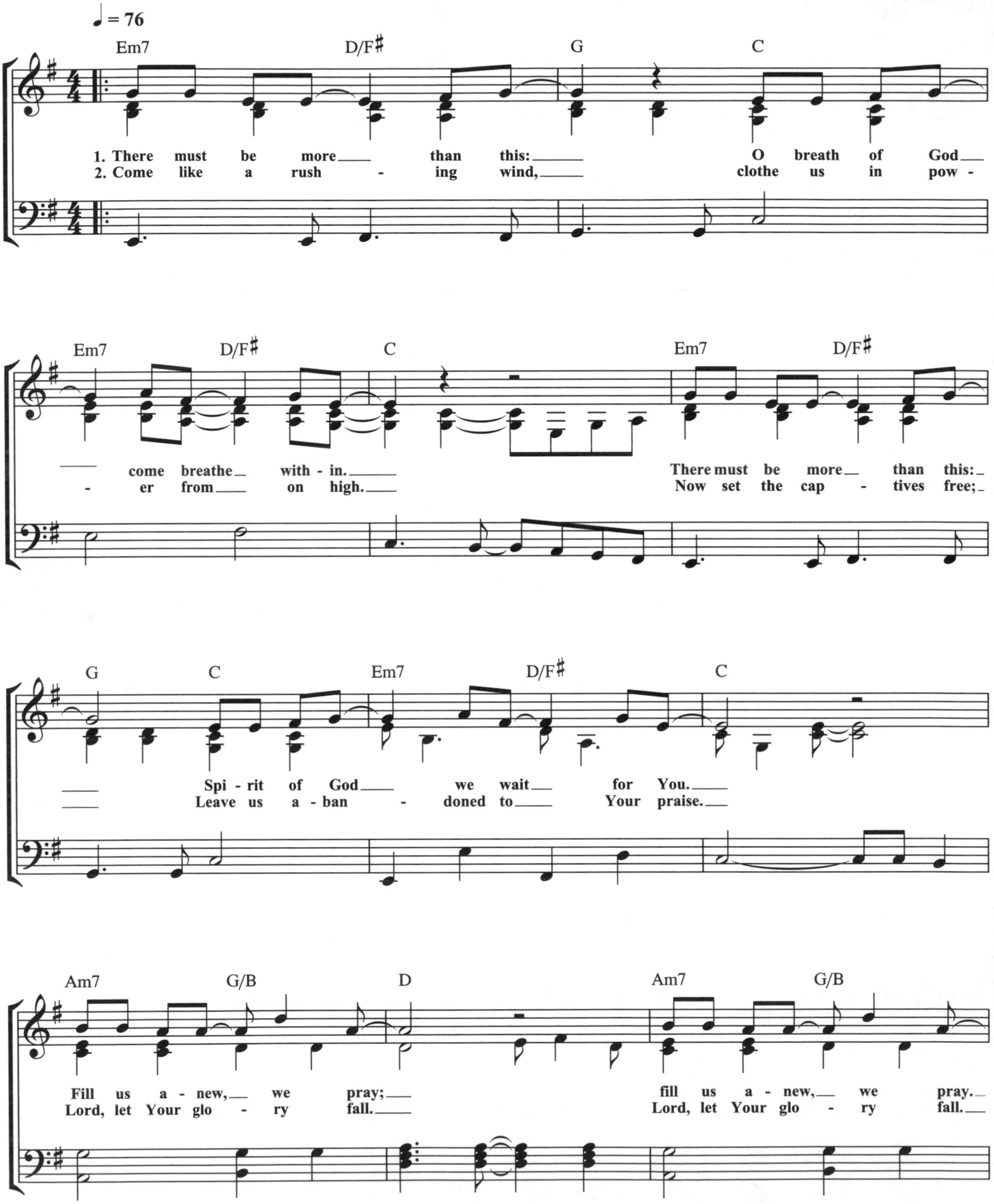
♩ = 76
Em7 D/F♯ G C
1. There must be more than this: O breath of God
2. Come like a rush - ing wind, clothe us in pow -
Em7 D/F♯ C Em7 D/F♯
come breathe with - in. There must be more than this:
- er from on high. Now set the cap - tives free;
G C Em7 D/F♯ C
Spi - rit of God we wait for You.
Leave us a - ban - doned to Your praise.
Am7 G/B D Am7 G/B
Fill us a - new, we pray; fill us a - new, we pray.
Lord, let Your glo - ry fall. Lord, let Your glo - ry fall.

D
G
D/F♯
Con - sum - ing Fire, fan in - to flame a
Em7
C
G
pas - sion for Your name. Spi - rit of God, fall in this
D/F♯
Em7
D/F♯
place. Lord, have Your way, Lord, have Your way with us.
C
G
8vb

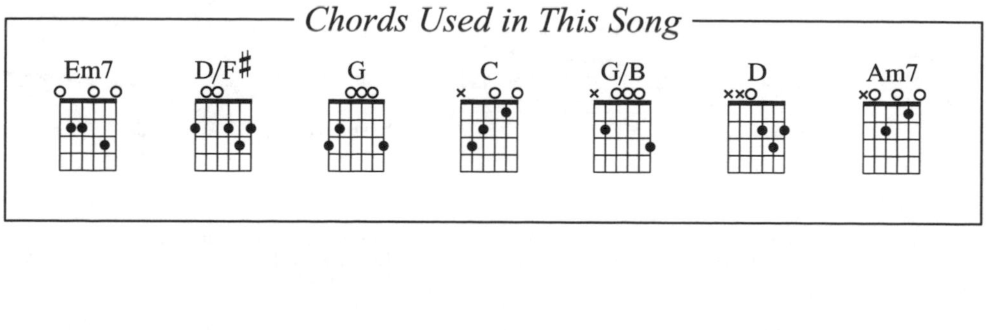
Chords Used in This Song
Em7
D/F♯
G
C
G/B
D
Am7

Communion

Words and Music by
MAC POWELL, DAVID CARR,
TAI ANDERSON, BRAD AVERY
and MARK LEE

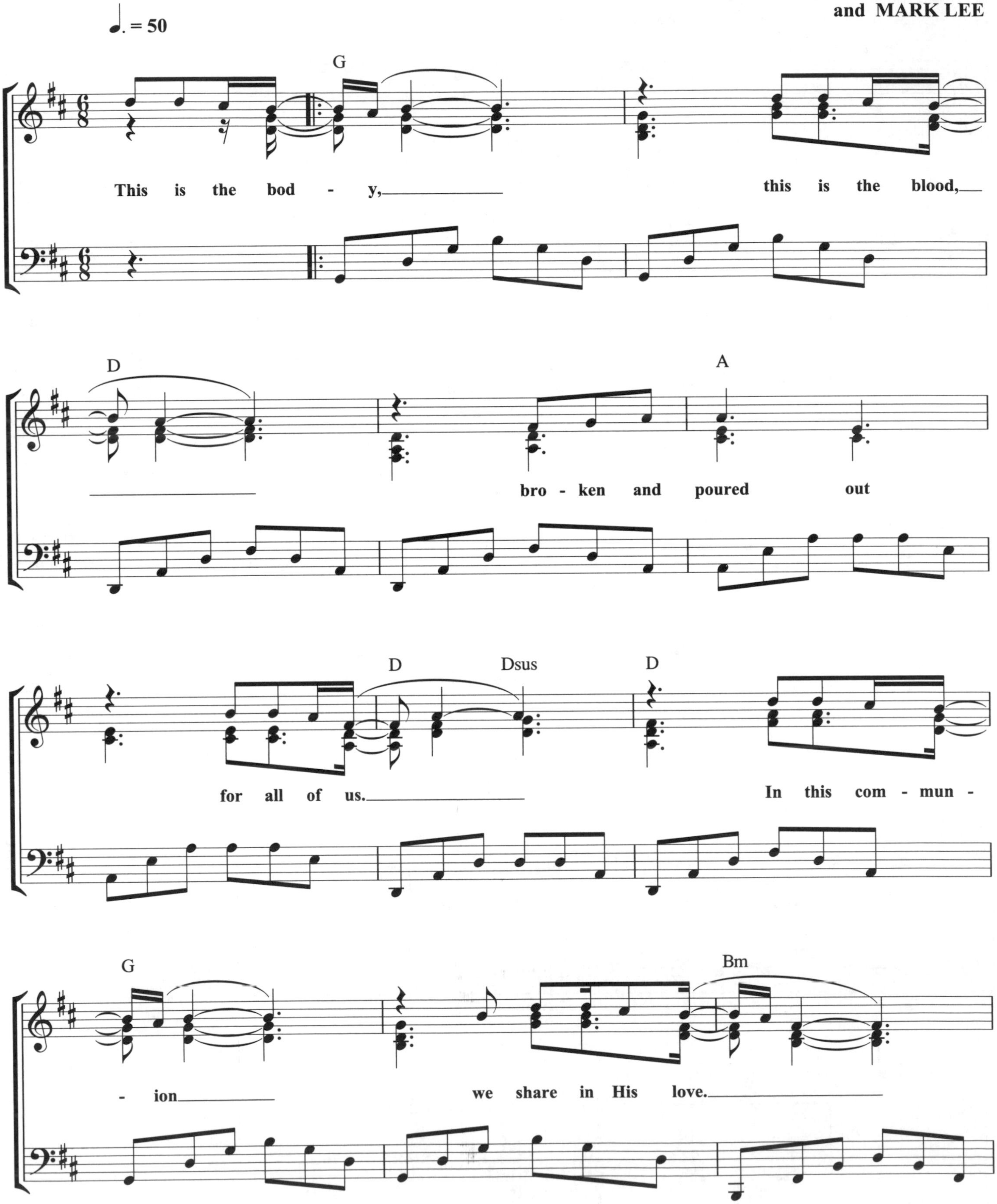
♩. = 50
G
This is the bod - y,
this is the blood,
D
A
bro - ken and poured out
D
Dsus
D
for all of us.
In this com - mun -
G
Bm
- ion
we share in His love.

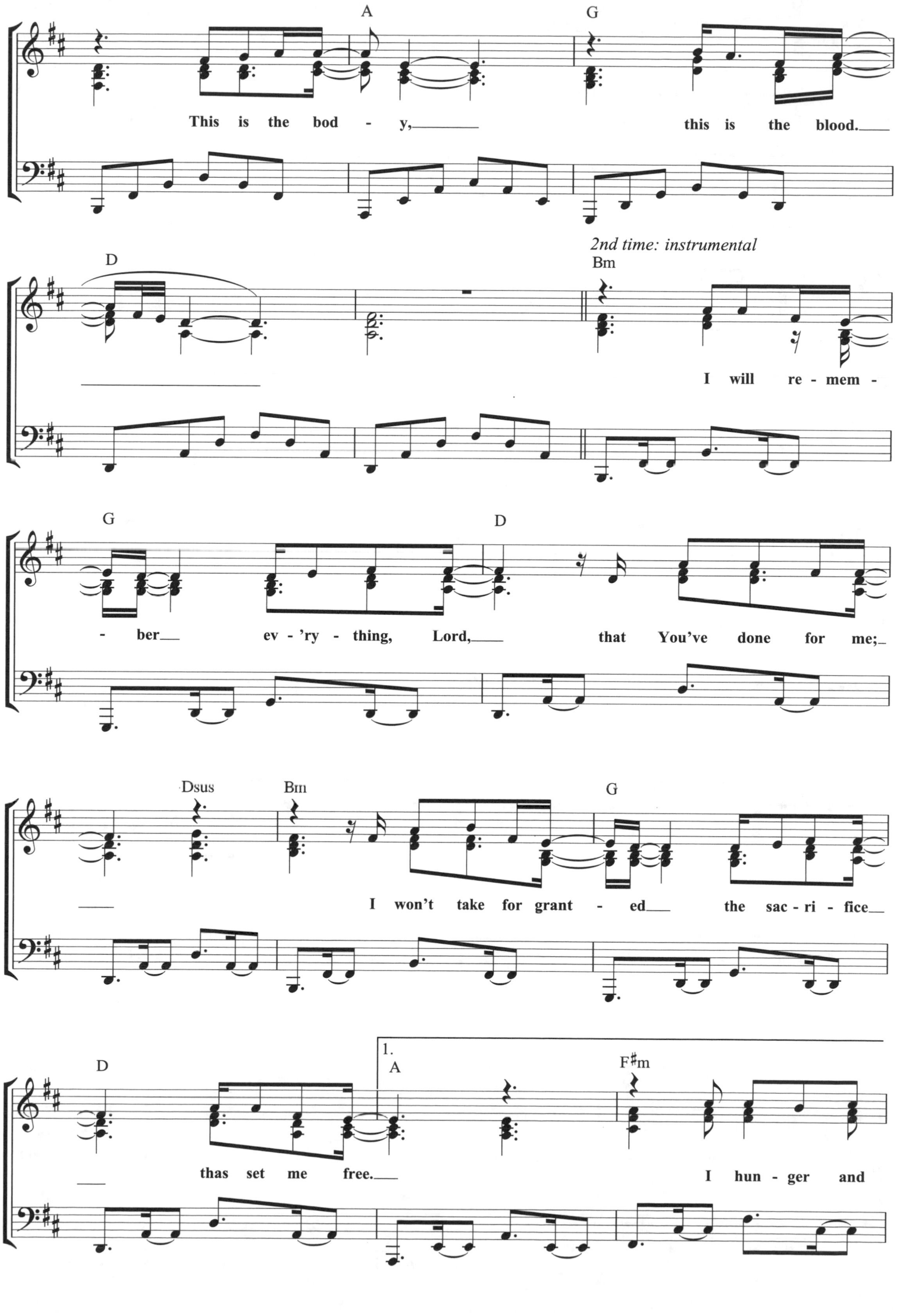
A
G
This is the bod - y,
this is the blood.
D
2nd time: instrumental
Bm
I will re - mem -
G
D
- ber ev - 'ry - thing, Lord,
that You've done for me;
Dsus
Bm
G
I won't take for grant - ed
the sac - ri - fice
D
1.
A
F♯m
thas set me free.
I hun - ger and

G
F#m
thirst for Your love; come fill me
A
2.
to - day. This is the bod-
F#m
G
F#m
We hun - ger and thirst for Your love, and Your right -
G
F#m
G
- eous - ness. We long for Your pres - ence here, Lord.
F#m
A
Be with us a - gain. This is the bod-

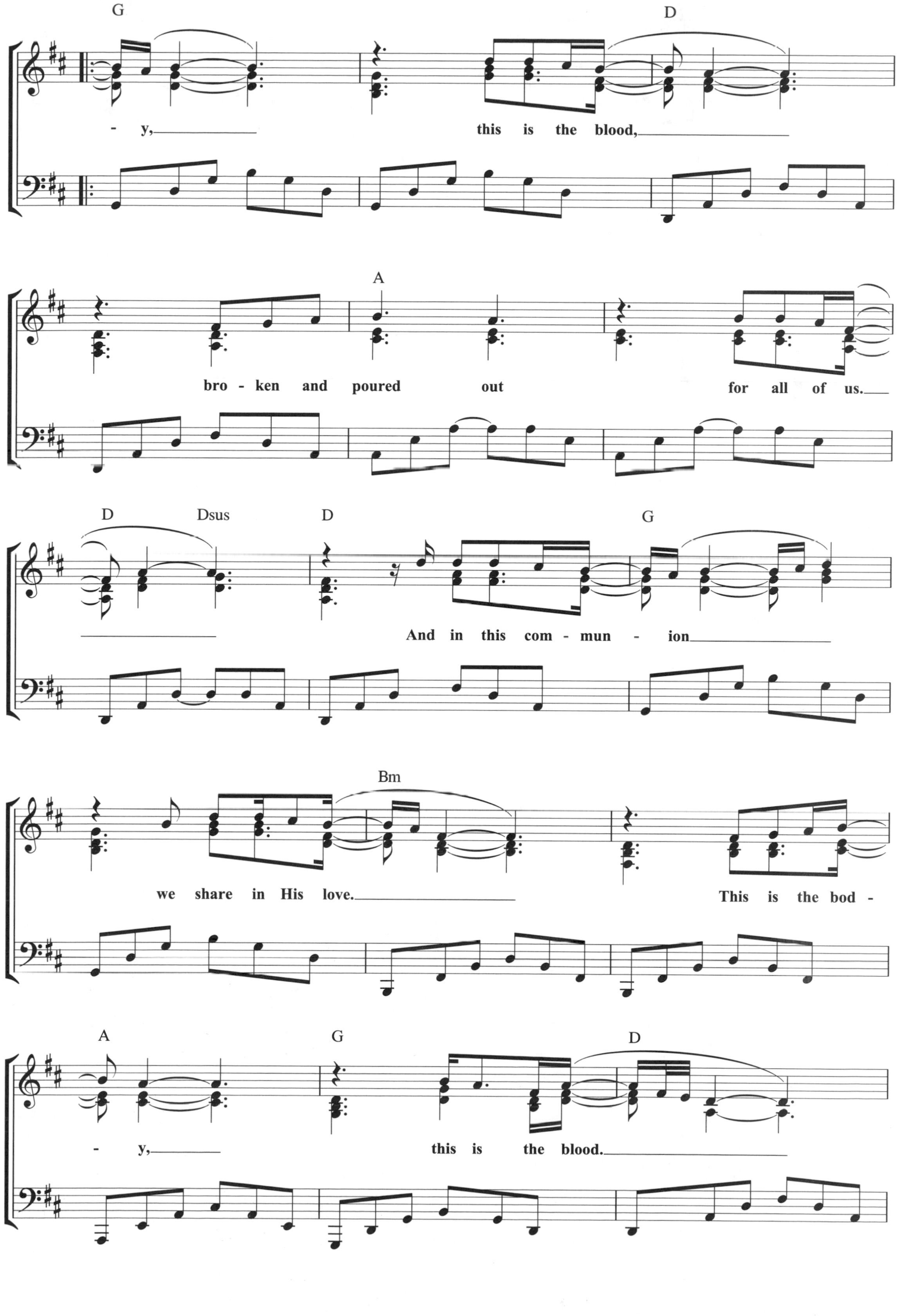
G
D
- y,
this is the blood,
A
bro - ken and poured out
for all of us.
D
Dsus
D
G
And in this com - mun - ion
Bm
we share in His love.
This is the bod -
A
G
D
- y,
this is the blood.

1.
2.
A
This is the bod-
This is the bod - y,
G
D
this is the blood.
This is the bod -
A
G
D
- y,
this is the blood.

Chords Used in This Song

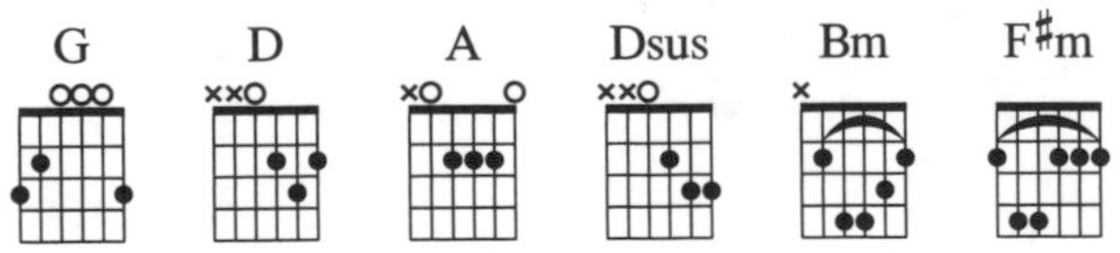
G
D
A
Dsus
Bm
F#m

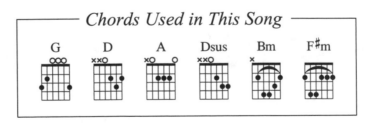

Cry in My Heart

Words and Music by
TIM NEUFELD and JON NEUFELD

♩ = 76
D
A
There's a cry in my heart for Your glo - ry to fall, for Your
Em7
Asus
A
pres - ence to fill up my sens - es. There's a
D
A
yearn - ing a - gain, a thirst for dis - ci - pline, a
Em7
Asus
A
hun - ger for things that are deep - er. Could You

Bm G D A
take me be - yond? Could You car - ry me through? If I
2nd time to CODA
Bm G D A
o - pen my heart could I go there with You?
G
For what do I have if I don't have You, Je -
D A
- sus? What in this life could mean an - y more?
Bm D/F# G
You are my rock, You are my glo -

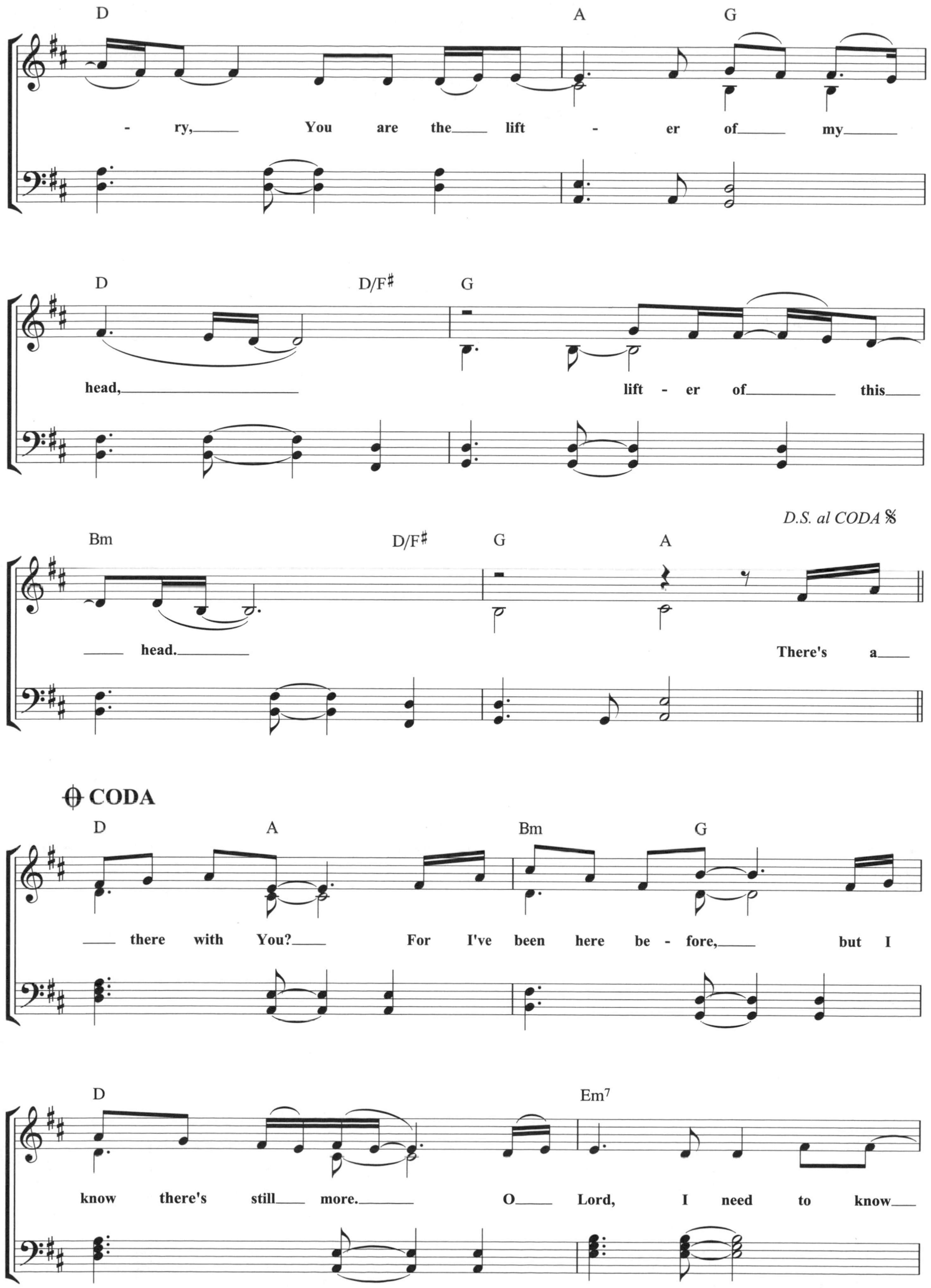
D A G
- ry, You are the lift - er of my
D D/F♯ G
head, lift - er of this
D.S. al CODA 𝄋
Bm D/F♯ G A
head. There's a
CODA
D A Bm G
there with You? For I've been here be - fore, but I
D Em7
know there's still more. O Lord, I need to know

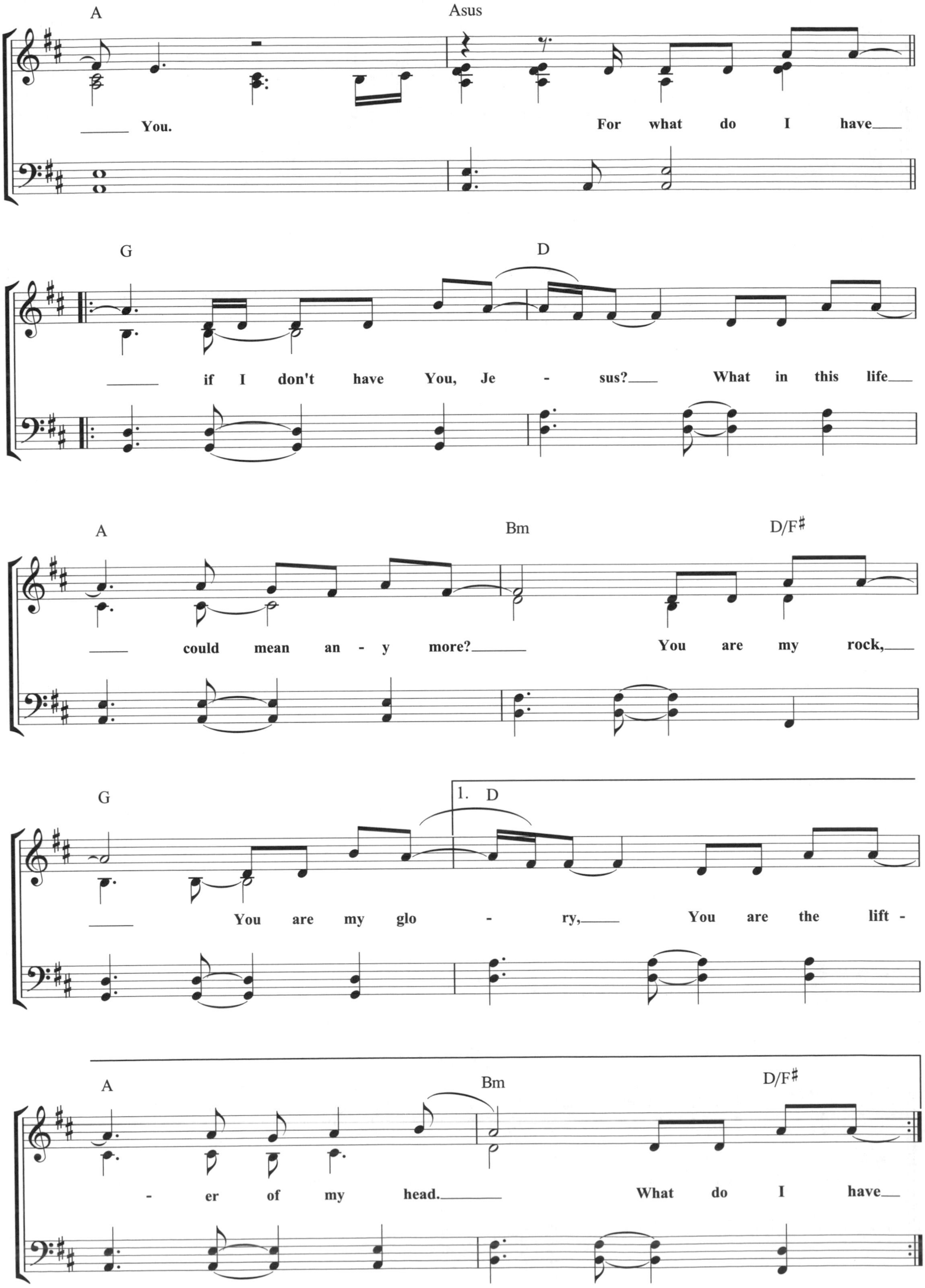
A
Asus
You. For what do I have
G
D
if I don't have You, Je - sus? What in this life
A
Bm
D/F#
could mean an - y more? You are my rock,
G
1. D
You are my glo - ry, You are the lift -
A
Bm
D/F#
- er of my head. What do I have

2.
D
A
– ry,
You are the lift - er of my
Bm
G
head,
lift - er of this
Bm
G
A
D
head.
Yeah.

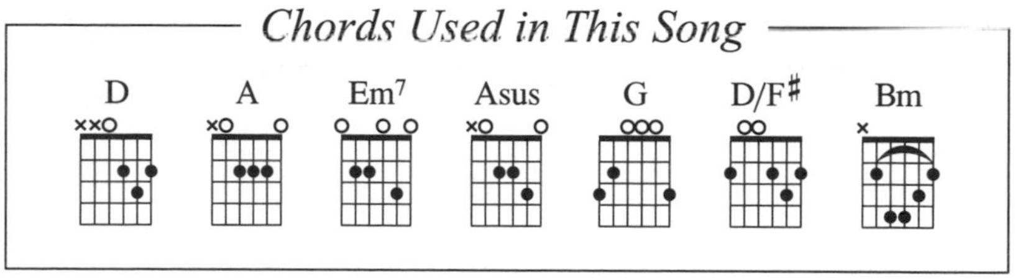
Chords Used in This Song
D
A
Em7
Asus
G
D/F♯
Bm

Dancing Generation

Words and Music by
MATT REDMAN

♩ = 138
D
Your mer - cy taught us how to dance, to
Bm
cel - e - brate with all we have, and we'll
G2 D2 D
dance to thank You for mer - cy.
F D
Your glo - ry taught us how to shout; We'll

Bm
lift Your name in all the earth, and we'll
G2
D2
D
shout to the praise of Your glo - ry.
F
Em
It's the o - ver - flow of a for -
D/F#
G
G2
G
giv - en soul. And now we've seen You God,
G6
Gmaj7
Asus
A
our hearts can - not stay si - lent. And we'll

D
Em7
be a danc - ing gen - er - a - tion, danc - ing be - cause of Your
G
great mer - cy, Lord, Your great mer - cy, Lord.
D Dsus D Dsus D
And we'll be a shout - ing
Em7
gen - er - a - tion, shout - ing be - cause of Your great glo - ry, Lord,
G
D Dsus
Your great glo - ry, Lord.

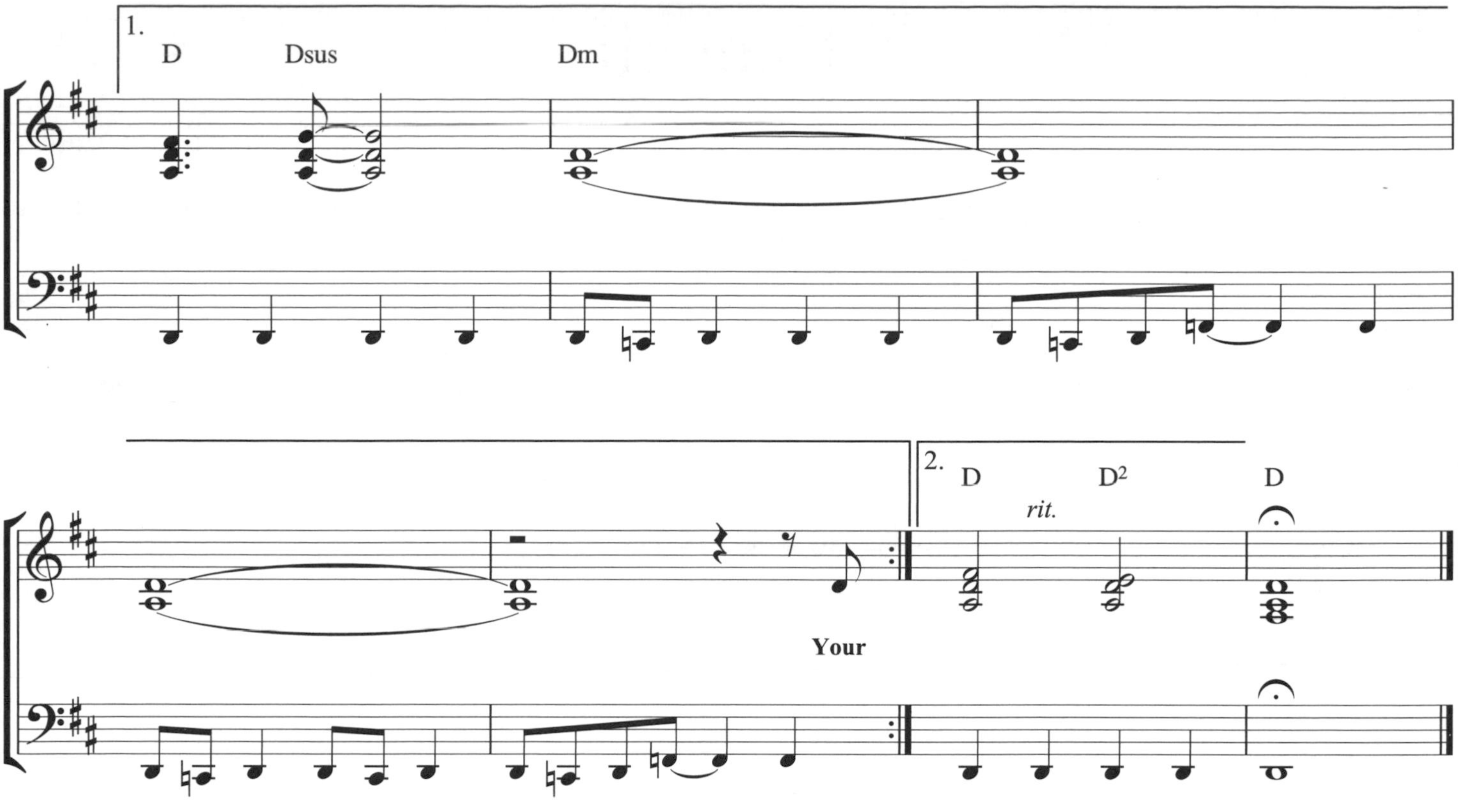

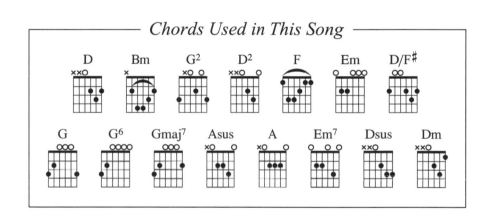

Chords Used in This Song

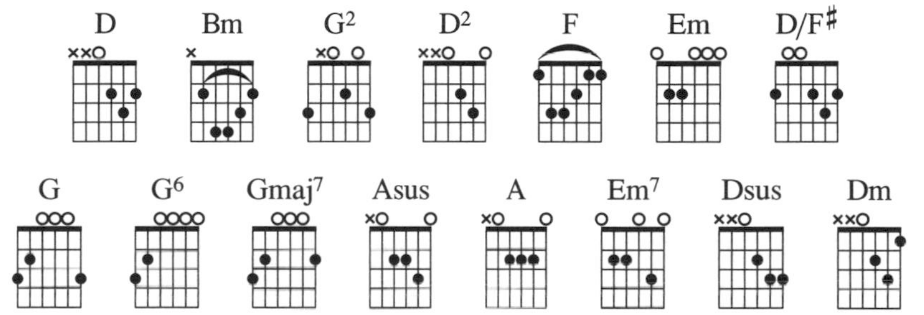

Enough

Words and Music by
CHRIS TOMLIN
and LOUIE GIGLIO

♩ = 78
A
D2/F♯
All of You___ is more than e - nough___
Esus
D2
A
D2/F♯
___ for all of me,___ for ev - 'ry thirst___
Esus
D2
A
D2/F♯
___ and ev - 'ry need.___ You___ sat - is - fy___
3rd time to CODA
4th time to CODA
Esus
D2
A/C♯
D2
___ me with Your love,___ and all I have___ in You___

Esus
A
D2/F♯
is more than e - nough.
Esus
D2
A
D2/F♯
Esus
D2
A
D2
1. You're my sup - ply,
2. You're my sac - ri - fice
Esus
A/C♯
D2
my breath of life; still more awe -
of great - est price; still more awe -
Bm7
Esus
A
D2
- some than I know. You're my re - ward,
- some than I know. You're my com - ing King,

Esus A/C♯ D2
worth liv - ing for; still more awe -
You are ev - 'ry - thing; still more awe -
1. 2.
D.S. al CODA
Bm7 Esus Bm7 Esus
- some than I know. And all of You - some than I know. And all of You
CODA
Esus A D2
More than all I want,
Esus D2 A/C♯ D2
more than all I need, You are more
Esus A D2
than e - nough for me. More than all I know,

Esus
D2
A/C♯
D2
more than all I can
You are more
1.
Esus
than e - nough.
2.
Esus
D.S. al CODA 𝄋
than e - nough. And all of You
CODA
Esus
A
is more than e - nough.

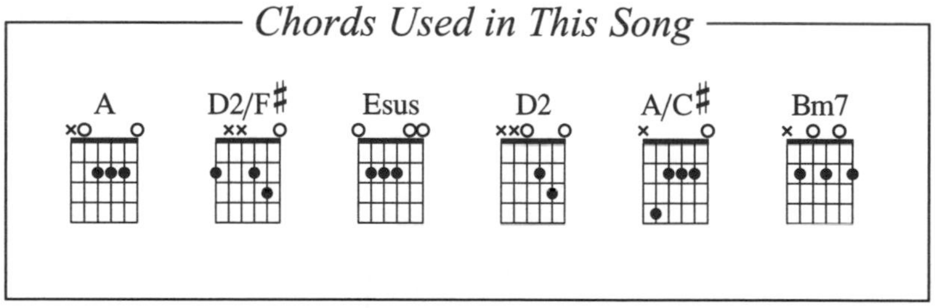
Chords Used in This Song
A
D2/F♯
Esus
D2
A/C♯
Bm7

Everlasting God

Words and Music by
BRENTON BROWN
and KEN RILEY

♩ = 108

Capo 3 (G)

Keyboard
(Guitar)
B♭ (G)
*opt. [B♭sus (Gsus)]
Strength will rise as we wait___ up - on the Lord, we will wait___ up - on the Lord, we will wait___ up - on the Lord.
Strength will rise as we wait___ up - on the Lord, we will wait___ up - on the Lord, we will wait___ up - on the Lord. Our God,___
[B♭/D (G/B)]
E♭ (C)

*All chords in brackets are optional.

Bb/D (G/B) Eb (C) F (D) Gm (Em) F (D) Bb/D (G/B) Eb (C)
You reign for - ev - er. Our Hope,
Bb/D (G/B) Eb (C) F (D) Gm (Em) F (D)
our strong De - liv - 'rer
Bb (G) Eb (C)
You are the ev - er - last - ing God, the ev -
Gm (Em)
- er - last - ing God You do not faint, You
Eb (C) F/Eb (D/C) Eb (C) Cm7/Eb (Am7/C) Bb (G)
won't grow wea - ry You're the de - fend -

E♭ (C)
- er of the weak, You com - fort those in need.
3rd time to CODA
Gm (Em) E♭ (C) F/E♭ (D/C)
You lift us up on wings like
1. E♭ (C) Cm7/E♭ (Am7/C)
ea - gles.
2. E♭ (C) Cm7/E♭ (Am7/C) B♭/D (G/B) E♭ (C)
ea - gles.
B♭/D (G/B) E♭ (C) F (D) Gm (Em) F (D) B♭/D (G/B) E♭ (C)
B♭/D (G/B) E♭ (C) F (D) Gm (Em) F (D) B♭/D (G/B) E♭ (C)
Our God,

Bb/D (G/B) Eb (C) F (D) Gm (Em) F (D) Bb/D (G/B) Eb (C)
You reign for - ev - er. Our Hope,
Bb/D (G/B) Eb (C) F (D) Gm (Em) F (D)
D.S. al CODA
our strong De - liv - 'rer.
CODA
Eb (C) Cm7/Eb (Am7/C) Bb (G) Bbsus (Gsus) Bb (G) Bbsus (Gsus)
ea - gles.
Bb (G) Bbsus (Gsus) Bb (G)
You are the ev -
Eb (C)
- er - last - ing God, the ev - er - last - ing God

Gm (Em)
Eb (C)
You do not faint, You won't grow
Bb (G)
wea - ry. You're the de - fend - er of the weak,
Eb (C)
Gm (Em)
You com - fort those in need. You lift
Eb (C)
Bb (G)
us up on wings like ea - gles.

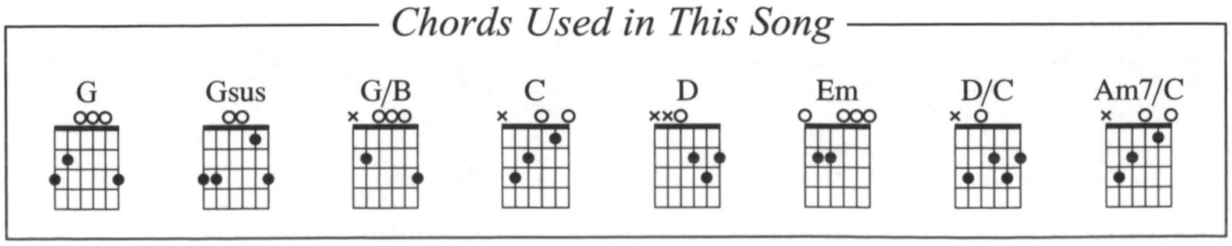
Chords Used in This Song
G
Gsus
G/B
C
D
Em
D/C
Am7/C

Facedown

Capo 6 (C)

Words and Music by
MATT and BETH REDMAN

♩ = 76
Keyboard
(Guitar)
E♭m
(Am)
B♭
(E)
1.2. Wel - comed in to the courts of the King, I've been
3. Who is there in the heav - ens like You, and up -
G♭maj7
(Cmaj7)
A♭
(D)
ush - ered in to Your pres - ence.
- on the earth, who's Your e - qual? You are
E♭m
(Am)
B♭
(E)
Lord, I stand on Your mer - ci - ful ground, yet with
far a - bove, You're the high - est of heights. We are
G♭maj7
(Cmaj7)
1. A♭
(D)
2.3. C♭maj7
(Fmaj7)
ev - 'ry step tread with rev - 'rence. rev - 'rence.
bow - ing down to ex alt You.

C♭6 (F6)
G♭2 (C2)
C♭2 (F2)
And I'll fall face - down as Your
E♭m7 (Am7)
D♭sus (Gsus)
C♭2 (F2)
G♭2 (C2)
glo - ry shines a round.
Yes, I'll fall face -
C♭ (F)
E♭m7 (Am7)
D♭sus (Gsus)
3rd time to CODA
C♭2 (F2)
down as Your glo - ry shines a-round.
1.
Repeat to beginning
2. D♭ (G)
C♭2 (F2)
A round,
a round.
D♭ (G)
C♭2 (F2)
D♭sus (Gsus)
So, let Your glo - ry shine a - round, let Your glo - ry shine a -

C♭2 (F2)
1. D♭ (G)
2. D♭ (G)
D.S. al CODA 𝄋
round, King of glo - ry, here be found, King of glo - ry. found, King of glo - ry.
CODA
D♭ (G)
C♭2 (F2)
So, let Your glo - ry shine a -
D♭ (G)
C♭2 (F2)
round, let Your glo - ry shine a - round, King of glo - ry, here be
1. D♭ (G)
2. D♭ (G)
found, King of glo - ry. found, King of glo - ry.

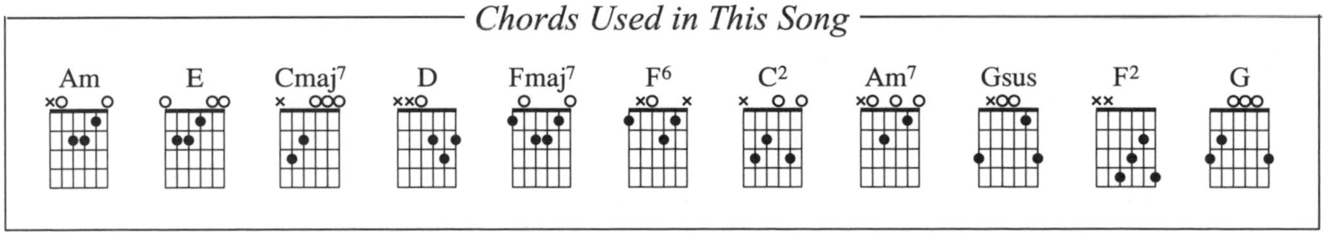

Chords Used in This Song
Am
E
Cmaj7
D
Fmaj7
F6
C2
Am7
Gsus
F2
G

Famous One

Words and Music by
CHRIS TOMLIN
and JESSE REEVES

= 70
G
G/B
C2
You are the Lord, the fa - mous One,
Em7
D
fa - mous One; great is Your name in all
C
G
the earth. The heav - ens de - clare
G/B
C2
You're glo - ri - ous, glo - ri - ous;

3rd time to CODA
Em7
D
G
great is Your fame be - yond the earth.
G/B
F2
C2
Am7
1. And for all You've done and
2. The Morn - ing Star is
Em7
C
yet to do, with ev - 'ry breath
shin - ing through, and ev - 'ry

G
I'm praising You. De-
eye is watching You. Re-
Am7
Em7
sire of nations and ev-'ry heart,
veal Thy nature and mir-a-cles.
C
You a-lone are God, You a-
You are beau-ti-ful, You are
Dsus
1.
2.
D.S. al CODA
lone are God.
beau-ti-ful.
CODA
G
the earth.

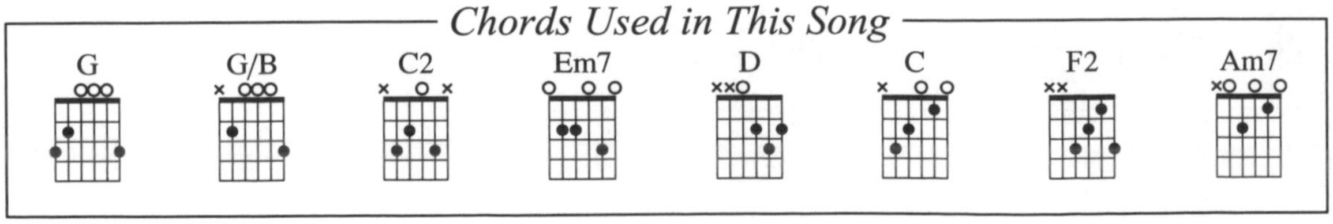
Chords Used in This Song
G
G/B
C2
Em7
D
C
F2
Am7

Filled With Your Glory

Words and Music by
TIM and JON NEUFELD

Capo 1 (G)
♩ = 120
Keyboard (Guitar)
A♭ (G)
1. In my heart, in my heart, there's a fi - re burn - ing,
(2. From the ends) of the earth, to the heights of Heav - en,
E♭sus (Dsus)
a pas - sion deep with - in my soul.
Your glo - ry, Lord, is far and wide.
D♭ (C)
Not slow - ing down, not grow - ing cold,
Through his - to - ry You reign on high.
B♭m7 (Am7)
E♭ (D)

A♭ (G)
an un - quench - a - ble flame___ that keeps burn -
From the depths___ of the sea___ to the moun -
E♭sus (Dsus)
ing___ bright - er, a love that's
tain's___ sum - mit, Your pow - er,
D♭ (C)
blaz - ing like___ the sun___ for who You
Lord, it knows___ no bounds.___ A high - er
B♭m7 (Am7)
E♭ (D)
are and what___ You've done.___
love can - not___ be found.___
A♭/C (G/B)
D♭ (C)
A♭/C (G/B)
And as___ the fire___ is rag -
So let___ the u - ni - verse___

E♭ (D)
B♭m7 (Am7)
D♭ (C)
- ing on, so Your praise
pro-claim Your great pow - er
A♭/C (G/B)
E♭sus (Dsus)
be-comes my song. The whole
and Your great name.
A♭ (G)
earth is filled with Your glo - ry, Lord;
E♭sus (Dsus)
An - gels and men a - dore.
sing on D.S. only: (Moun - tains bow and o - ceans roar.)
D♭ (C)
B♭m7 (Am7)
Cre - a - tion longs for what's

E♭sus
(Dsus)
A♭
(G)
in store. May You be
E♭
(D)
hon - ored and glo - ri - fied, ex -
Cm7
(Bm7)
D♭
(C)
alt - ed and lift - ed high.
B♭m7
(Am7)
E♭sus
(Dsus)
3rd time to CODA
Here at Your feet I lay my life.
1.
A♭
(G)

D.S. al CODA 𝄋
2.
2. From the ends
The whole
CODA
A♭
(G)

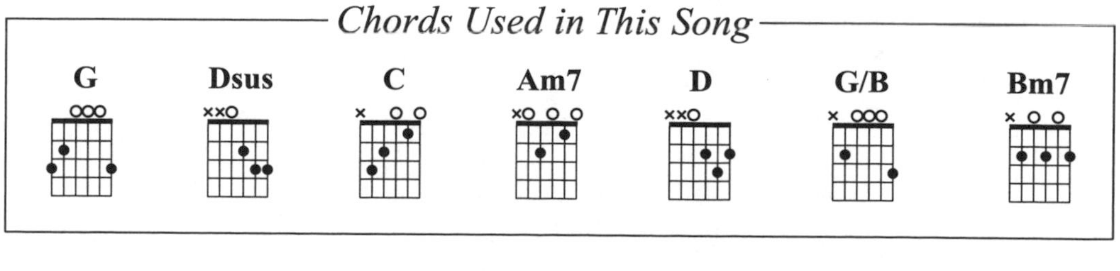
Chords Used in This Song
G
Dsus
C
Am7
D
G/B
Bm7

Father, Spirit, Jesus

Words and Music by
MARK HALL, CHAD CATES
and DAVID HUNT

Capo 2 (A)
♩ = 118
Keyboard
(Guitar)
B7 (A7)
Lord, the wor - ship we bring is more than songs that we
3
F♯m (Em)
sing, it's a re - flec - tion of our ev - er - chang - ing
E (D)
lives;
2. (hearts)
the best we have to of -
B7 (A7)
- fer.
We don't just lift up our hands,

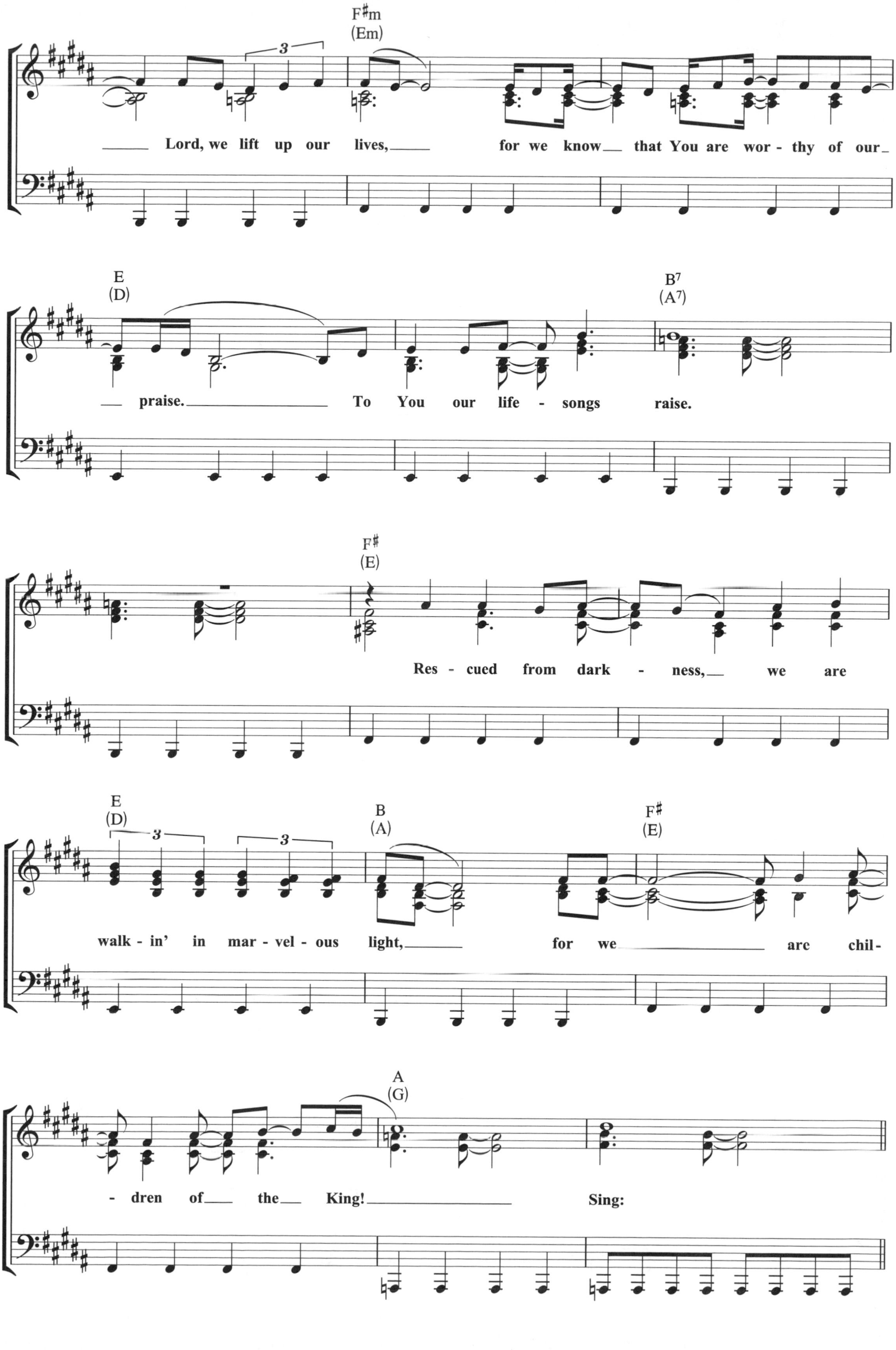
F♯m
(Em)
3
Lord, we lift up our lives, for we know that You are wor - thy of our
E
(D)
B7
(A7)
praise. To You our life - songs raise.
F♯
(E)
Res - cued from dark - ness, we are
E
(D)
3
3
B
(A)
F♯
(E)
walk - in' in mar - vel - ous light, for we are chil -
A
(G)
- dren of the King! Sing:

B (A)
E (D)
You ___ are wor - thy ___ of all hon - or,
C♯m (Bm)
E (D)
glo - ry, ___ praise, and pow - er; King of the na - tions. ___
B7 (A7)
B (A)
You ___ are
E (D)
ho - ly ___ God, al - might - y. Clothed in ___ bril - liant
C♯m (Bm)
E (D)
B7 (A7)
maj - es - ty; Fa - ther, Spir - it, Je - sus! ___

1.
F♯m
(Em)
E
(D)
2.
F♯
(E)
E
(D)
Res - cued from dark - ness, we are walk - in' in mar - vel - ous
B
(A)
F♯
(E)
light, for we are chil - dren of the King!
A
(G)
B/A
(A/G)
E/A
(D/G)
Sing,
sing:

B
(A)
E
(D)
You are wor - thy of all hon - or,
C♯m
(Bm)
E
(D)
glo - ry, praise, and pow - er; King of the na - tions.
B7
(A7)
B
(A)
You are
E
(D)
ho - ly God, al - might - y. Clothed in bril - liant
C♯m
(Bm)
E
(D)
1.
B7
(A7)
maj - es - ty; Fa - ther, Spir - it, Je - sus!

Chords Used in This Song

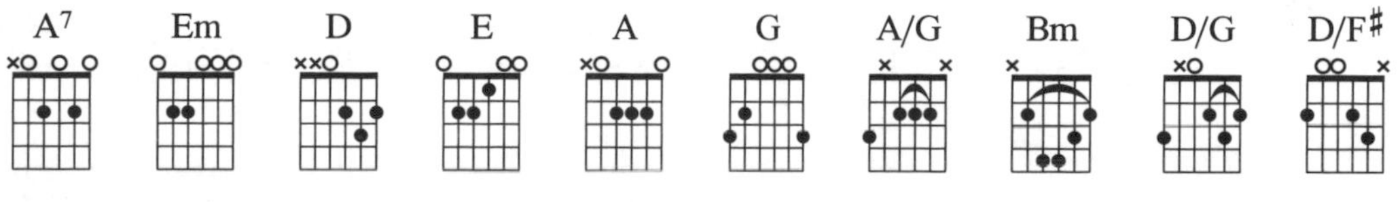

For Your Glory

Words and Music by
MATT MAHER

♩ = 132
E A E
There is a time to live, there is a time
There is a time to sow, there is a time
B E A
to die. There is a time to laugh,
to reap. A time for vic - to - ry,
C♯m B E
there is a time to cry. There is a time
a time to claim de - feat. A time to be
A E B
to dance, a time for joy's em - brace,
re - newed, a time to be re - born.

E/G♯ A C♯m
and in___ all sea - sons, God__ we hum - bly seek__
and in___ all sea - sons, God__ we bow__ be - fore__
B A B
___ Your face.___
___ Your throne.___ This is___ our of - fer - ing to You,
A/C♯ B E
this is___ our of - fer - ing.___ Ev - 'ry - thing I am is
A C♯m B
for Your glo - ry, Ev - 'ry - thing I am for You, Lord,

E A
Ev - 'ry - thing I am is for Your glo - ry, Ev - 'ry - thing I am for
C♯m B
1.
E E2
You, Lord,
Esus
2.
A2 B
The earth stands still with -
F♯m E/G♯ A2 B
out You. We could on - ly move be - cause You

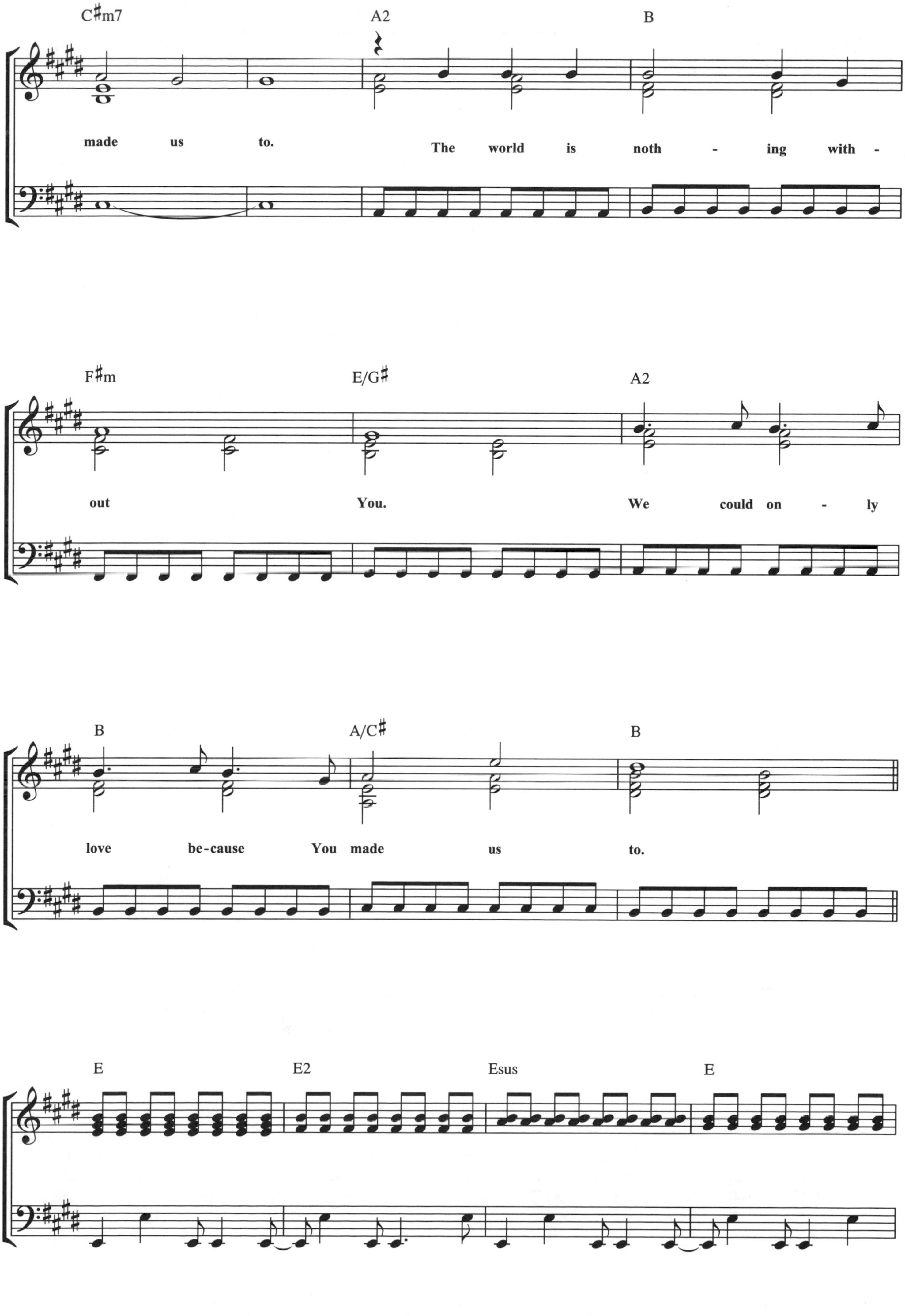
C♯m7
A2
B
made us to.
The world is noth - ing with -
F♯m
E/G♯
A2
out You.
We could on - ly
B
A/C♯
B
love be-cause You made us to.
E
E2
Esus
E

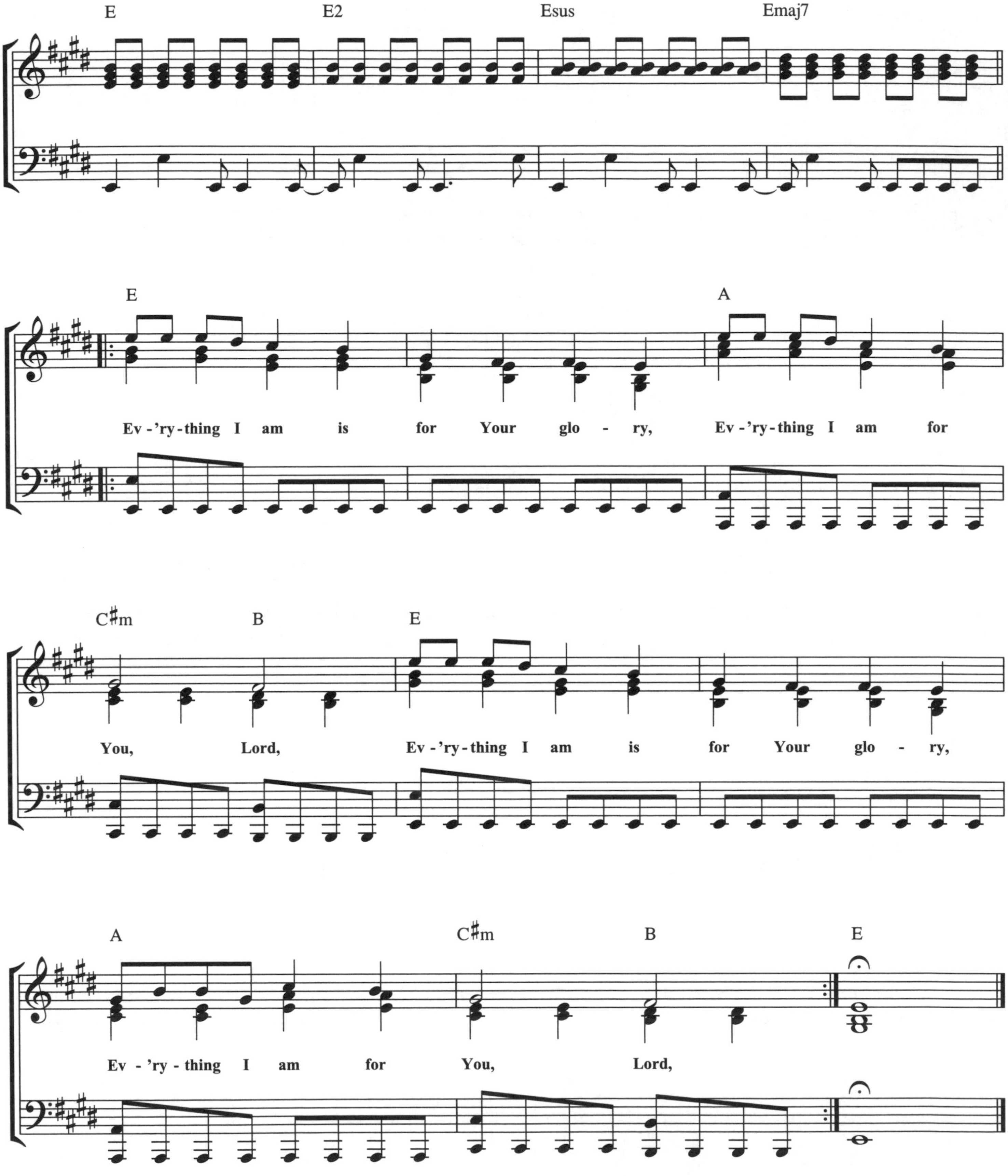
E E2 Esus Emaj7
E A
Ev-'ry-thing I am is for Your glo-ry, Ev-'ry-thing I am for
C#m B E
You, Lord, Ev-'ry-thing I am is for Your glo-ry,
A C#m B E
Ev-'ry-thing I am for You, Lord,

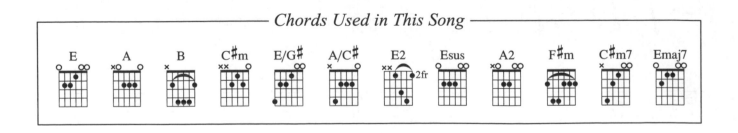

Chords Used in This Song

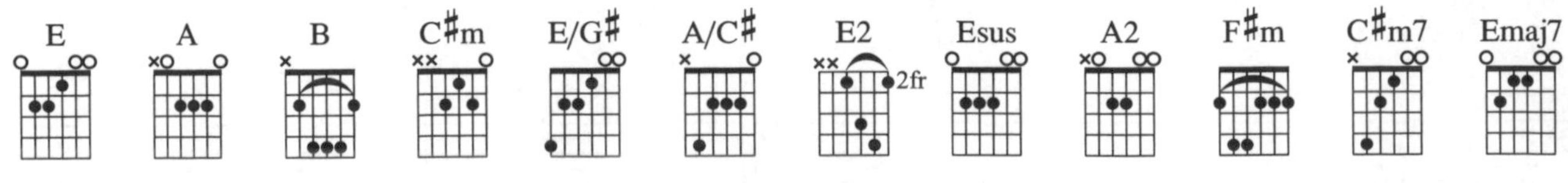

Forever

Words and Music by
CHRIS TOMLIN

♩ = 120
A
1. Give thanks to the Lord our God and King; His
2. With a might - y hand and out - stretched arm; His
3. From the ris - ing to the set - ting sun His
love en - dures for - ev - er.
love en - dures for - ev - er.
love en - dures for - ev - er. And by the
D
For He is good, He is a - bove all things; His
For the life that's been re - born; His
grace of God we will car - ry on; His
A
love en - dures for - ev - er. Sing
love en - dures for - ev - er.
love en - dures for - ev - er.

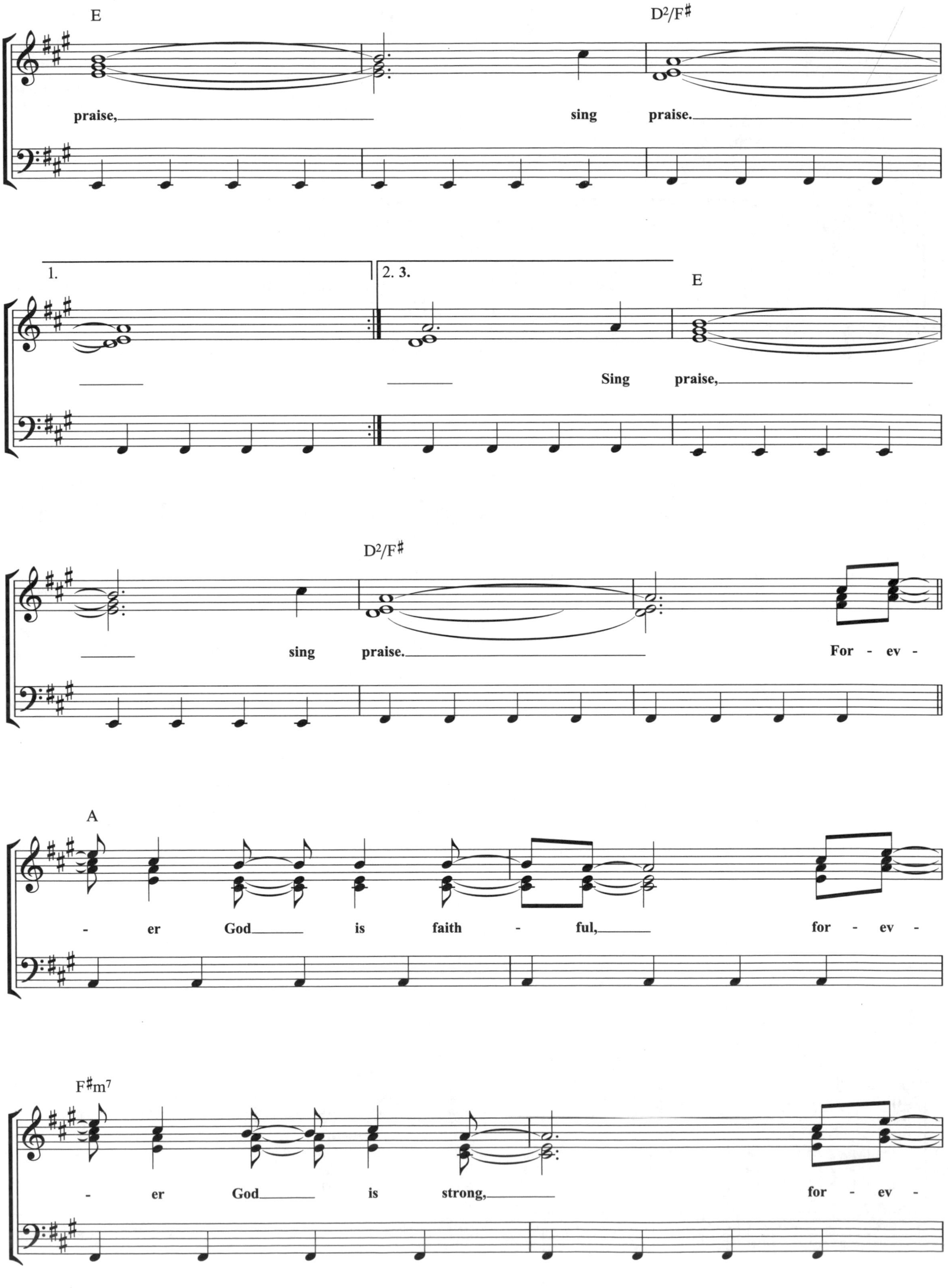
E
D2/F#
praise, sing praise.
1.
2. 3.
E
Sing praise,
D2/F#
sing praise. For - ev -
A
- er God is faith - ful, for - ev -
F#m7
- er God is strong, for - ev -

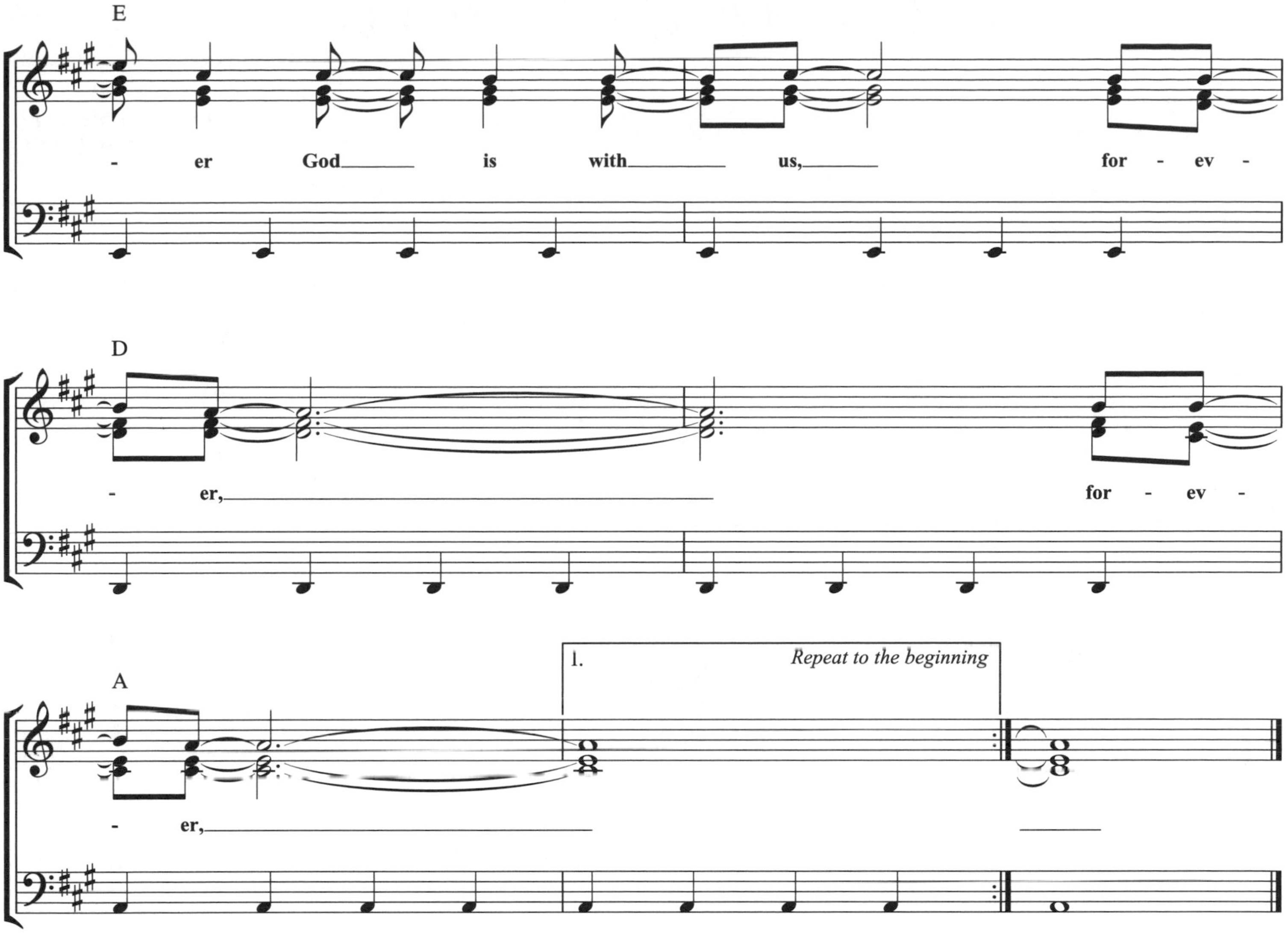
E
- er God is with us, for - ev -
D
- er, for - ev -
A
- er,
1.
Repeat to the beginning

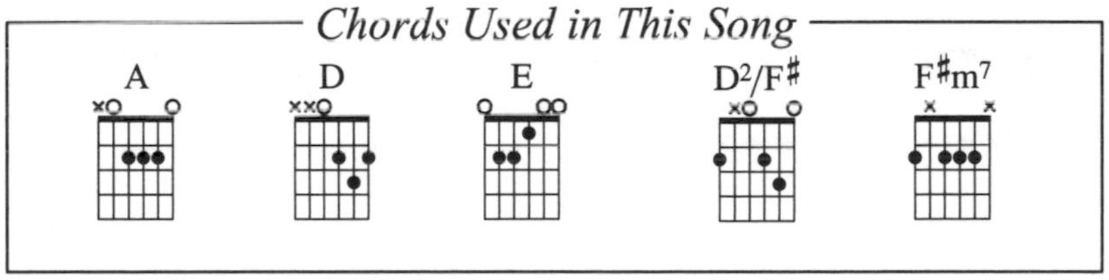
Chords Used in This Song
A
D
E
D2/F#
F#m7

Give Us Clean Hands

Words and Music by
CHARLIE HALL

Capo 1 (G)
♩ = 78
Keyboard
(Guitar)
A♭ (G)
E♭ (D)
A♭/C (G/B)
We bow our hearts, we bend our knees;
D♭ (C)
A♭ (G)
D♭/E♭ (C/D)
Oh Spir - it, come make us hum - ble.
A♭ (G)
E♭ (D)
A♭/C (G/B)
We turn our eyes from e - vil things;
D♭ (C)
Oh Lord, we cast down our i - dols. Give us clean__ hands,__

A♭ (G)
E♭ (D)
give us pure hearts; let us
A♭ (G)
D♭ (C)
not lift our souls to an - oth - er. Give us clean hands,
A♭ (G)
E♭ (D)
give us pure hearts; let us
Fm (Em)
E♭ (D)
A♭ (G)
not lift our souls to an - oth - er. And O God, let us be
E♭ (D)
a gen - er - a - tion that seeks, that seeks Your face,

Fm (Em)
E♭ (D)
A♭ (G)
__ O__ God__ of Ja - cob.__ And O God, let us be__
E♭ (D)
__ a gen - er - a - tion that seeks,__ that seeks Your face,__
Fm (Em)
E♭ (D)
D♭ (C)
__ O__ God__ of Ja - cob.__
A♭ (G)

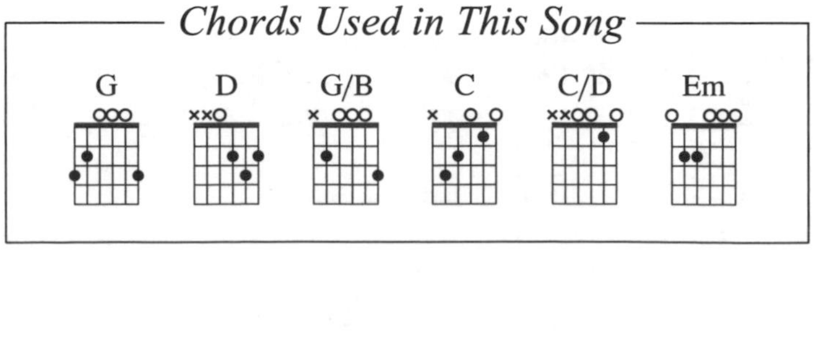

Chords Used in This Song
G
D
G/B
C
C/D
Em

Glory
(God, You Are My God)

Words and Music by
JOHNNY PARKS

♩ = 138
D
E
1. God, You are my God; there's
2. Death is o - ver - come, for -
G
A
no one else like You. You
giv - en is my sin.
D
E
glad - ly gave Your blood to
Heav - en is my home; You've
G
C
A
bring me back to You.
wel - comed me in.

D
E
I will sing Your praise,
I can't wait to hear the
G
A
I will lift Your name, I'll
saints join in one song, as we
D
E
glad - ly give You all to
praise the lov - ing Son who's
G
A
see Your king - dom reign. And I won't
giv - en us His all.
G
D/F♯
be a - shamed when I lift up Your name to let all

Em7
Asus
the world see. You are the King. And I won't
G
D/F♯
be a - shamed when I lift up Your name to all the
Em7
Asus
world to see You are the King.
D
We give You glo - ry,
E
G
glo - ry to You.

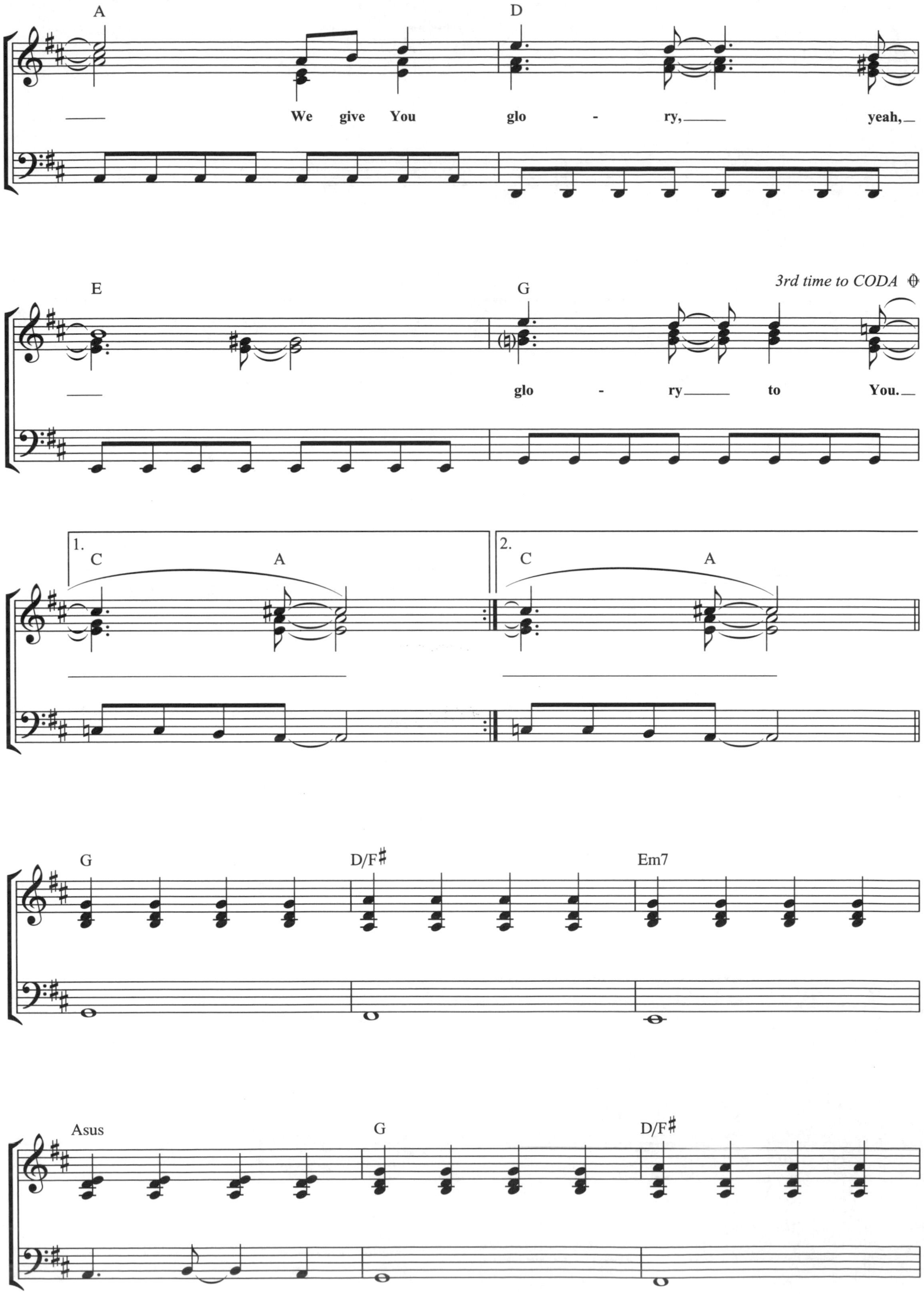
A
D
We give You glo - ry,
yeah,
E
G
3rd time to CODA
glo - ry to You.
1.
C
A
2.
C
A
G
D/F♯
Em7
Asus
G
D/F♯

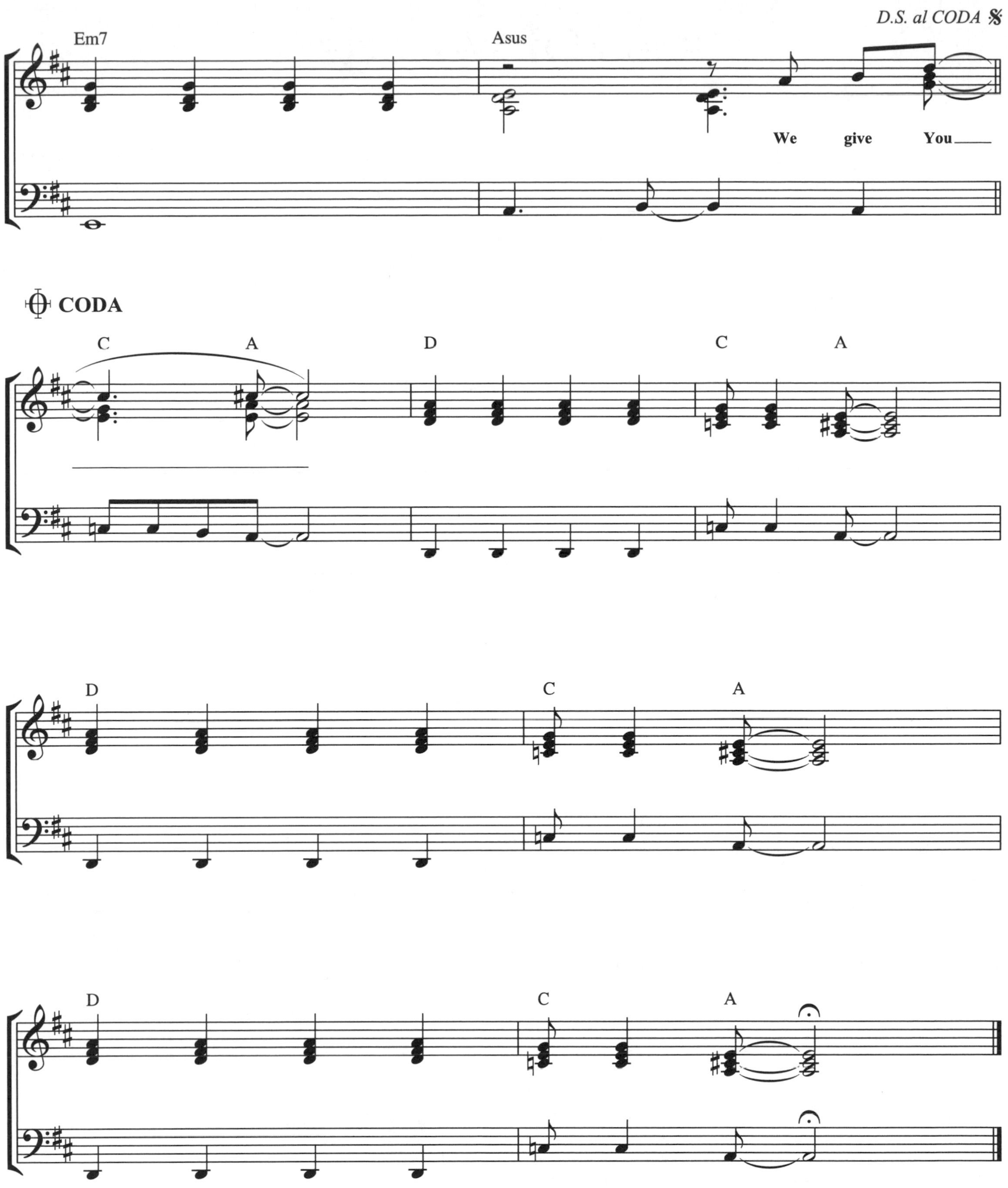
D.S. al CODA
Em7
Asus
We give You
CODA
C
A
D
C
A
D
C
A
D
C
A

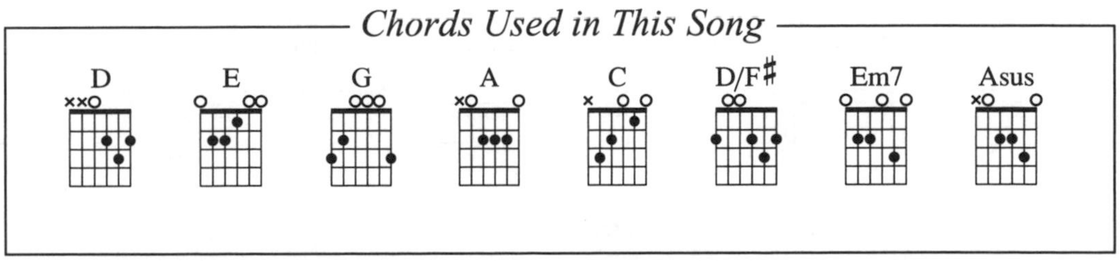
Chords Used in This Song
D
E
G
A
C
D/F♯
Em7
Asus

God Of Wonders

Words and Music by
MARC BYRD and
STEVE HINDALONG

Capo 1 (A)

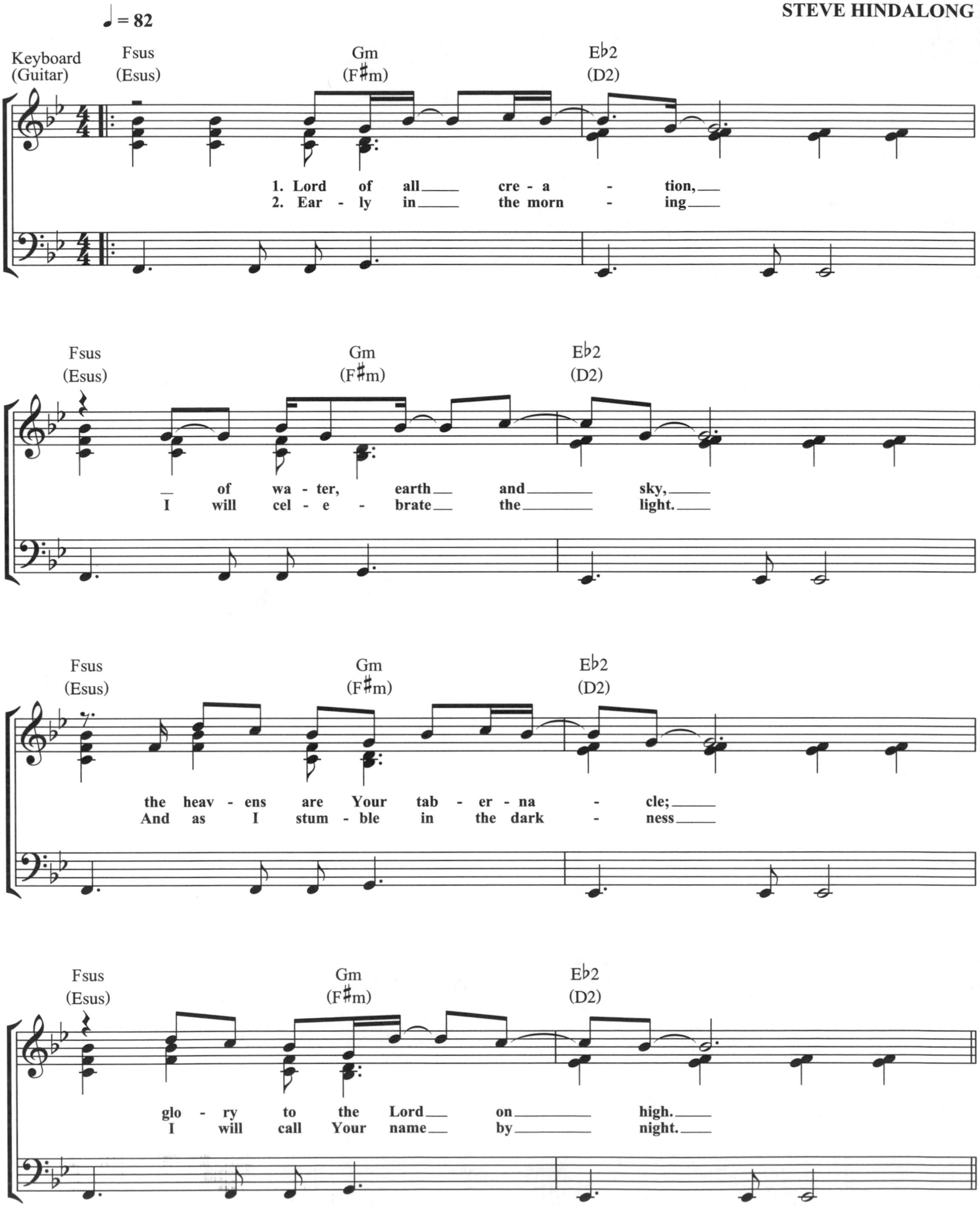
♩ = 82
Keyboard
(Guitar)
Fsus
(Esus)
Gm
(F♯m)
E♭2
(D2)
1. Lord of all ___ cre - a - tion, ___
2. Ear - ly in ___ the morn - ing ___
Fsus
(Esus)
Gm
(F♯m)
E♭2
(D2)
___ of wa - ter, earth ___ and ___ sky, ___
I will cel - e - brate ___ the ___ light. ___
Fsus
(Esus)
Gm
(F♯m)
E♭2
(D2)
the heav - ens are Your tab - er - na - cle; ___
And as I stum - ble in the dark - ness ___
Fsus
(Esus)
Gm
(F♯m)
E♭2
(D2)
glo - ry to the Lord ___ on ___ high. ___
I will call Your name ___ by ___ night. ___

B♭
(A)
God of won - ders be - yond our gal - ax - y,
F
(E)
You are
Cm7
(Bm7)
ho - ly,
E♭2
(D2)
ho - ly;
the
B♭
(A)
u - ni - verse de - clares Your maj - es - ty.
F
(E)
You are
Cm7
(Bm7)
ho - ly,
E♭2
(D2)
ho - ly;
Lord of heav - en and earth,

1.
Lord of heav - en and earth.
Fsus (Esus)
Gm (F♯m)
E♭2 (D2)
Fsus (Esus)
Gm (F♯m)
E♭2 (D2)
2.
Cm7 (Bm7)
Hal - le - lu - jah! to the
E♭2 (D2)
Cm7 (Bm7)
Lord of heav - en and earth. Hal - le - lu - jah! to the

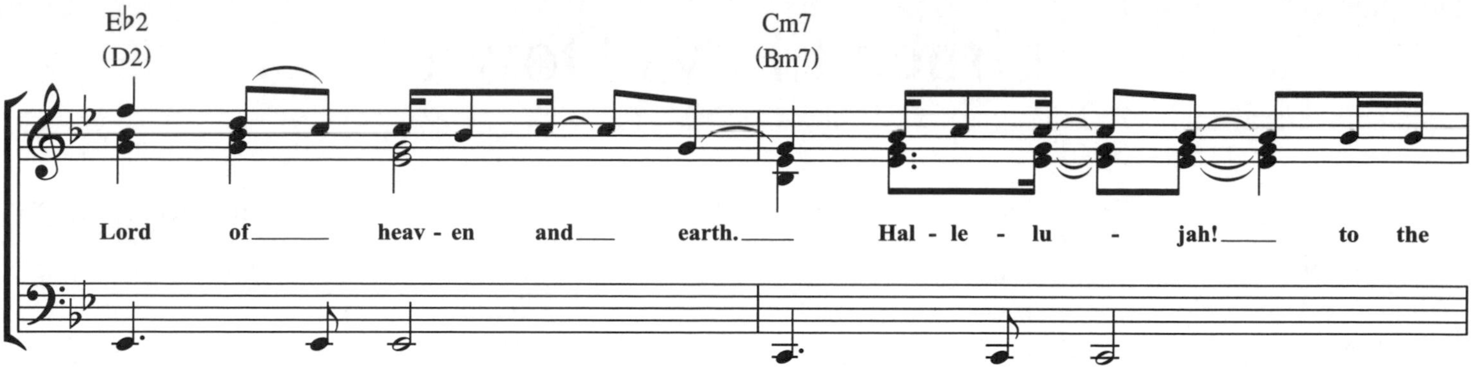
E♭2
(D2)
Cm7
(Bm7)
Lord of heav - en and earth. Hal - le - lu - jah! to the

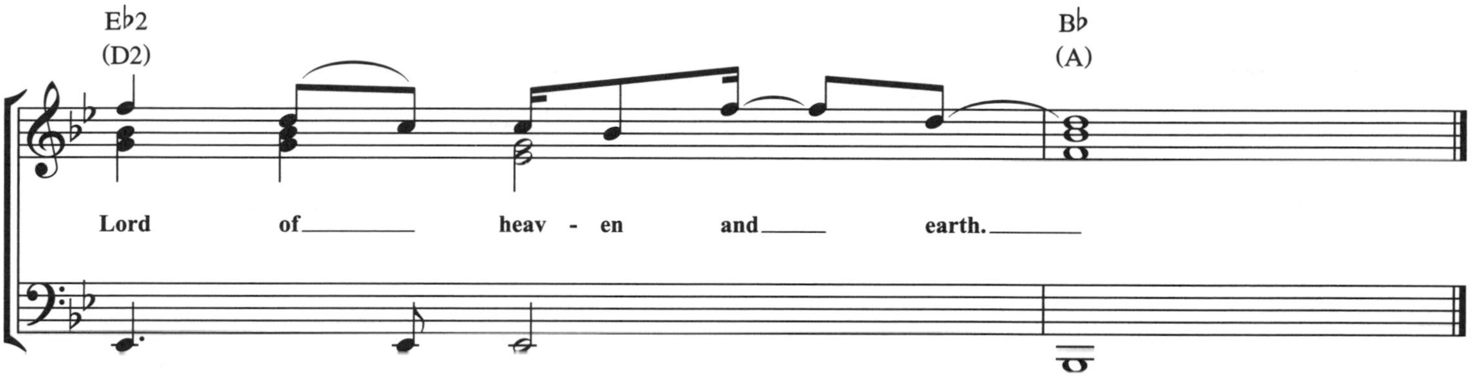
E♭2
(D2)
B♭
(A)
Lord of heav - en and earth.

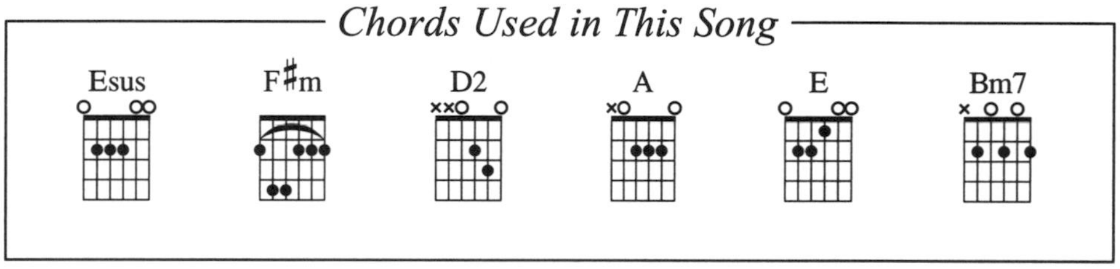
Chords Used in This Song
Esus
F♯m
D2
A
E
Bm7

Grace Flows Down

Words and Music by
DAVID BELL, LOUIE GIGLIO
and ROD PADGETT

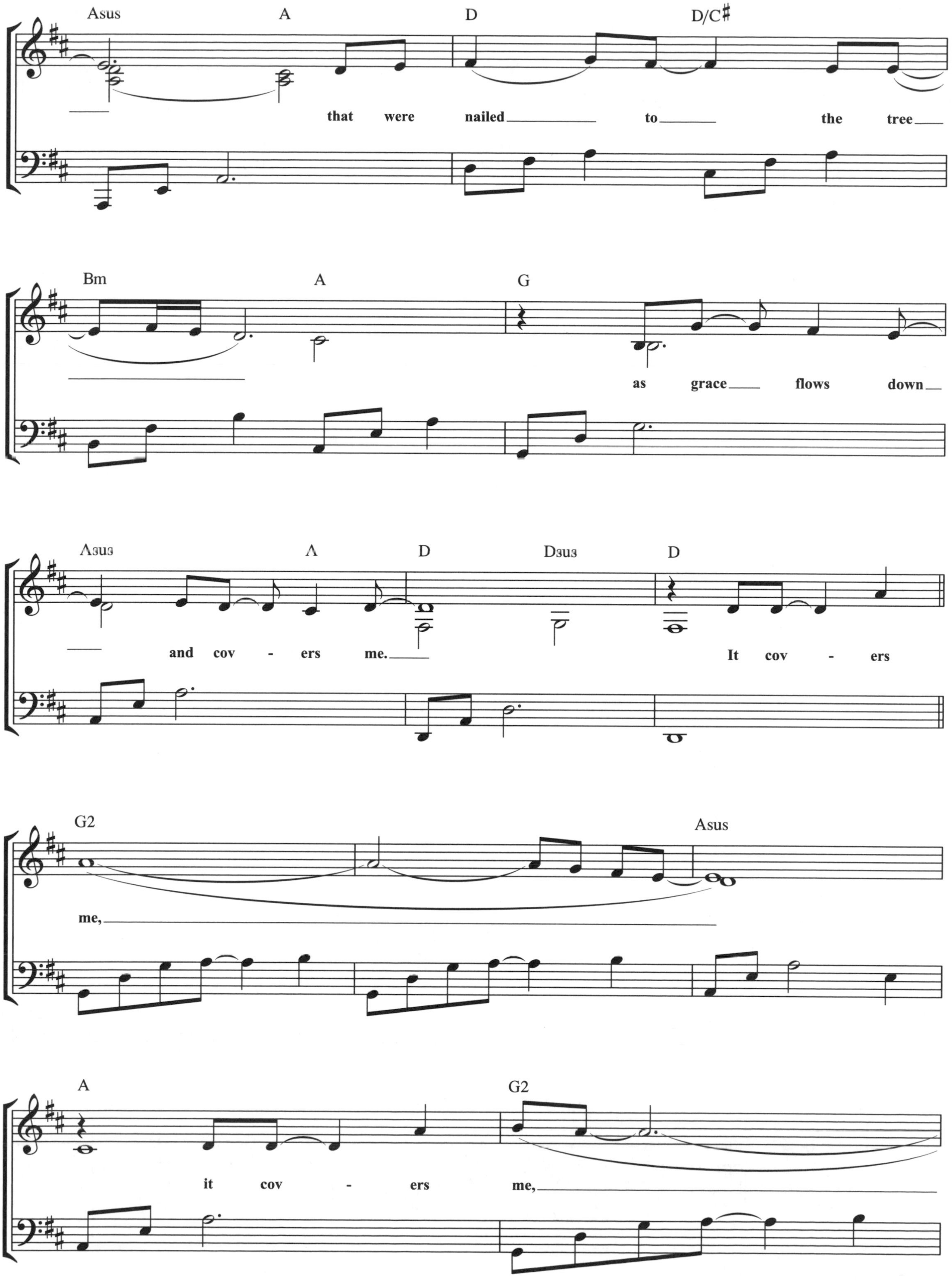
Asus
A
D
D/C♯
that were nailed to the tree
Bm
A
G
as grace flows down
Asus
A
D
Dsus
D
and cov - ers me.
It cov - ers
G2
Asus
me,
A
G2
it cov - ers me,

Chords Used in This Song

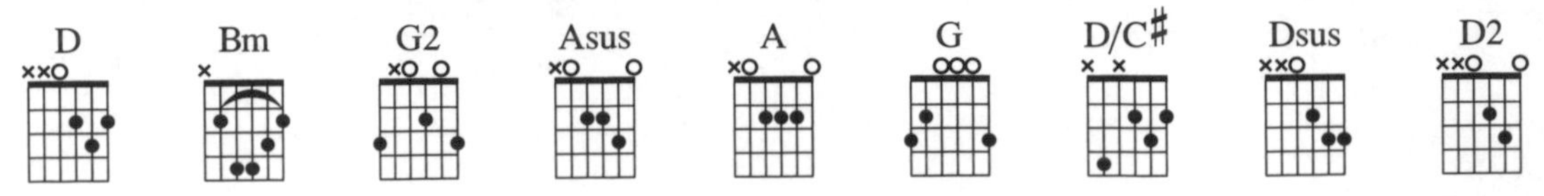

Great Is The Lord

Words and Music by
MICHAEL W. SMITH
and DEBORAH D. SMITH

Moderately fast, ♩. = 62

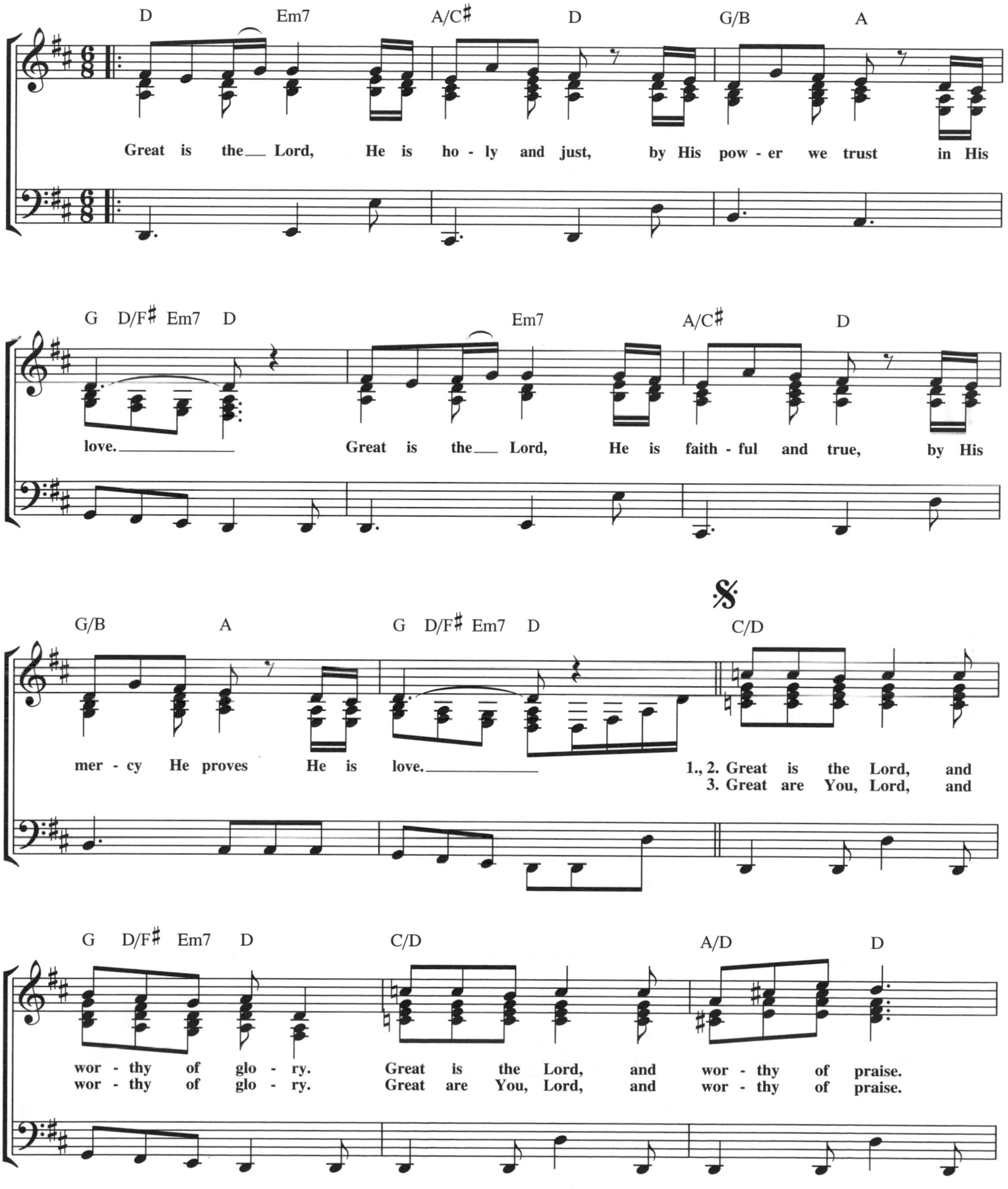
D Em7 A/C♯ D G/B A
Great is the Lord, He is ho - ly and just, by His pow - er we trust in His
G D/F♯ Em7 D Em7 A/C♯ D
love. Great is the Lord, He is faith - ful and true, by His
G/B A G D/F♯ Em7 D C/D
mer - cy He proves He is love.
1., 2. Great is the Lord, and
3. Great are You, Lord, and
G D/F♯ Em7 D C/D A/D D
wor - thy of glo - ry. Great is the Lord, and wor - thy of praise.
wor - thy of glo - ry. Great are You, Lord, and wor - thy of praise.

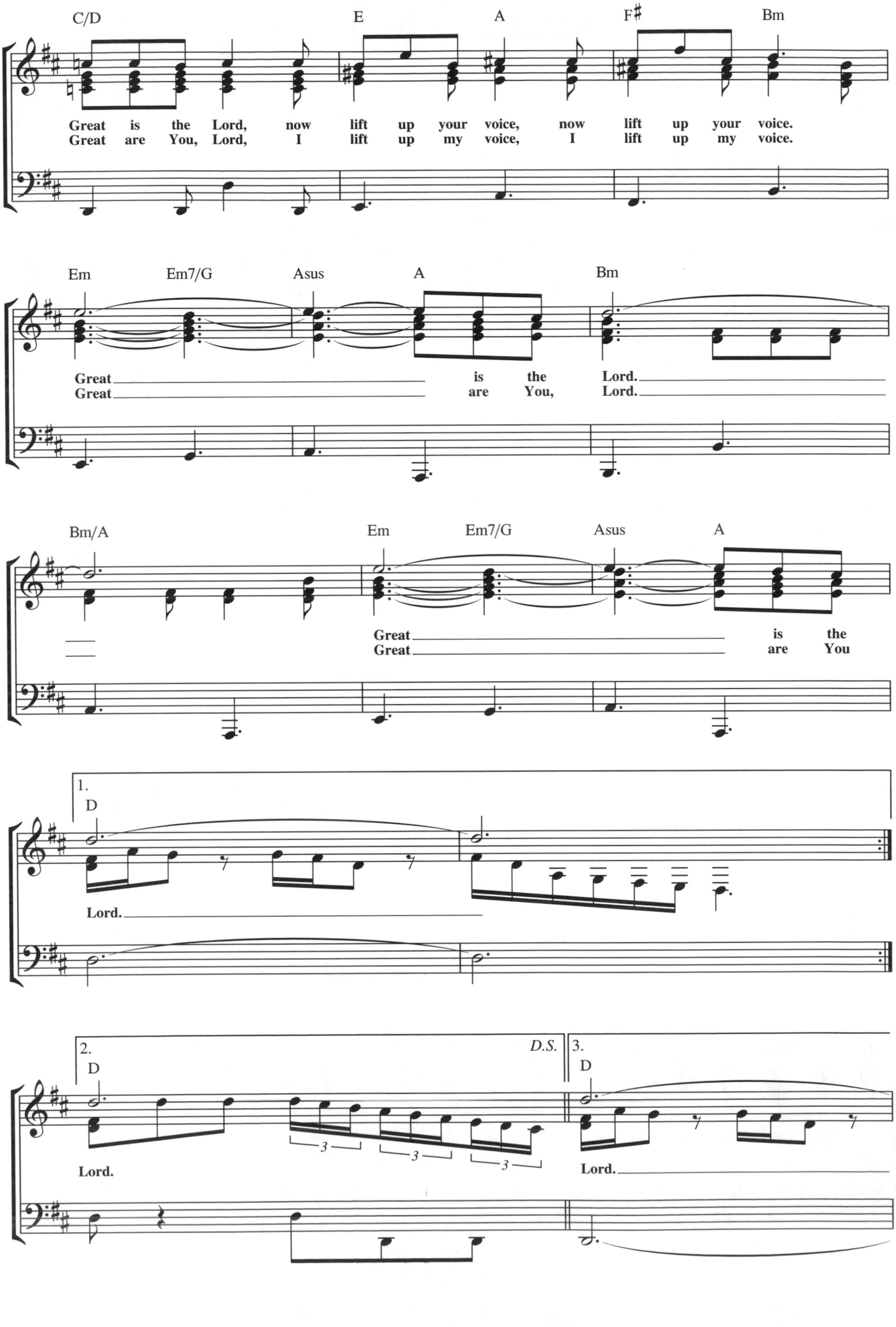
C/D E A F♯ Bm
Great is the Lord, now lift up your voice, now lift up your voice.
Great are You, Lord, I lift up my voice, I lift up my voice.
Em Em7/G Asus A Bm
Great is the Lord.
Great are You, Lord.
Bm/A Em Em7/G Asus A
Great is the
Great are You
1.
D
Lord.
2.
D
D.S.
3.
D
Lord.
3
3
3
Lord.

B♭/D
Great are you,
Lord.
Great are you,
G/D
Lord.
Great are you,
Lord.
D A D A
D A D A D

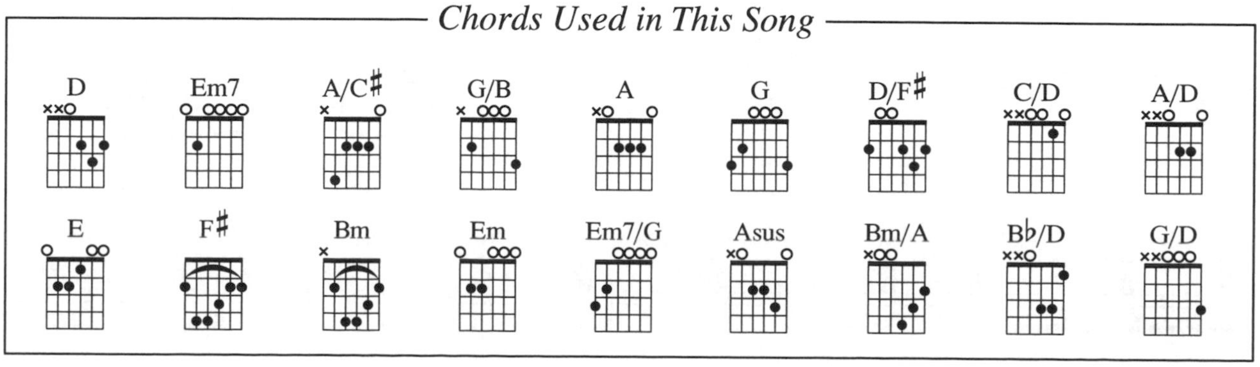
Chords Used in This Song
D
Em7
A/C♯
G/B
A
G
D/F♯
C/D
A/D
E
F♯
Bm
Em
Em7/G
Asus
Bm/A
B♭/D
G/D

He Reigns

Words and Music by
PETER FURLER
and STEVE TAYLOR

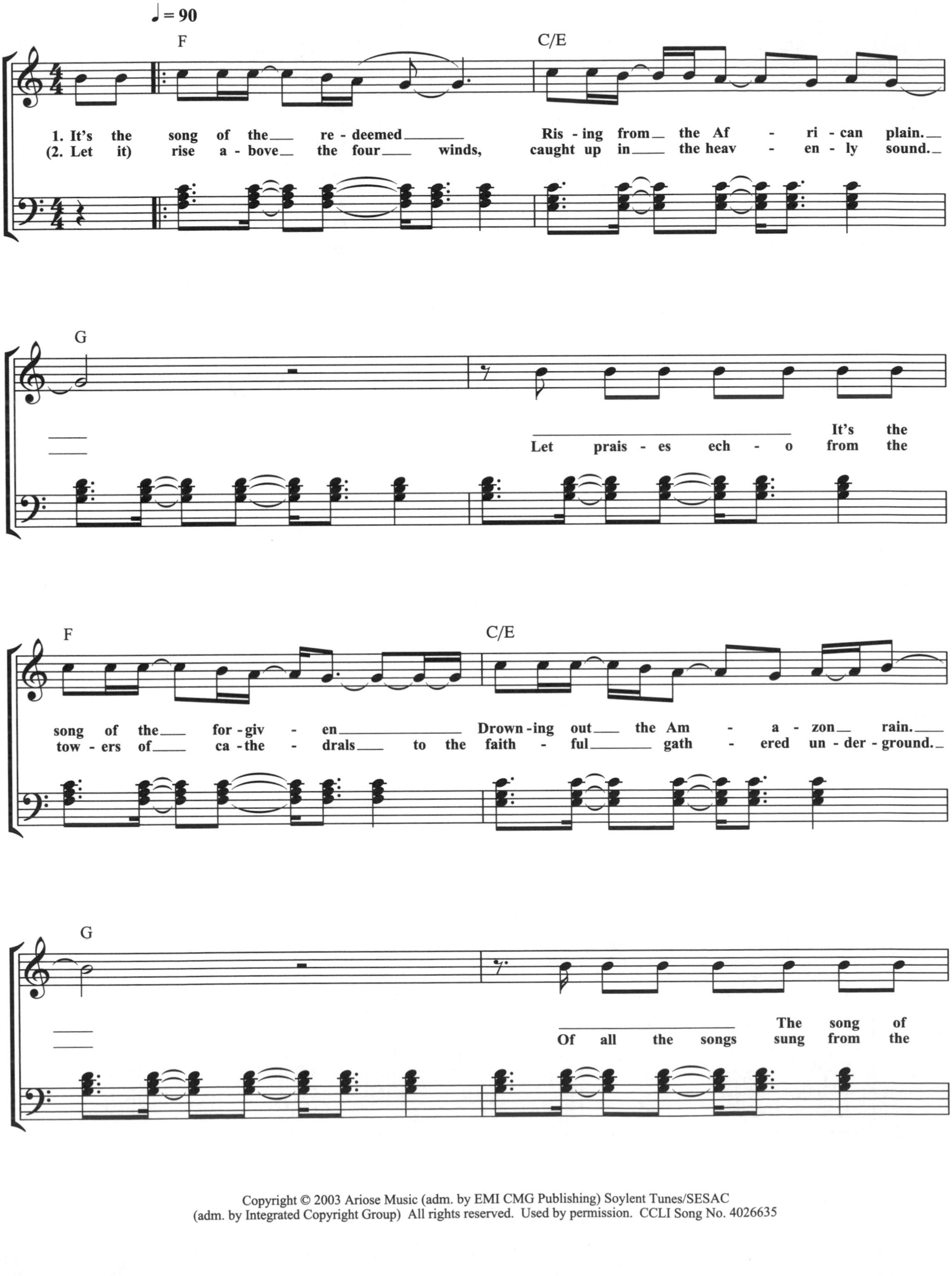
♩ = 90
F
C/E
1. It's the song of the re - deemed Ris - ing from the Af - ri - can plain.
(2. Let it) rise a - bove the four winds, caught up in the heav - en - ly sound.
G
It's the
Let prais - es ech - o from the
F
C/E
song of the for - giv - en Drown - ing out the Am - a - zon rain.
tow - ers of ca - the - drals to the faith - ful gath - ered un - der - ground.
G
The song of
Of all the songs sung from the

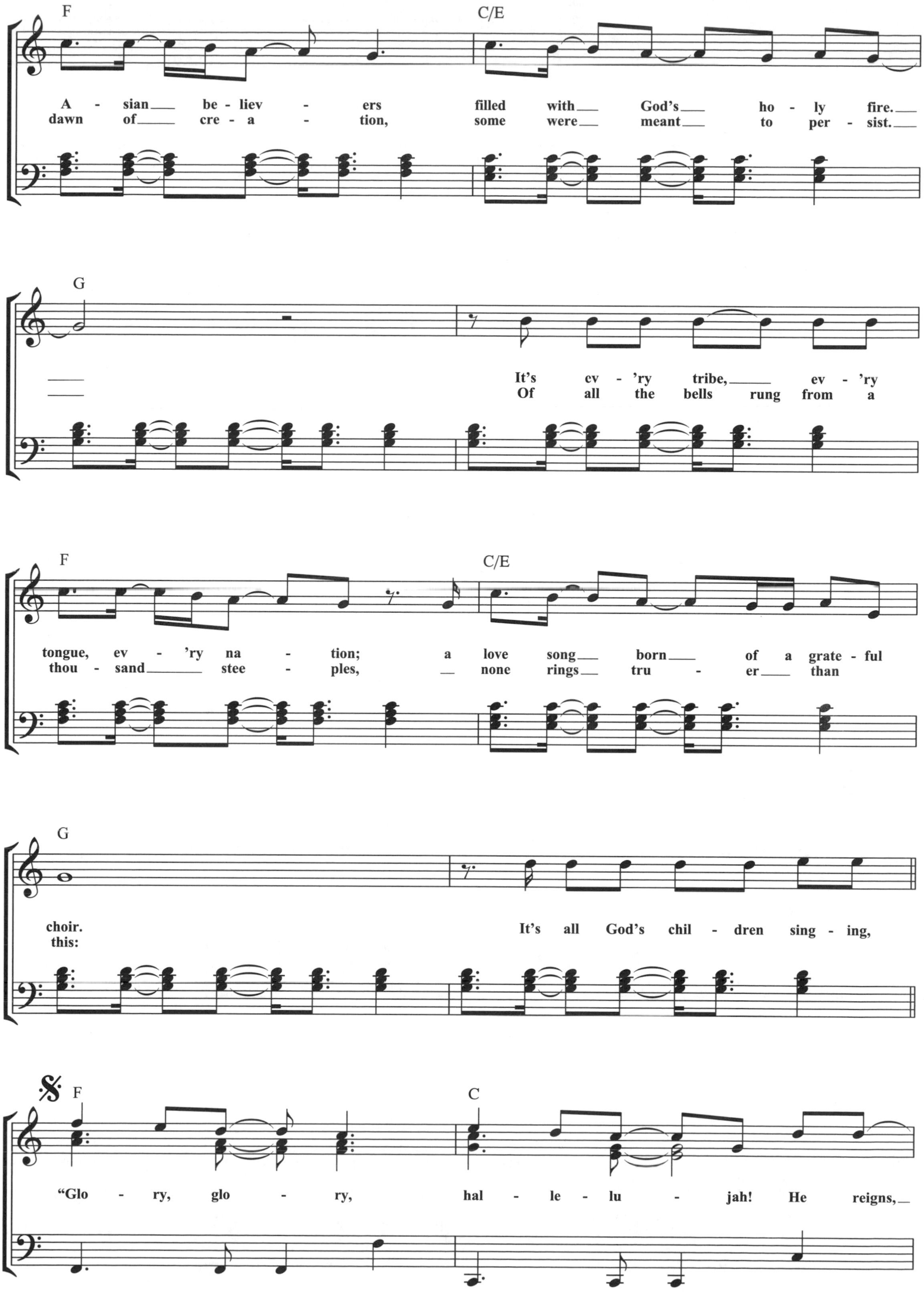
F
C/E
A - sian be - liev - ers filled with God's ho - ly fire.
dawn of cre - a - tion, some were meant to per - sist.
G
It's ev - 'ry tribe, ev - 'ry
Of all the bells rung from a
F
C/E
tongue, ev - 'ry na - tion; a love song born of a grate - ful
thou - sand stee - ples, none rings tru - er than
G
choir.
this:
It's all God's chil - dren sing - ing,
F
C
"Glo - ry, glo - ry, hal - le - lu - jah! He reigns,

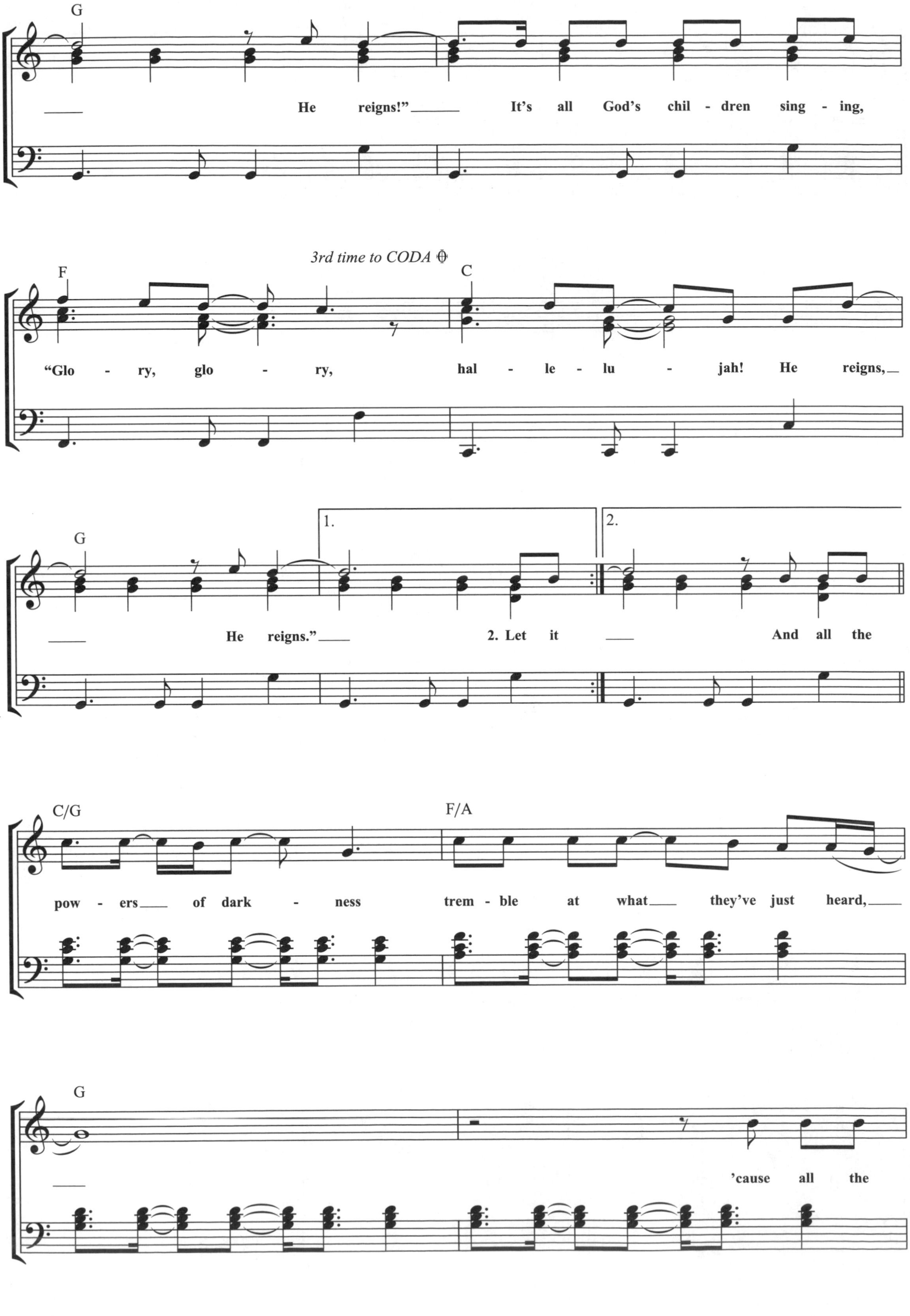
G
He reigns!" It's all God's chil - dren sing - ing,
3rd time to CODA
F
C
"Glo - ry, glo - ry, hal - le - lu - jah! He reigns,
G
1.
2.
He reigns." 2. Let it And all the
C/G
F/A
pow - ers of dark - ness trem - ble at what they've just heard,
G
'cause all the

C/G
F/A
pow - ers of dark - ness can't drown out a sin - gle
G
D.S. al CODA
word. It's all God's chil - dren sing - ing,
CODA
C
G
hal - le - lu - jah! He reigns,

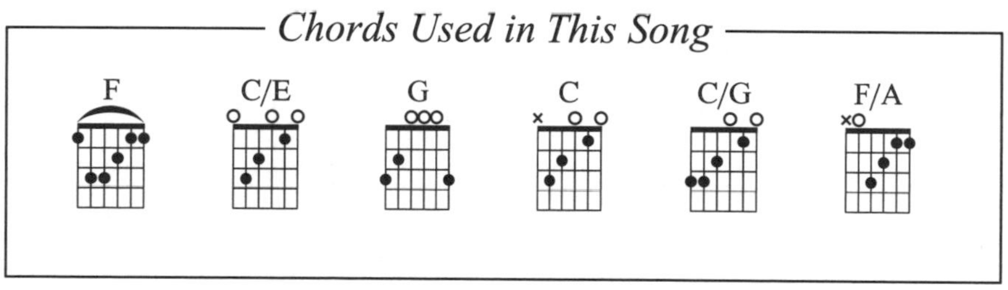
Chords Used in This Song
F
C/E
G
C
C/G
F/A

Healing Rain

Words and Music by
MARTIN SMITH
MICHAEL W. SMITH
and MATT BRONLEEWE

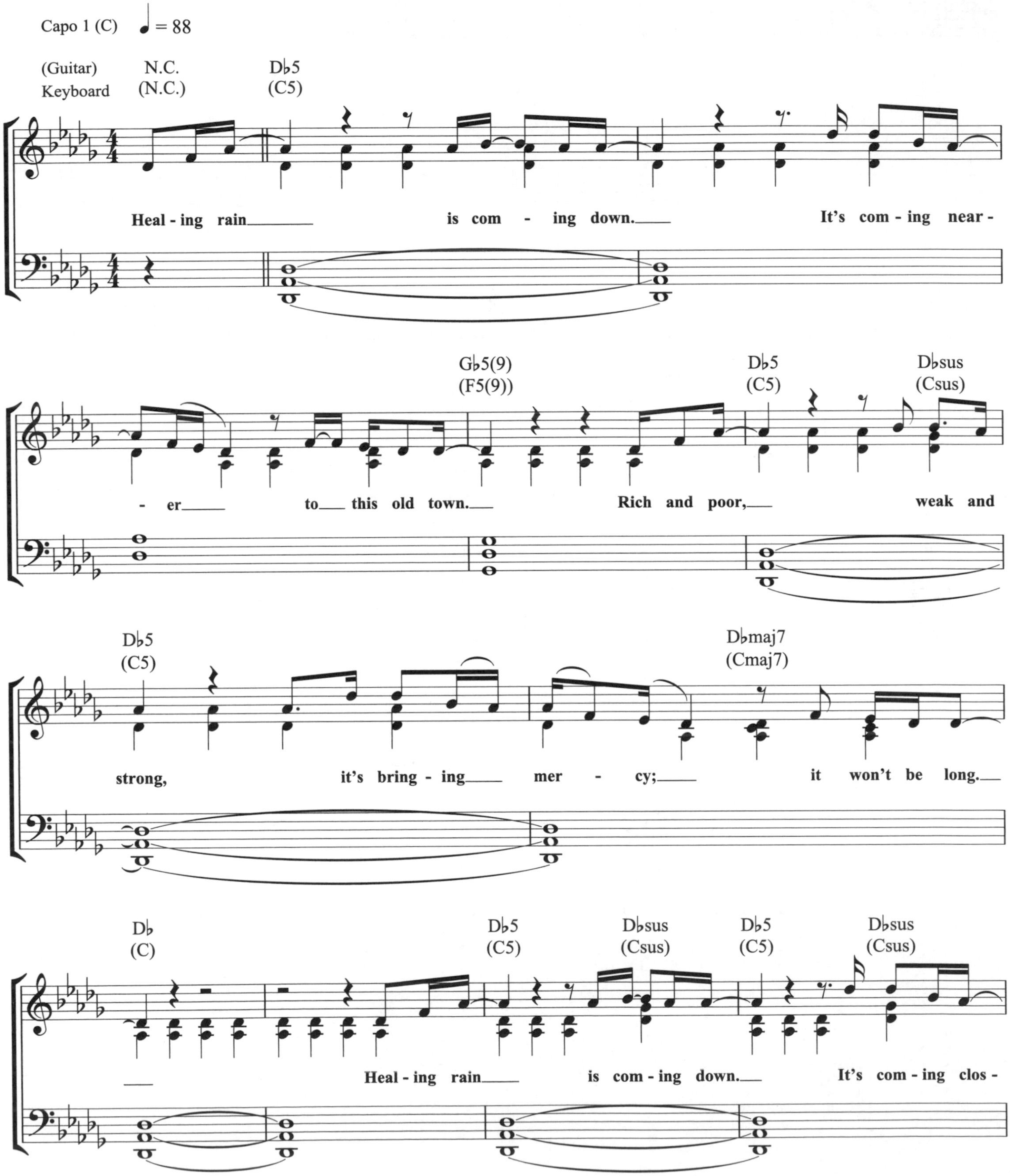
Capo 1 (C) ♩ = 88
(Guitar)
Keyboard
N.C.
(N.C.)
D♭5
(C5)
Heal - ing rain is com - ing down. It's com - ing near -
G♭5(9)
(F5(9))
D♭5
(C5)
D♭sus
(Csus)
- er to this old town. Rich and poor, weak and
D♭5
(C5)
D♭maj7
(Cmaj7)
strong, it's bring - ing mer - cy; it won't be long.
D♭
(C)
D♭5
(C5)
D♭sus
(Csus)
D♭5
(C5)
D♭sus
(Csus)
Heal - ing rain is com - ing down. It's com - ing clos -

D♭5 (C5) D♭maj7 (Cmaj7) G♭5(9) (F5(9)) D♭5 (C5) D♭sus (Csus)
- er___ to the lost and found.___ Tears of joy___ and tears of
D♭5 (C5) D♭sus (Csus) D♭5 (C5) D♭maj7 (Cmaj7) D♭5 (C5) D♭/F (C/E)
shame are washed for - ev - er___ in Je - sus' name.___ Heal - ing rain,___
A♭ (G) B♭m (Am)
___ it comes with fire. So let it fall___
G♭ (F) D♭ (C) D♭/F (C/E)
___ and take___ us high - er. The heal - ing rain,___
A♭ (G) B♭m (Am) G♭ (F)
2nd time to CODA
___ I'm not___ a - fraid to be washed_

D♭/A♭ (C/G) A♭ (G) D♭sus (Csus)
in heav - en's rain. Lift your
D♭maj7/F (Cmaj7/E) G♭2 (F2) D♭5 (C5) G♭2 (F2) D♭ (C) D♭maj7 (Cmaj7)
heads, let us re - turn to the mer - cy seat where time be - gan.
G♭5(9) (F5(9)) D♭5 (C5) G♭2 (F2) D♭5 (C5) G♭ (F)
And in your eyes I see the pain. Come soak this
D♭ (C) D♭maj7 (Cmaj7) D♭ (C) D♭/F (C/E)
dry heart with heal - ing rain. And on - ly You,
A♭ (G) B♭m (Am) G♭ (F)
the Son of Man, can take a lep - er and let him

D♭ (C) D♭/F (C/E) A♭ (G) B♭m (Am) G♭ (F)
— stand. So lift your hands, — they can — be — held by — some - one —
D♭/A♭ (C/G) A♭ (G) D♭ (C) D♭/F (C/E)
D.S. al CODA
— great - er, — the great — I AM. Heal - ing rain, —
CODA
D♭/A♭ (C/G) A♭ (G) B♭m (Am) G♭ (F) D♭/A♭ (C/G) A♭ (G)
— in heav - en's rain, — to be washed — in — heav - en's rain. —
D♭ (C) A♭ (G) B♭m (Am)
G♭ (F) D♭ (C) A♭ (G)
Heal - ing rain is fall - ing down. — Heal - ing rain is fall - ing down. —

Bbm (Am)
I'm not a - fraid.
Gb (F)
I'm not a - fraid.
Db/F (C/E)
Heal - ing rain is fall - ing down.
Ab (G)
Heal - ing rain is fall - ing down.
Bbm (Am)
I'm not a - fraid.
Gb (F)
I'm not a - fraid.
Db/F (C/E)
Heal - ing rain is fall - ing down.
Gb (F)
Ab (G)
Heal - ing rain is fall - ing down.
Bbm (Am)
I'm not a - fraid.
Gb/Bb (F/A)
I'm not a - fraid.
Gb (F)

D♭
(C)
B♭m
(Am)
A♭
(G)
Heal-ing rain_ is fall - ing down. Heal-ing rain_ is fall - ing down.___
D♭/F
(C/E)
G♭
(F)
I'm not a-fraid.___ I'm not a-fraid.___
D♭
(C)
A♭
(G)
Heal-ing rain_ is fall - ing down.__ Heal-ing rain_ is fall - ing down.
B♭m
(Am)
G♭
(F)
D♭
(C)
I'm not a-fraid._ I'm not a-fraid.__ I'm not a-fraid.____

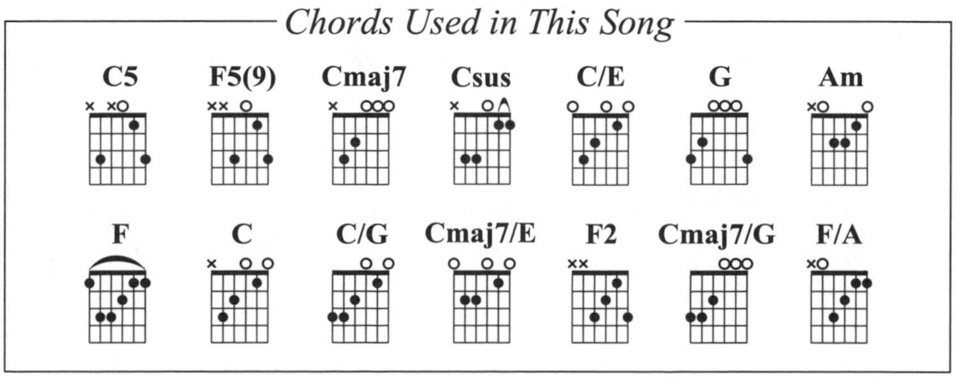
Chords Used in This Song
C5
F5(9)
Cmaj7
Csus
C/E
G
Am
F
C
C/G
Cmaj7/E
F2
Cmaj7/G
F/A

Here I Am to Worship

Words and Music by
TIM HUGHES

Capo 1 (E)

♩ = 84
Keyboard
(Guitar)
F (E) C (B) Gm7 (F♯m7)
1. Light of the World, You stepped down in - to dark - ness,
2. King of all days, oh so high - ly ex - al - ted,
F (E) C (B) B♭ (A)
o - pened my eyes, let me see.
glo - rious in heav - en a - bove.
F (E) C (B) Gm7 (F♯m7)
Beau - ty that made this heart a - dore You,
Hum - bly You came to the Earth You cre - at - ed,
F (E) C (B) B♭ (A)
hope of a life spent with You.
all for love's sake be - came poor.

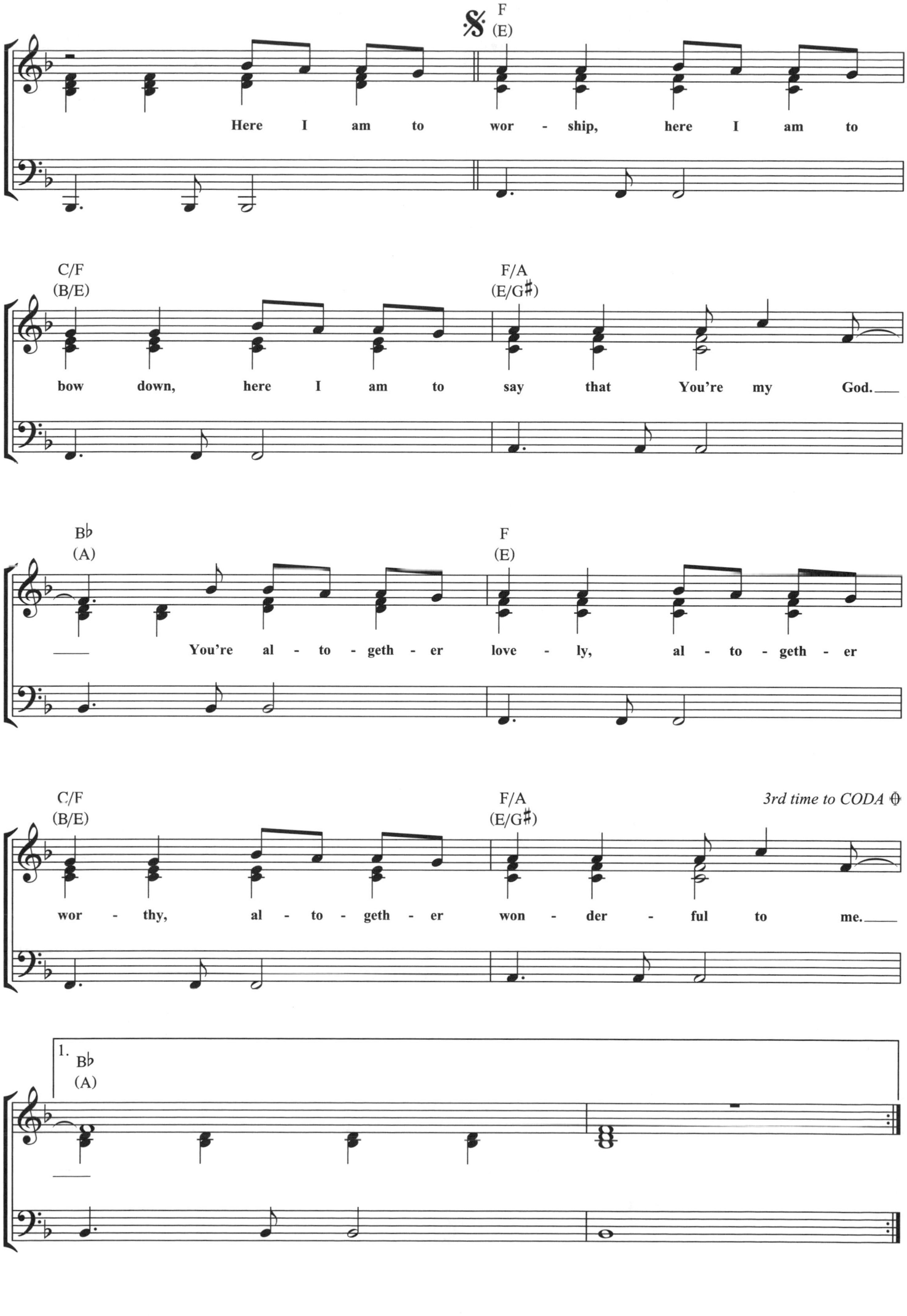
F
(E)
Here I am to wor - ship, here I am to
C/F
(B/E)
bow down, here I am to
F/A
(E/G♯)
say that You're my God.
B♭
(A)
You're al - to - geth - er
F
(E)
love - ly, al - to - geth - er
C/F
(B/E)
wor - thy, al - to - geth - er
F/A
(E/G♯)
won - der - ful to me.
3rd time to CODA
1.
B♭
(A)

2. B♭ (A) C (B) F/A (E/G♯)
And I'll nev - er know how much
B♭ (A) C (B) F/A (E/G♯)
it cost to see my sin up - on
1. B♭ (A) 2. B♭ (A)
that cross. I'll nev - that cross. I'll nev -
C/E (B/D♯) F (E) B♭2 (A2)
- er know how much it cost to see
C/E (B/D♯) F (E) 1. B♭2 (A2)
my sin up - on that cross. I'll nev -

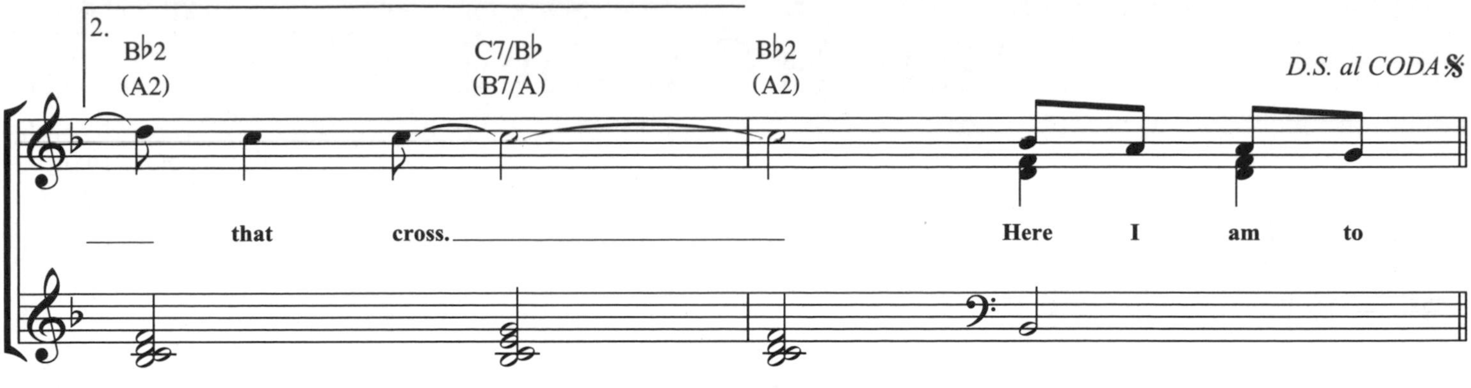
2.
B♭2
(A2)
C7/B♭
(B7/A)
B♭2
(A2)
D.S. al CODA
that
cross.
Here
I
am
to

CODA
B♭2
(A2)

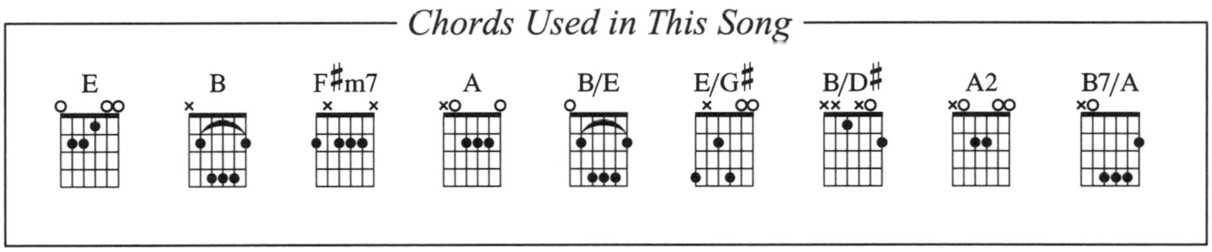
Chords Used in This Song
E
B
F♯m7
A
B/E
E/G♯
B/D♯
A2
B7/A

Here Is Our King

Words and Music by
DAVID CROWDER

♩ = 132
Capo 3 (G)
Keyboard (Guitar)
B♭/D (G/B) E♭2 (C2) B♭/D (G/B)
From wher - ev - er spring ar - rives to heal the ground
E♭2 (C2) B♭/D (G/B) E♭2 (C2)
From wher - ev - er search - ing comes,
B♭/D (G/B) E♭2 (C2) B♭/D (G/B)
the look it - self,
a trace of what
E♭2 (C2) B♭/D (G/B) E♭2 (C2)
we're look - ing for
so be qui - et now
and

B♭/D (G/B) E♭2 (C2) F (D)
wait. The o - cean
E♭2 (C2) F (D) E♭2 (C2)
is grow - ing,
F (D) E♭2 (C2)
the tide is com - ing in; here it is.
N.C. B♭ (G) B♭/D (G/B)
Here is our King, here is our Love, here is our
E♭2 (C2) B♭ (G)
God who's come to bring us back to Him. He is the One,

Bb/D (G/B)
Eb2 (C2)
He is Je - sus, Je - sus.
Bb/D (G/B)
Eb2 (C2)
Bb/D (G/B)
And what was said to the rose to make it un - fold
Eb2 (C2)
Bb/D (G/B)
Eb2 (C2)
was said to me here in my chest.
Bb/D (G/B)
Eb2 (C2)
Bb/D (G/B)
So be qui - et now and rest.
Eb2 (C2)
F (D)
Eb2 (C2)
The o - cean

F (D) Eb2 (C2) F (D)
is grow - ing, the tide is com -
Eb2 (C2) Bb (G)
- ing, here it is. Here is our King, {here / He} is our
Bb/D (G/B) Eb2 (C2)
Love, {here / He} is our God who's come to bring us back to Him.
Bb (G) Bb/D (G/B) 1. Eb2 (C2)
He is the One, He is Je - sus.
2. Eb2 (C2)
And He is our - sus, Je - sus, our

Gm7 (Em7) F/A (D/F♯) B♭ (G) Cm7 (Am7)
Maj - es - ty, fi -
B♭/D (G/B) E♭2 (C2) Gm7 (Em7) F/A (D/F♯)
nal - ly. Here. Here is our
B♭ (G) B♭/D (G/B) E♭2 (C2)
King, here is our Love, here is our God who's come to bring us back to Him.
B♭ (G) B♭/D (G/B) E♭2 (C2)
He is the One, He is Je - sus, He is Je -
B♭ (G) B♭/D (G/B)
- sus. And He is our King, He is our Love, He is our

Eb2
(C2)
Bb
(G)
God who's come to bring us back to Him. He is the One,
Bb/D
(G/B)
Eb2
(C2)
Gm7
(Em7)
He is Jesus, He is Jesus, our Maj -
F/A
(D/F#)
Bb
(G)
Eb2
(C2)
Gm7
(Em7)
es - ty, fi -
F/A
(D/F#)
Eb2
(C2)
Bb
(G)
nal - ly, You.

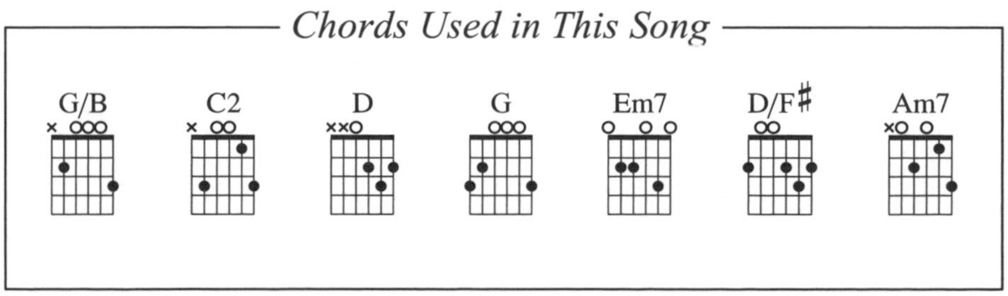
Chords Used in This Song
G/B
C2
D
G
Em7
D/F#
Am7

He Is Exalted

Words and Music by
TWILA PARIS

Capo 1 (G)
♩. = 60
Keyboard
(Guitar)
A♭ (G) D♭ (C)
He is ex - alt - ed, the King is ex - al - ted on high, and I will
B♭m (Am) E♭/G (D/F♯) A♭ (G)
praise Him. He is ex - al - ted, for - ev - er ex - al - ted and
B♭m7 (Am7) Cm7 (Bm7) D♭ (C) E♭/G (D/F♯) F (E)
I will praise His Name For
B♭m7 (Am7) A♭ (G) E♭/G (D/F♯) A♭ (G) D♭ (C) A♭/C (G/B)
He is the Lord, for - ev - er His truth shall reign.

2nd time, D.S. al CODA 𝄋
B♭m7 (Am7) A♭ (G) E♭/G (D/F♯) A♭ (G) D♭ (C) A♭/C (G/B)
Hea - ven and earth re - joice in His ho - ly Name.
3rd time to CODA 𝄌
B♭m7 (Am7) A♭ (G) E♭/G (D/F♯) A♭ (G)
He is ex - al - ted the King is ex - al - ted on high.
(He is ex - al - ted. He is ex - al - ted.)
D♭ (C)
𝄌 CODA
E♭/G (D/F♯) D♭ (C)
King is ex - al - ted on high.
A♭/C (G/B) D♭ (C)

Chords Used in This Song

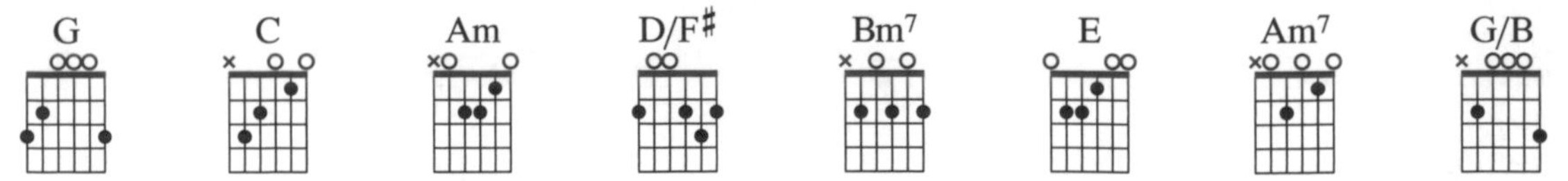

Holy Ground

Words and Music by
GERON DAVIS

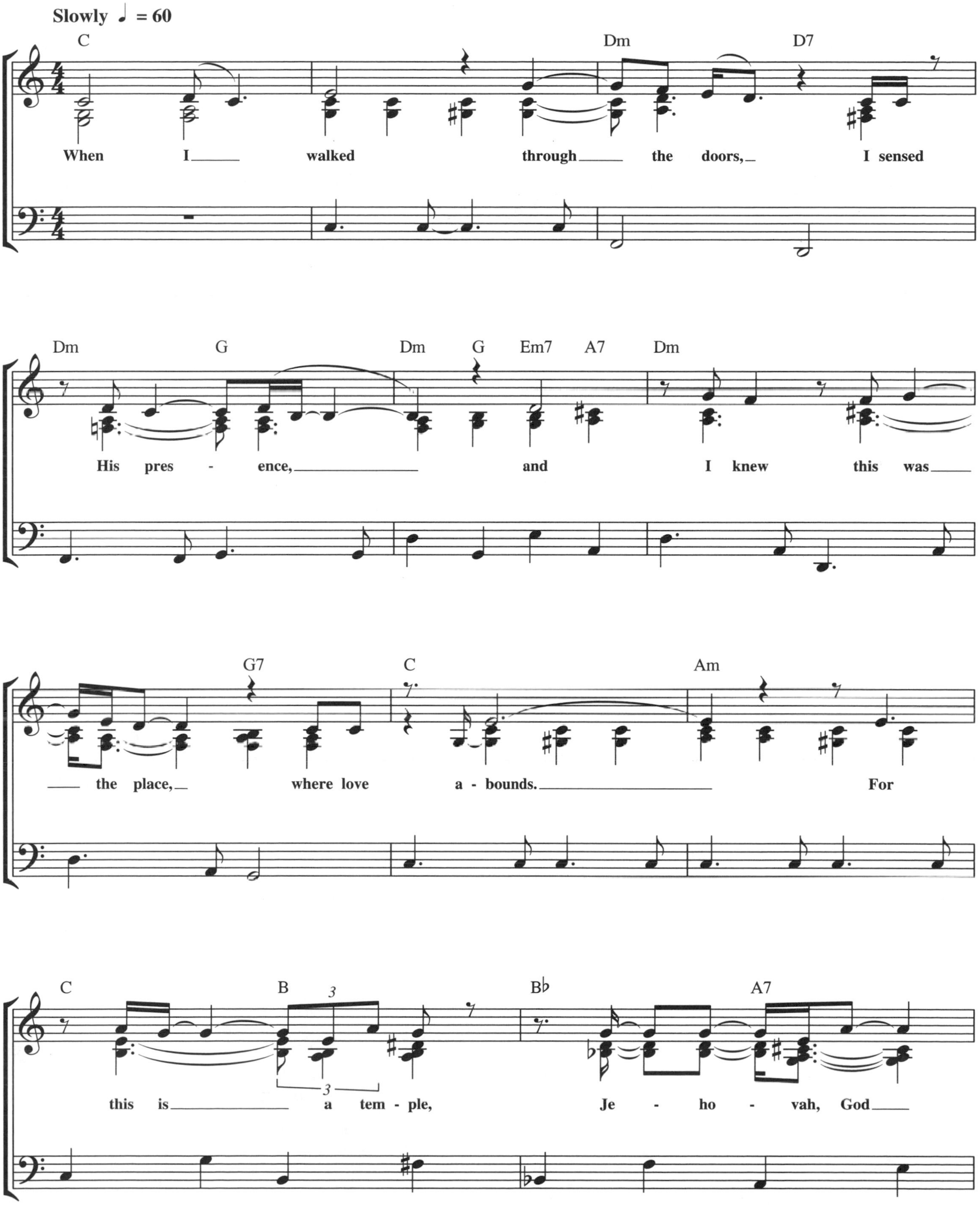
Slowly ♩ = 60
C Dm D7
When I walked through the doors, I sensed
Dm G Dm G Em7 A7 Dm
His pres - ence, and I knew this was
G7 C Am
the place, where love a - bounds. For
C B B♭ A7
this is a tem - ple, Je - ho - vah, God
3
3

Dm
Ab
a - bides here, and we are
C Am Dm G
standing in His presence on a holy
C G7 C
ground. We are stand - ing
Am
on a ho - ly ground, and
C A7
I know there are an - gels all

Dm Bb G7 C Am
a - round. Let us praise
G C F C Dm Am Fm/Ab
Je - sus now, for we
G A7 Dm7 G7 Ab
are stand - ing in His pres - ence on ho - ly ground.
F G7 C Am Ab
*
In His pres - ence I know there is joy be -
Dm7 G Dm G7 Em A7 Dm
yond all meas - ure. And at His feet sweet peace

*At this point, the recorded version modulates from C to D♭

G7 C G♭7
of mind can still be found.
F B♭ G7 C B
For when we have a need,
B♭ A7 Dm Em F
He is still the an - swer, oh, reach out and
C Am7 Dm G7 C
claim it. For we are stand - ing on ho - ly ground.
G7 C Dm C F
Lead vocal ad lib.: We are stand - ing on ho - ly

C F C Em
ground, and I know, and I know there're
A Dm B♭ G C
an - gels all a - round. Let us
Am Dm Gm C F C
praise Je - sus now,
Am Fm/A♭ C A7 Dm G7
for we are stand - ing in His pres - ence on ho - ly
C B♭m7 E♭m7 A♭m7 A7 D/A
ground.
Choir: Let us
Lead vocal: (Let us praise

D Bm Em7 Am7 D7 G D
praise let us praise God now,
Bm Edim D Gm D/A
for we are stand - ing,
we are stand - ing in
Em D/F♯ Gm D/A
we are stand - ing,
His pres - ence in His ho - ly won - der - ful
Em Gm D/A
we are stand - ing,
pres - ence He loves us in our
Em Gm D/A
we are stand - ing,
hour of sor - row He's our hope, our hope

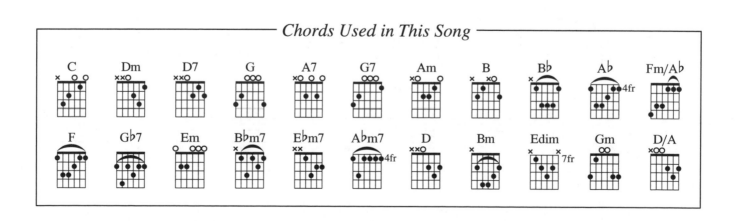

Chords Used in This Song

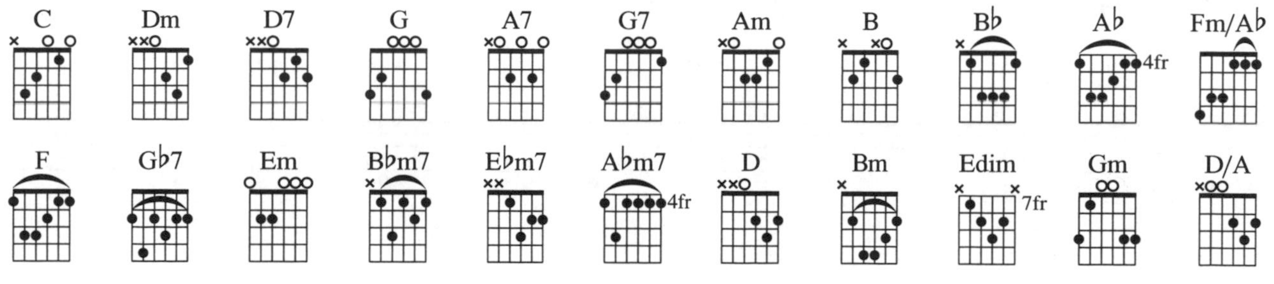

Holy Is the Lord

Words and Music by
CHRIS TOMLIN
and LOUIE GIGLIO

♩ = 84
A
D2
Esus
We stand and lift up our hands, for the joy
A/C♯
D2
Esus
of the Lord is our strength.
A
D2
Esus
We bow down and wor - ship Him now; How great,
A/C♯
D2
Esus
how awe - some is He. And to - geth - er we sing,

B7
D2
ev - 'ry - one
B7
D2
sing:
Ho - ly is the Lord
A/C♯
D2
Esus
God Al - might - y;
The earth
F♯m7
D2
E
is filled with His glo - ry.
Ho - ly is the Lord
A/C♯
D2
Esus
God Al - might - y;
The earth

F♯m7
D2
Esus
is filled with His glo - ry, the earth
3rd time to CODA
F♯m7
D2
Esus
is filled with His glo - ry.
1.
E
2.
E
It is ris -
A
E/G♯
- ing up all a - round; It's the an -
G2
D
- them of the Lord's re - nown. It's ris -

A
E/G♯
ing up all a - round; It's the an -
G2
D
them of the Lord's re - nown. It is ris -
A/C♯
E
G2
ing up all a - round; It's the an - them of the Lord's
D/F♯
A
re - nown. It's ris - ing up all
E/G♯
G2
a - round; It's the an - them of the Lord's

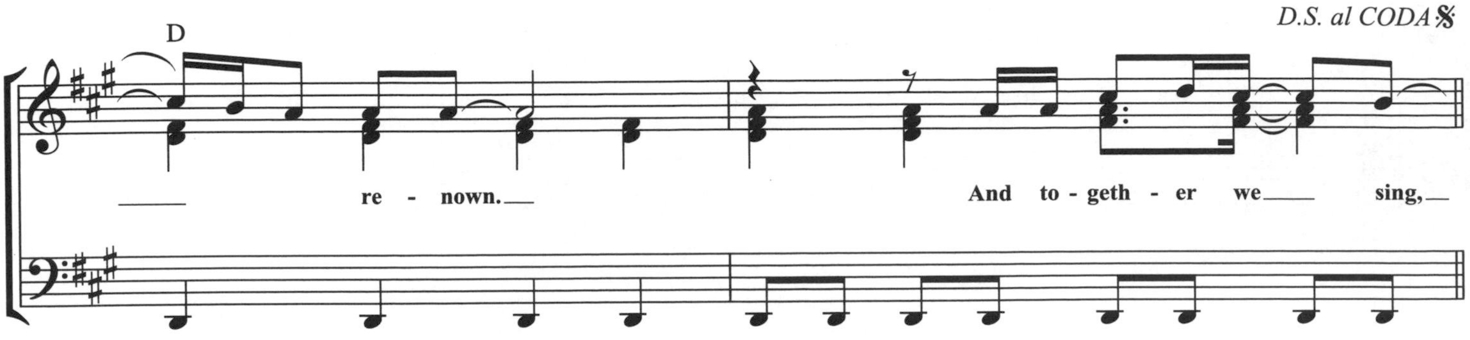
D.S. al CODA
D
re - nown.
And to - geth - er we sing,

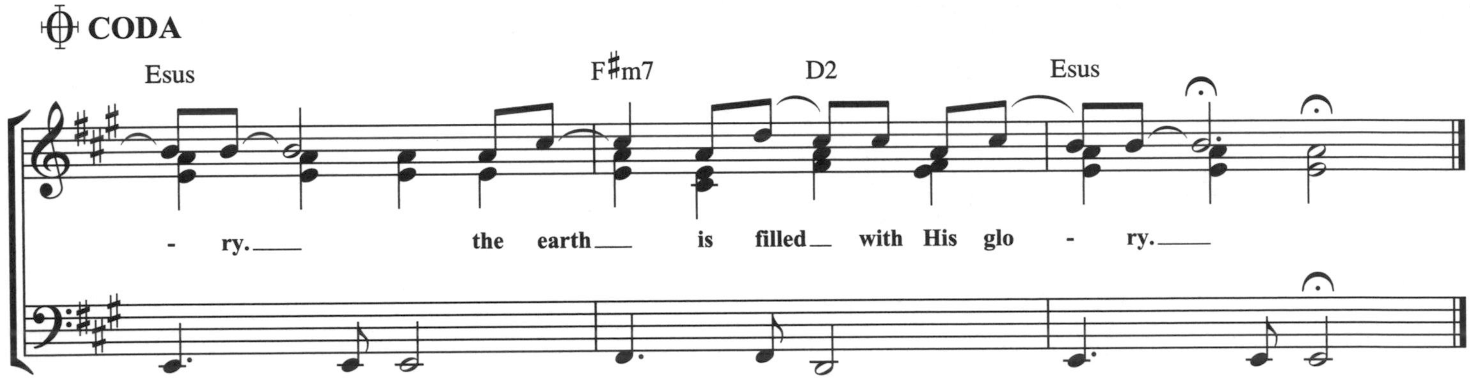
CODA
Esus
F♯m7
D2
Esus
- ry.
the earth is filled with His glo - ry.

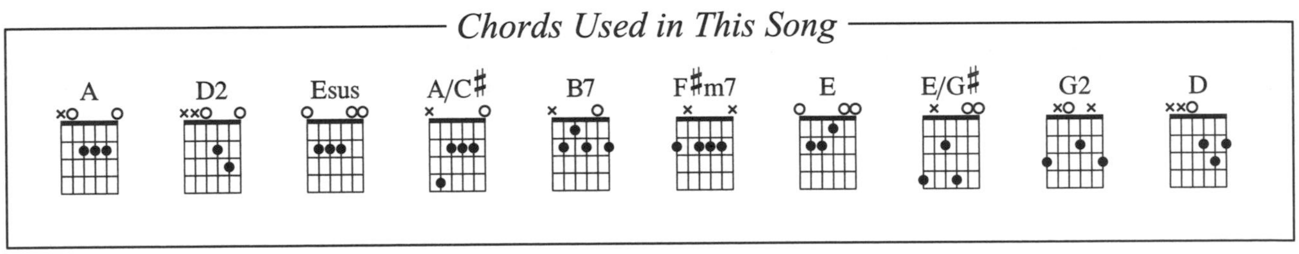
Chords Used in This Song
A
D2
Esus
A/C♯
B7
F♯m7
E
E/G♯
G2
D

How Great Is Our God

Words and Music by CHRIS TOMLIN,
JESSE REEVES and ED CASH

♩ = 76
C
G/B
The splen - dor of the King
(And) age to age He stands and
Am7
clothed in maj - es - ty let all the earth re - joice,
time is in his hands, be - gin - ning and the End,
Fmaj7
G
all the earth re - joice. He wraps
Be - gin - ning and the End. The God -
C
G/B
Him - self in light, and
head, three in one, and

Am7
dark - ness tries to hide, and trem - bles at His voice,
Fa - ther and Spir - it and Son, The Li - on and the Lamb,
Fmaj7
G
trem - bles at His voice. How great
Li - on and the Lamb.
C
G/B
Am7
is our God! Sing with me: How great is our God!
C/G
Fmaj7
Gsus
G
And all will see how great, how great is our God.
C
1.
2.
And 'Cause You're the Name a - bove all

G/B Am7 C/G
names, and wor - thy of all praise. And my
Fmaj Gsus G C
heart will sing: How great is our God.
C G/B
You're the Name a - bove all names, and
Am7 C/G F
wor - thy of all praise. And my heart will sing: How great
Gsus G C
is our God. How great

G/B Am7
is our God! Sing with me: How great is our God!
C/G Fmaj7 Gsus G
And all will see how great, how great is our God.
C
Then sings my soul, my
F C
Savior God, to Thee, How great Thou
1.
G F C
art, how great Thou art.

Chords Used in This Song

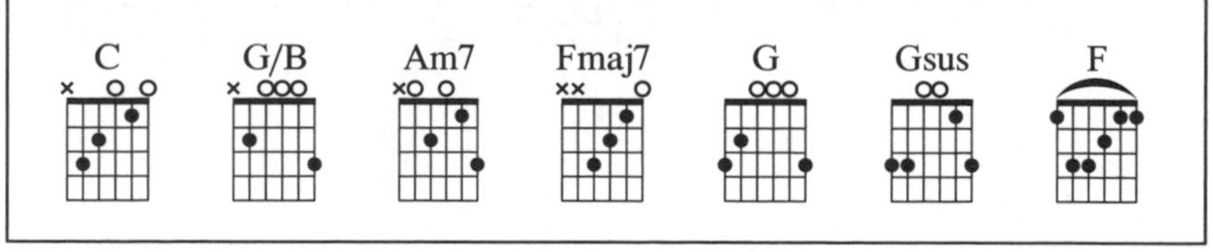

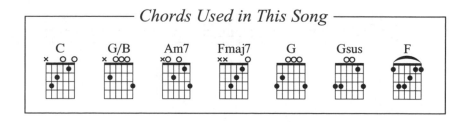

How Deep the Father's Love For Us

Words and Music by
STUART TOWNEND

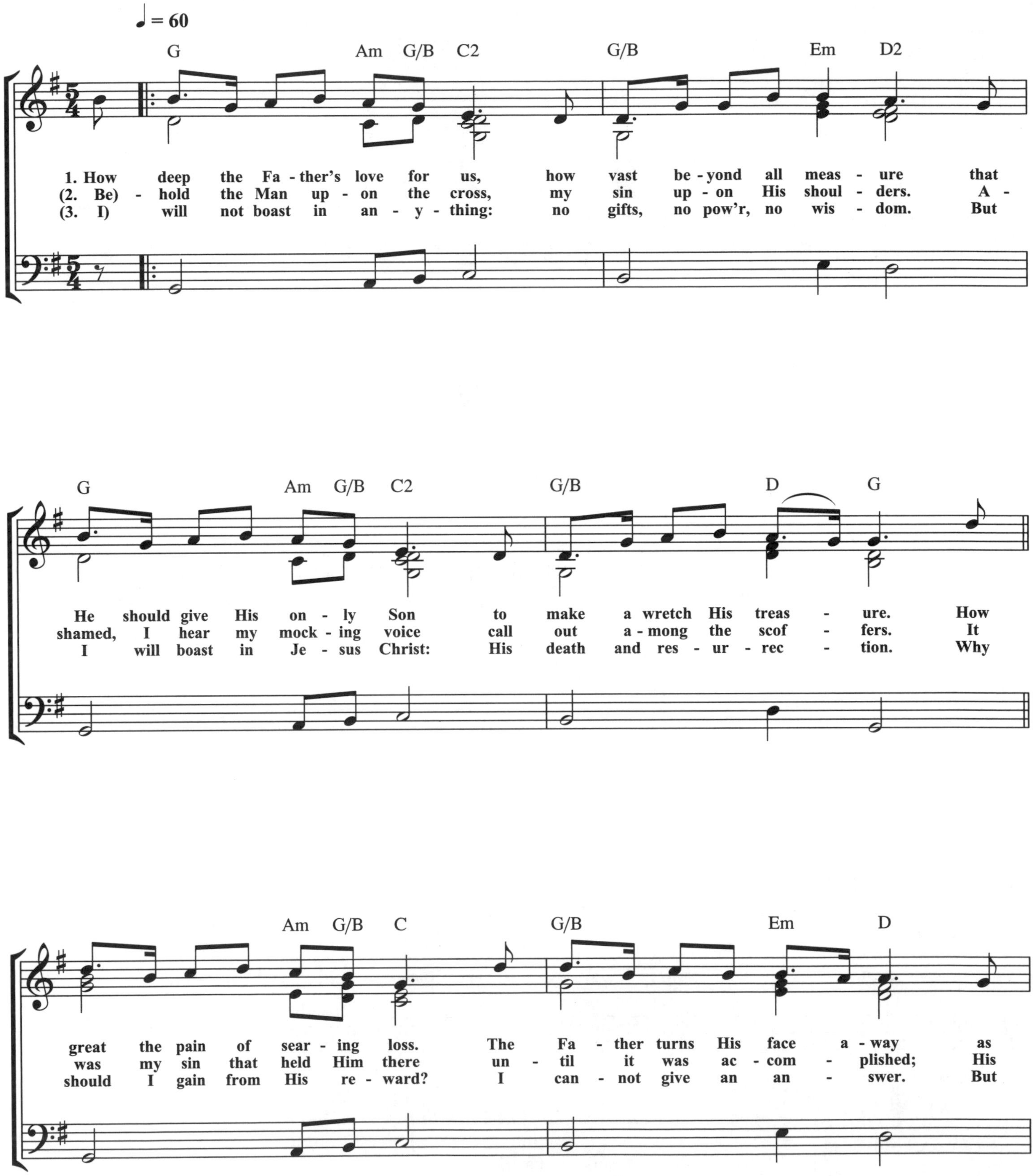
♩ = 60
G Am G/B C2 G/B Em D2
1. How deep the Fa - ther's love for us, how vast be - yond all meas - ure that
(2. Be) - hold the Man up - on the cross, my sin up - on His shoul - ders. A -
(3. I) will not boast in an - y - thing: no gifts, no pow'r, no wis - dom. But
G Am G/B C2 G/B D G
He should give His on - ly Son to make a wretch His treas - ure. How
shamed, I hear my mock - ing voice call out a - mong the scof - fers. It
I will boast in Je - sus Christ: His death and res - ur - rec - tion. Why
Am G/B C G/B Em D
great the pain of sear - ing loss. The Fa - ther turns His face a - way as
was my sin that held Him there un - til it was ac - com - plished; His
should I gain from His re - ward? I can - not give an an - swer. But

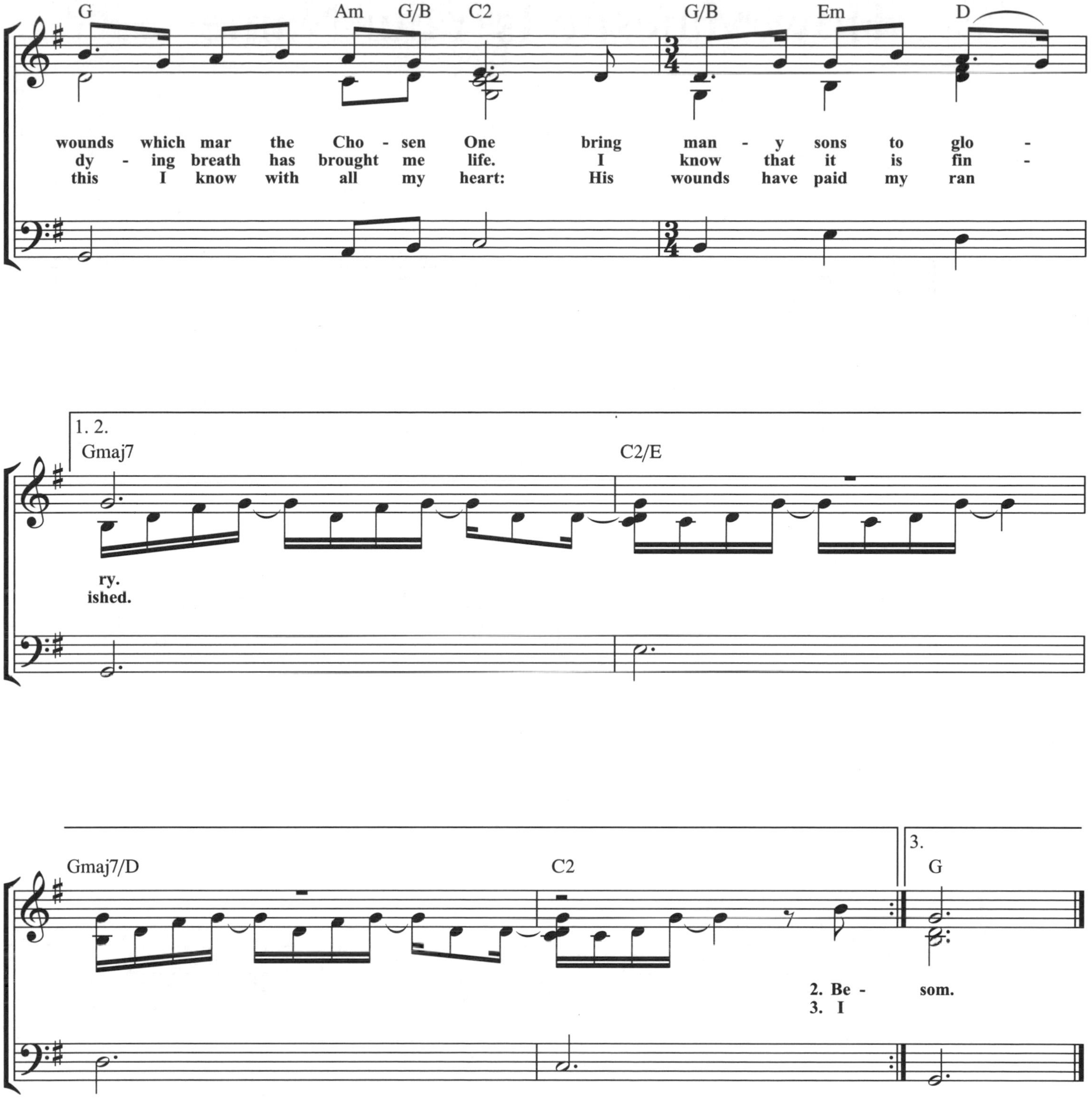
G Am G/B C2 G/B Em D
wounds which mar the Cho - sen One bring man - y sons to glo -
dy - ing breath has brought me life. I know that it is fin -
this I know with all my heart: His wounds have paid my ran
1. 2.
Gmaj7 C2/E
ry.
ished.
Gmaj7/D C2
3.
G
2. Be - som.
3. I

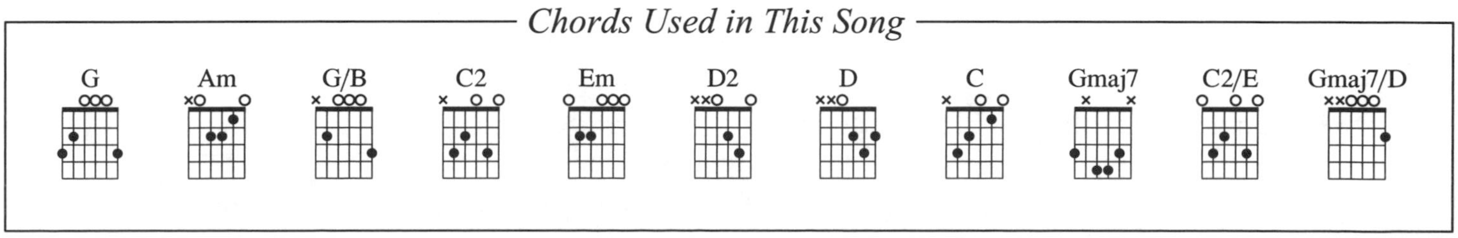
Chords Used in This Song
G Am G/B C2 Em D2 D C Gmaj7 C2/E Gmaj7/D

How Majestic Is Your Name

Words and Music by
MICHAEL W. SMITH

Moderate Samba ♩= 88

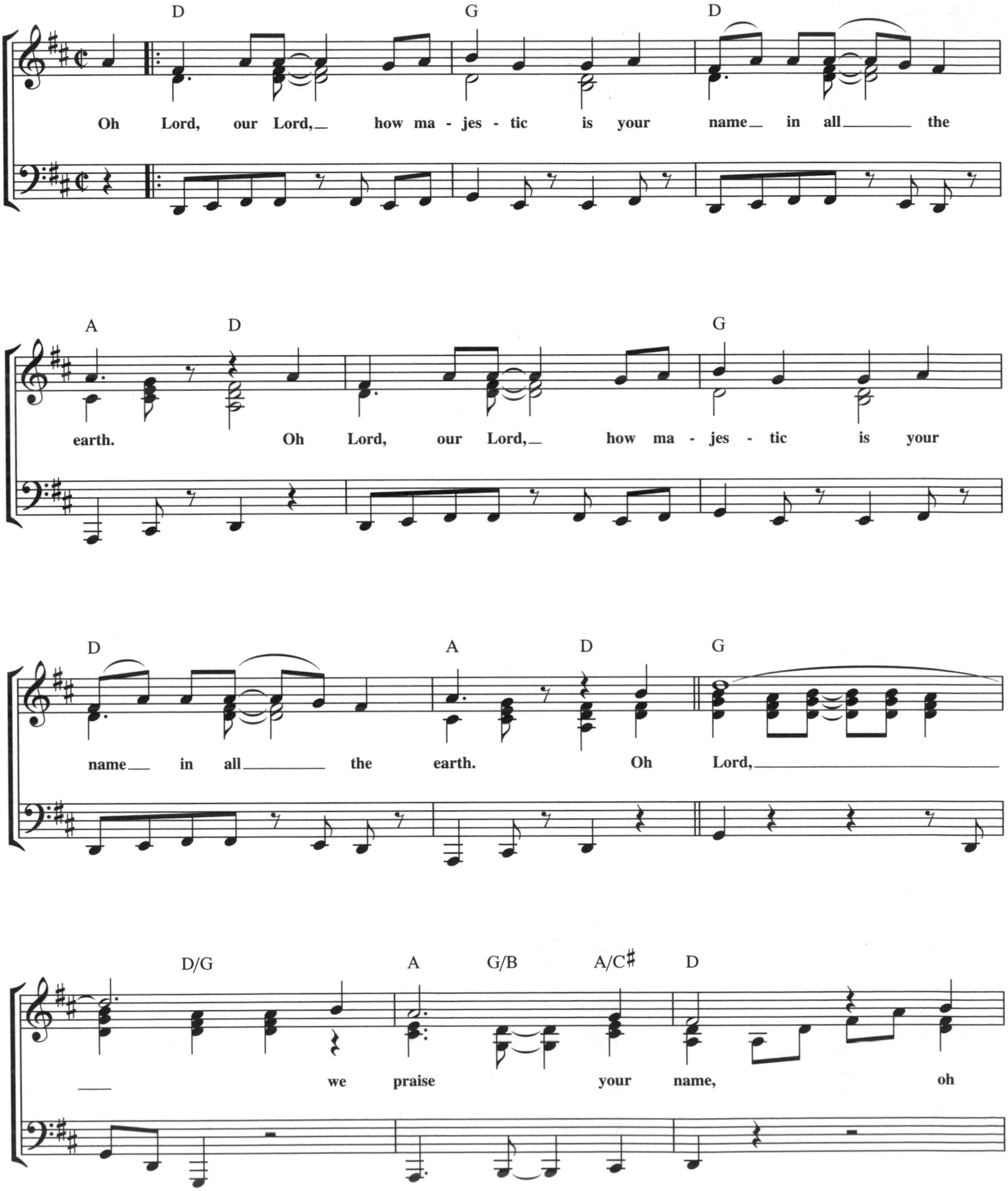
D G D
Oh Lord, our Lord, how ma - jes - tic is your name in all the
A D G
earth. Oh Lord, our Lord, how ma - jes - tic is your
D A D G
name in all the earth. Oh Lord,
D/G A G/B A/C♯ D
we praise your name, oh

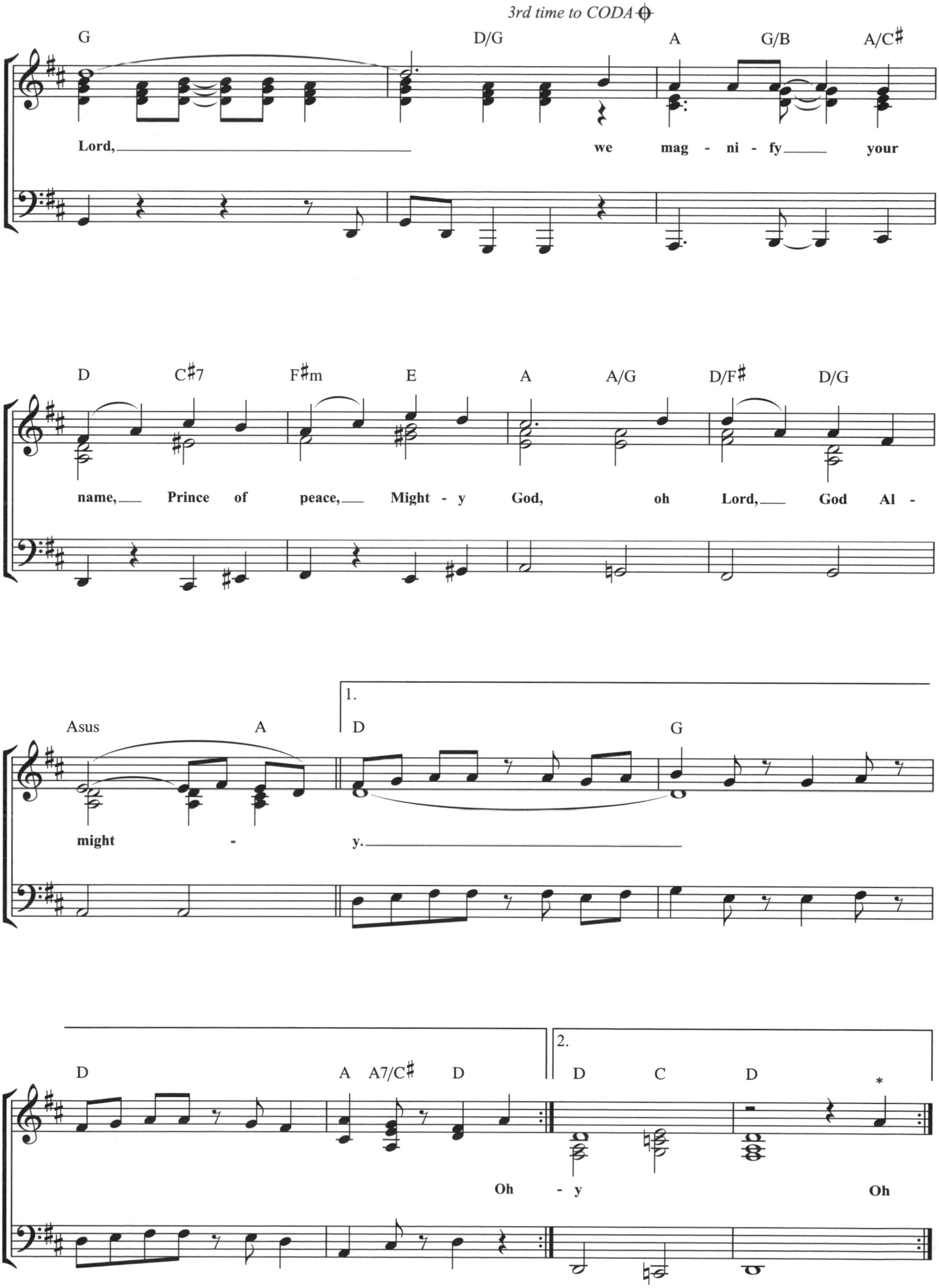
3rd time to CODA
G D/G A G/B A/C♯
Lord, we mag - ni - fy your
D C♯7 F♯m E A A/G D/F♯ D/G
name, Prince of peace, Might - y God, oh Lord, God Al -
Asus A
might - y.
1.
D G
D A A7/C♯ D
2.
D C D
Oh - y
*
Oh

*At this point the recorded version of the song modulates up ½-step to E♭.

CODA
A G/B A/C♯ D G
mag - ni - fy your name. Oh Lord,
D/G A G/B A/C♯ D
we praise your name, oh
G D/G A G/B A/C♯
Lord, we mag - ni - fy your
D C♯7 F♯m E A A/G D/F♯ D/G
name, Prince of peace, Might - y God, oh Lord, God Al -
Asus A D A D A D A D C♯7
might - y. Prince of

F#m E A A/G D/F# D/G Asus
peace, Might - y God, oh Lord, God Al - might -
D G D
y.
G D G
D A A7/C# D

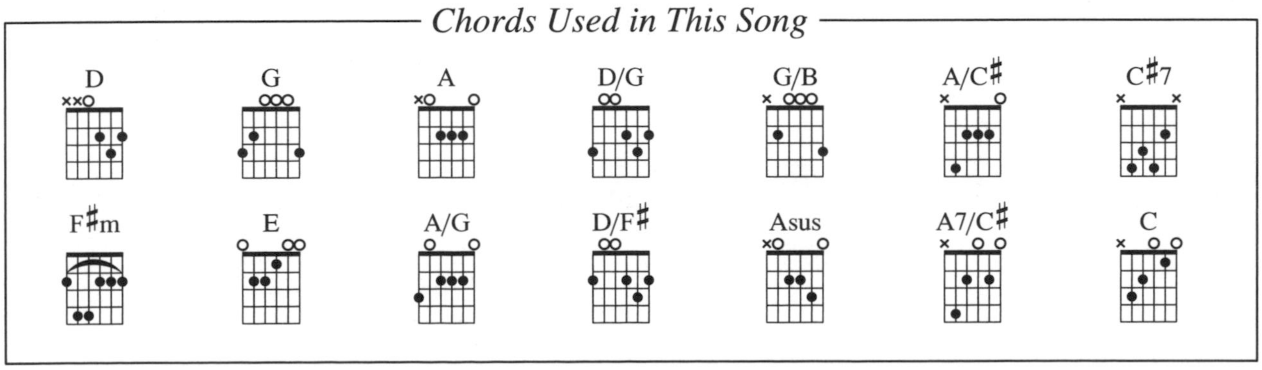
Chords Used in This Song
D G A D/G G/B A/C# C#7
F#m E A/G D/F# Asus A7/C# C

I Could Sing Of Your Love Forever

Words and Music by
MARTIN SMITH

♩ = 85
E
G♯m
O - ver the moun - tains and the sea Your riv - er runs with love for me,
F♯m7
A2
B
and I will o - pen up my heart, and let the Heal - er set me free.
E
G♯m
I'm hap - py to be in the truth, and I will dai - ly lift my hands,
F♯m7
A2
E/B
B7sus
for I will al - ways sing of when Your love came down.

E
B
I could sing of Your love___ for - ev - er,
C♯m
A2
B7sus
I could sing of Your love___ for - ev - er,
E
B
B♯dim
I could sing of Your love___ for - ev - er,
2nd time to CODA
C♯m
A2
B7sus
I could sing of Your love___ for - ev - er.
F♯m7
A2
Oh, I feel___ like danc - ing;___

C♯m7
G♯m
it's fool - ish - ness, I know.
F♯m7
A2
But when the world has seen the light, they will dance
D.S. al CODA
B7sus
with joy like we're danc - ing now.
CODA
A2
B7sus
F♯
for - ev - er. I could sing of Your love
C♯
D♯m
for - ev - er, I could sing of Your love

Chords Used in This Song

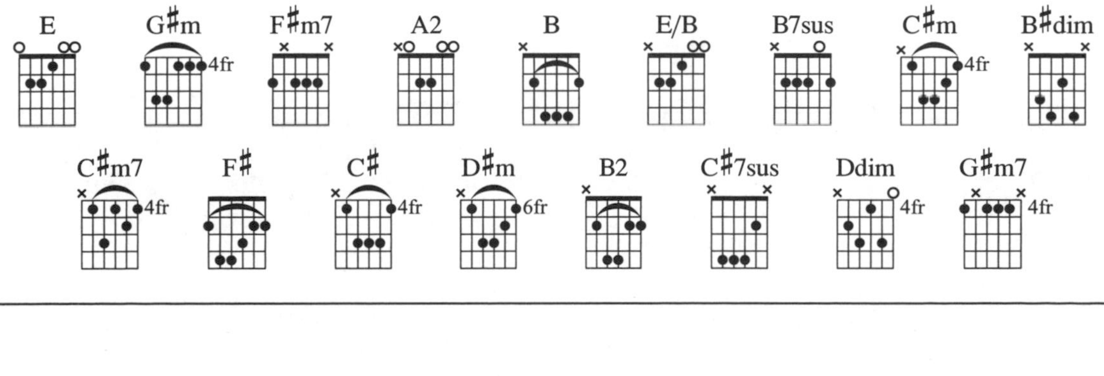

I Will Exalt Your Name

Words and Music by
JEFFREY B. SCOTT

Capo 2 (D)
♩ = 92
Keyboard
(Guitar)
B (A)
A2 (G2)
E (D)
I will ex - alt Your name. I will ex - alt Your name. I will ex - alt Your name, oh, my God.
last time to CODA
1.
I will ex - alt.
2.
C♯m7 (Bm7)
Amaj7 (Gmaj7)
Nev - er be - fore, nev - er a - gain,

E (D)
Esus (Dsus)
E (D)
C#m7 (Bm7)
Amaj7 (Gmaj7)
B (A)
will there be one
like You.
E (D)
D.S. al CODA
I will ex - alt
CODA
B (A)
A2 (G2)
E (D)
I will ex - alt Your name.

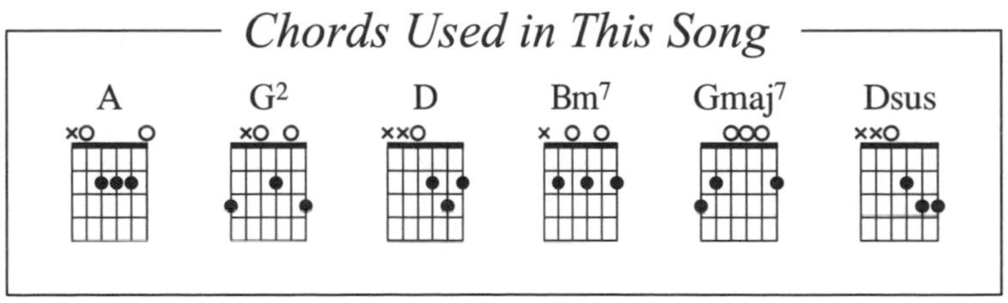
Chords Used in This Song
A
G2
D
Bm7
Gmaj7
Dsus

I Still Believe

Words and Music by
JEREMY CAMP

Moderately ♩.=56
Capo 1 (D)
Keyboard (Guitar)
Eb (D) Eb/D (D/C#) Eb/G (D/F#) Ab (G)
The scat - tered words, and emp - ty thoughts,
Eb (D) Eb/D (D/C#) Eb/G (D/F#) Ab (G)
seem to pour from my heart,
Eb (D) Eb/D (D/C#) Eb/G (D/F#) Ab (G) Eb (D) Eb/D (D/C#)
I've nev - er felt so torn be - fore. Seems I don't know where to start,
Eb/G (D/F#) Ab (G) Cm (Bm) Bb (A)
but it's now that I feel Your grace

Ab
(G)
— fall like rain, — from ev - 'ry
Cm
(Bm)
Bb
(A)
Ab
(G)
fin - ger - tip — washing a - way — my pain —
Eb
(D)
Eb/D
(D/C#)
'Cause I still be - lieve — in Your
Ab
(G)
Eb
(D)
faith - ful - ness, — 'cause I still be - lieve —
Eb/D
(D/C#)
Ab
(G)
— in Your — truth. —

E♭ (D) E♭/D (D/C♯) A♭ (G)
'Cause I still be - lieve in Your Ho - ly word,
E♭ (D) E♭/G (D/F♯) A♭ (G)
To Coda
e - ven when I don't see I still be - lieve.
E♭ (D) E♭/D (D/C♯) E♭/G (D/F♯) A♭ (G) E♭ (D) E♭/D (D/C♯) E♭/G (D/F♯) A♭ (G)
E♭ (D) E♭/D (D/C♯) E♭/G (D/F♯) A♭ (G)
Though the ques - tions still fog up my mind, with
E♭ (D) E♭/D (D/C♯) E♭/G (D/F♯) A♭ (G)
prom - is - es I still seem to bear, or

E♭ (D) E♭/D (D/C♯) E♭/G (D/F♯) A♭ (G)
e - ven when an - swers slow - ly un - wind. It's
E♭ (D) E♭/D (D/C♯) E♭/G (D/F♯) A♭ (G)
my heart I see you pre - pare, but it's now
Cm (Bm) B♭ (A)
that I feel Your grace
A♭ (G) Cm (Bm)
fall like rain, from ev - 'ry fin - ger - tip
B♭ (A) A♭ (G)
D.S. al CODA
wash - ing a - way my pain.

CODA
Cm (Bm) Bb (A) Ab (G) Bb (A)
Well, the
on - ly place I can go is in - to Your arms, where I throw
to You my fee - ble prayers. Well, in
bro - ken - ness I can see, that this was Your will for me,

A♭ (G)
E♭/G (D/F♯)
help me to know that You're near, yeah.
B♭ (A)
E♭ (D)
'Cause I still be - lieve
E♭/D (D/C♯)
A♭ (G)
in Your faith - ful - ness,
E♭ (D)
E♭/D (D/C♯)
A♭ (G)
'cause I still be - lieve in Your truth.
E♭ (D)
E♭/D (D/C♯)
'Cause I still be - lieve in Your

A♭ (G)
E♭/G (D/F♯)
Ho - ly word,
e - ven when I don't see
A♭ (G)
B♭ (A)
E♭ (D)
E♭/D (D/C♯)
1–3.
E♭/G (D/F♯)
A♭ (G)
Repeat 3 times
I still be - lieve.
Lead vocal ad lib.
'Cause I still be - lieve,
4.
E♭/G (D/F♯)
A♭ (G)
Repeat and Fade
'Cause I still be - lieve,
I still be - lieve.

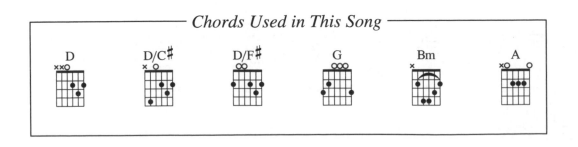

Chords Used in This Song

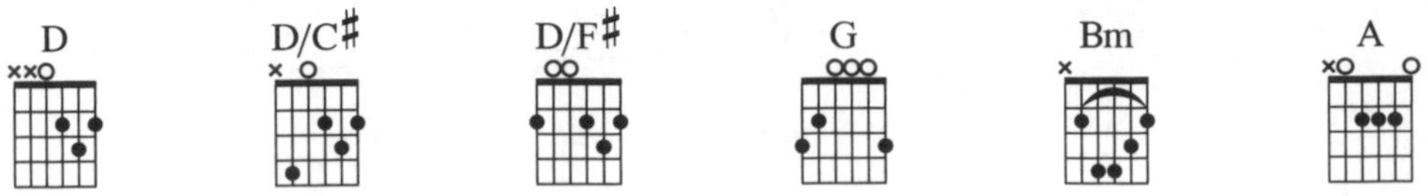

In Christ Alone

Words and Music by
KEITH GETTY and
STUART TOWNEND

♩ = 80
D G C D C D G C D C D G
1. In Christ a - lone my hope is found, He is my light, my strength, my song; this cor - ner - stone, this sol - id ground, firm through the fierc - est drought and storm. What heights of
(2. In Christ a - lone,) who took on flesh, full - ness of God in help - less Babe! This gift of love and right - eous - ness, scorned by the ones He came to save. 'Til on that
(3. There in the ground) His bod - y lay, Light of the world by dark - ness slain; then, burst - ing forth in glo - rious day, up from the grave He rose a - gain! And as He

C C/E D G/B
love, what depths of peace, when fears are
cross as Je - sus died, the wrath of
stands in vic - to - ry, sin's curse has
C C/E D
stilled, when striv - ings cease. My com - fort - er,
God was sat - is - fied. For ev - 'ry sin
lost its grip on me; for I am His
G C D
my all in all, here in the
on Him was laid; here in the
and He is mine, bought with the
C D
love of Christ I stand.
death of Christ I
pre - cious blood of
1.
G D
C Em7 D
2. In Christ a - lone
2. 3.
G
live.
Christ.

D
Am
C
G
D
Am
2nd time to CODA
D.S. al CODA
C
D
3. There in the ground
CODA
E/G♯
E
A
D
4. No guilt in life, no fear in

E D E A
death, this is the pow'r of Christ in me; from life's first
D E D E
cry to fi - nal breath, Je - sus com - mands my des - ti -
A D D/F♯ E A/C♯
ny. No pow'r of hell, no scheme of man, can ev - er
D D/F♯ E A D
pluck me from His hand; 'til He re - turns or calls me
E D E
home, here in the pow'r of Christ I'll

Chords Used in This Song

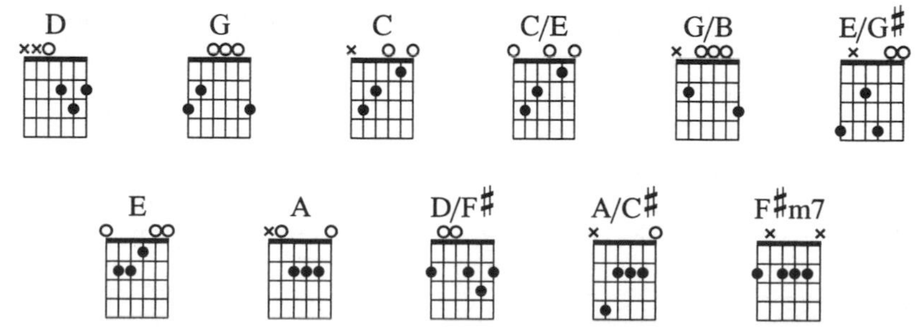

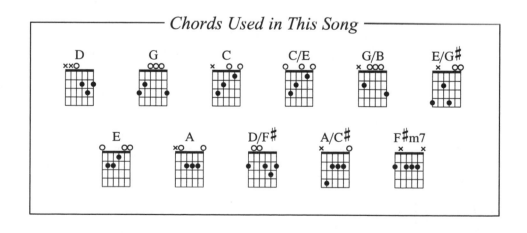

In the Cross Alone I Glory

Words and Music by
BRIAN PETAK

♩ = 82
Dm F Am Dm
1. In the cross a - lone I glo - ry re - cog -
(2.) cross a - lone I glo - ry, ev - er
(3.) cross a - lone I glo - ry, hold - ing
F G C Dm F B♭
ni - tion lay - ing down. Great - est trea - sures count as
reach - ing for the prize. Pres - sing on and lay - ing
fast the word of life. Toil - ing not in vain but
Am B♭ C Dm
worth - less stand - ing next to Heav - ens crowns,
hold of that for which my sav - ior died,
be - ing poured out as a sac - ri - fice,
3rd time to CODA
1.
B♭ C F Fsus4 F
stand - ing next to Heav - ens crowns.
that for which my sav - ior died.
poured out as a sac - ri - fice.
2. In the

2.
Fsus4 F Bb2 C F
In the cross a - lone I glo - ry; noth-ing
Bb C Dm Bb2
of my own to give. On - ly that which Christ has
A/C# Dm Bb2 Dm
of - fered for my soul that I may live
Bb2 C F Fsus4 F
D.S. al CODA
for my soul that I may live. In the
CODA
F Fsus4 F Em G C
fice. Nev - er will I seek the

Bm Em G A Dsus4 D Em
glo - ry that was nev - er meant for me. Al - ways
G C Bm C D
heav - en - ward re - flect - ing, all to Je - sus to re -
Em C D Em D
ceive, all to Je - sus to re - ceive,
C D G Gsus4 G
all to Je - sus to re - ceive. In the
C2 D G C D
cross a - lone I glo - ry; noth - ing of my own to

Em C B/D♯ Em
give. On - ly that which Christ has of - fered.
C Em 1. C D
for my soul that I may live. for my soul that I
G Gsus4 G 2. C D
may live. In the for my soul that I may
Em D C D G Gsus4 G
live, for my soul that I may live.

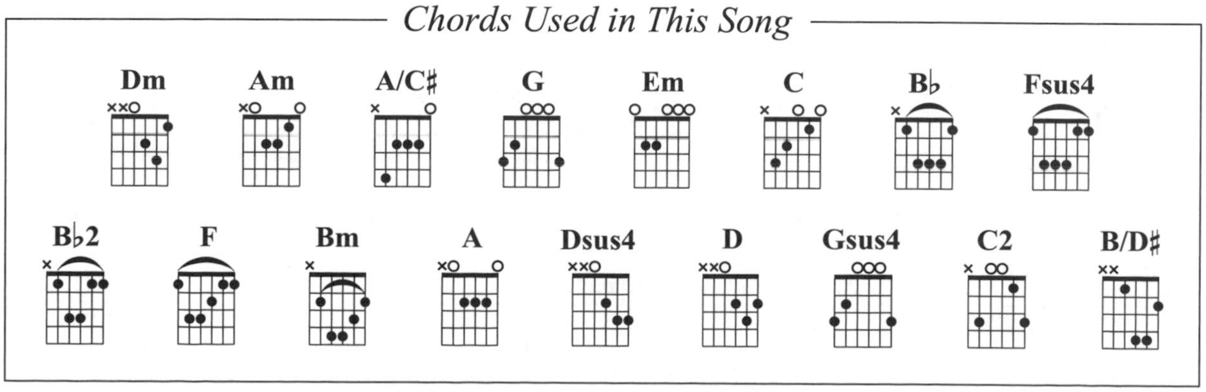
Chords Used in This Song
Dm Am A/C♯ G Em C B♭ Fsus4
B♭2 F Bm A Dsus4 D Gsus4 C2 B/D♯

In The Presence Of Jehovah (Psalm 130)

Words and Music by
GERON DAVIS
and BECKY DAVIS

Freely, with much rubato (♩ = ca. 78)

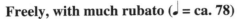

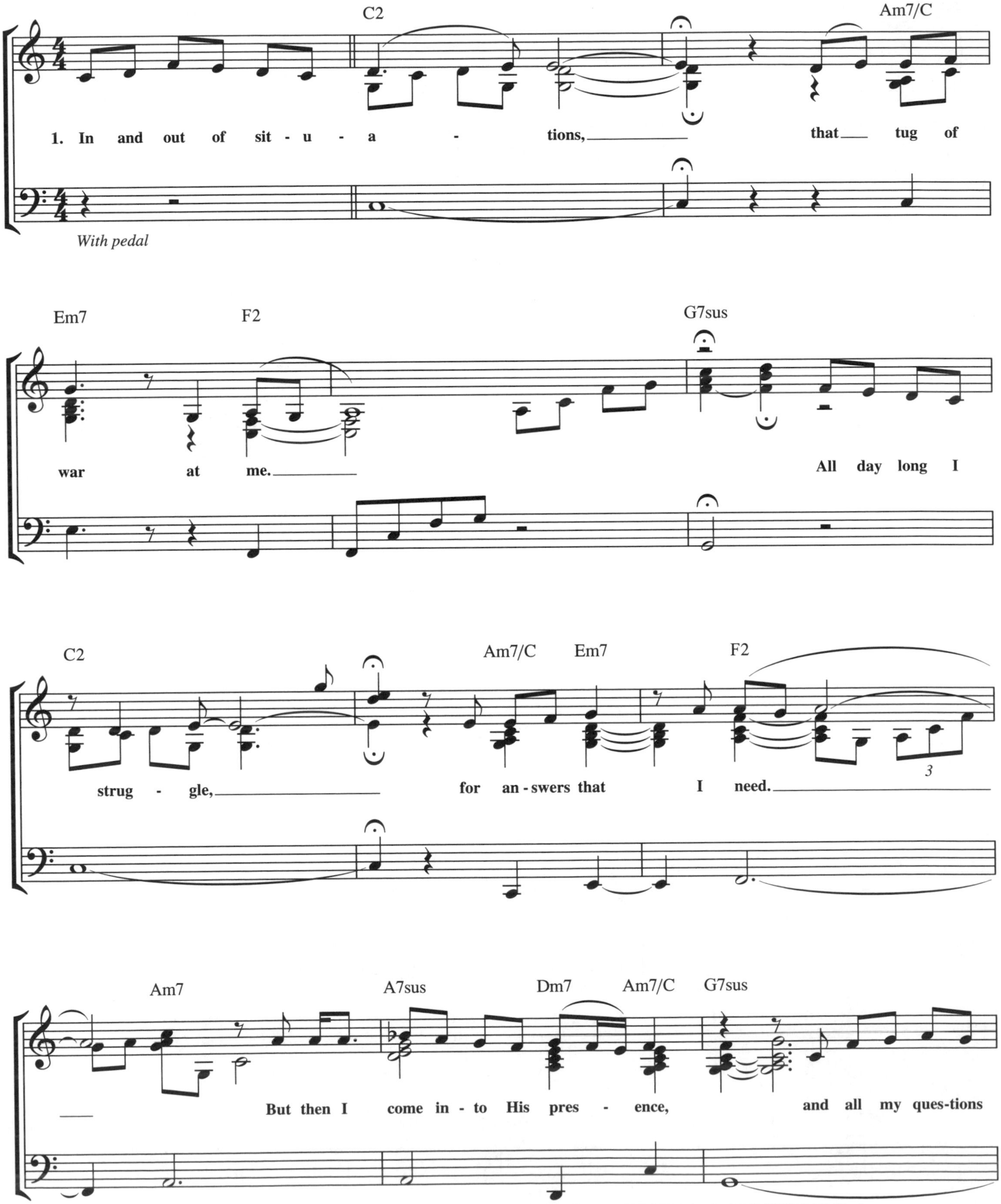
C2
Am7/C
1. In and out of sit - u - a - tions, that tug of
With pedal
Em7
F2
G7sus
war at me. All day long I
C2
Am7/C
Em7
F2
strug - gle, for an - swers that I need.
3
Am7
A7sus
Dm7
Am7/C
G7sus
But then I come in - to His pres - ence, and all my ques-tions

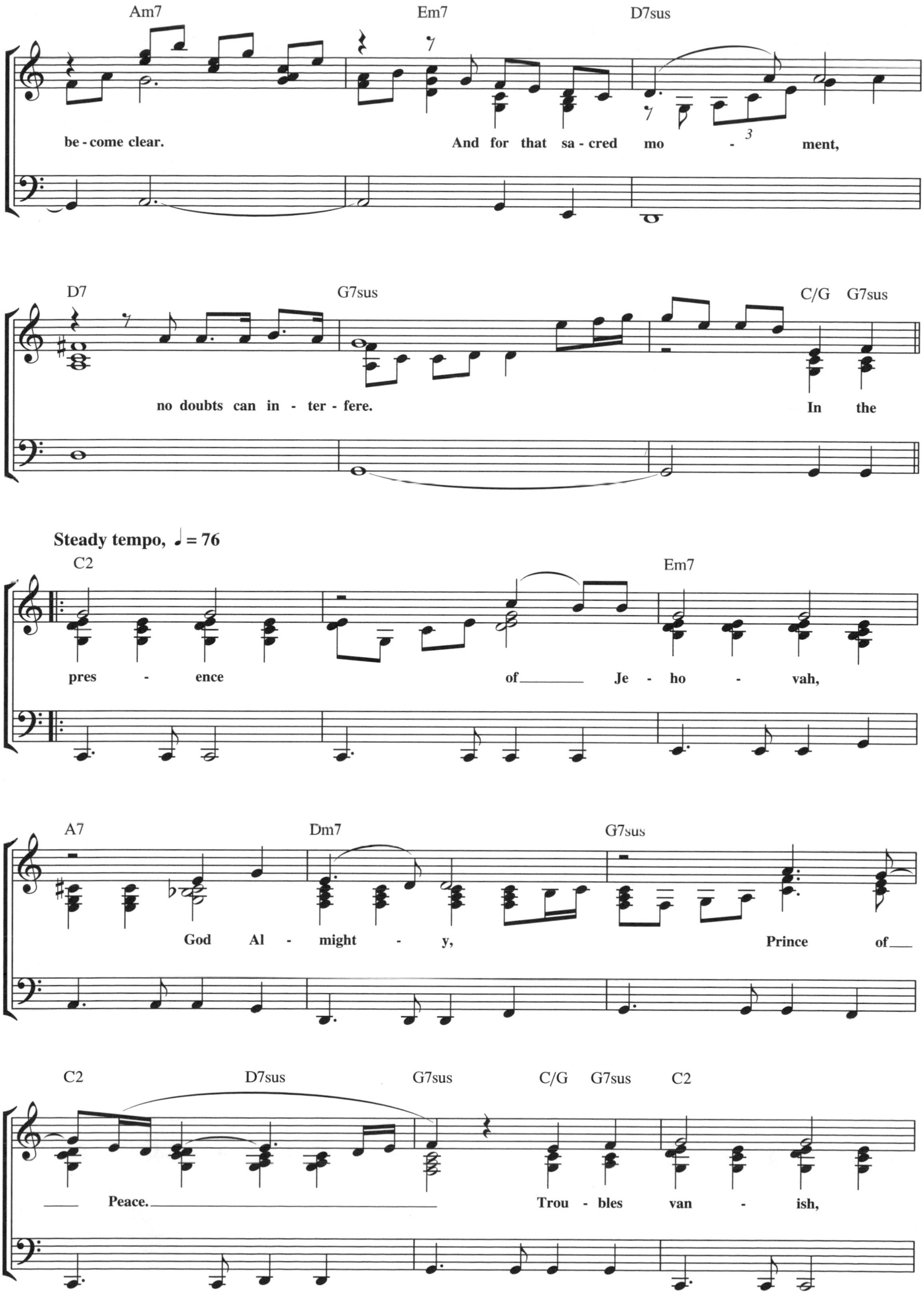
Am7 Em7 D7sus
be-come clear. And for that sa-cred mo - ment,
D7 G7sus C/G G7sus
no doubts can in - ter - fere. In the
Steady tempo, ♩ = 76
C2 Em7
pres - ence of Je - ho - vah,
A7 Dm7 G7sus
God Al - might - y, Prince of
C2 D7sus G7sus C/G G7sus C2
Peace. Trou - bles van - ish,

Em7
A7
hearts are mend - ed, in the
2nd time, to CODA
Dm7
G7sus
C2
pres - ence of the King.
*
G7sus
C/G
G7sus
C2
Through His love the Lord pro - vid - ed
Em7
F2
a place for us to rest.
G7sus
C2
A place to find the an - swers

*At this point, the recorded version modulates from C to D♭.

Em7 F2
in the ho - ur of dis - tress.
Em7 A7 Dm7
Now there's nev - er an - y rea - son
G7sus Em7
for you to give up in des - pair,
Am7 G/B C2 D7sus
just slip a - way and breathe His name,
D7 G7sus C/G G7sus
*
He will sure - ly meet you there. In the

*At this point, the recorded version modulates from D♭ to D.

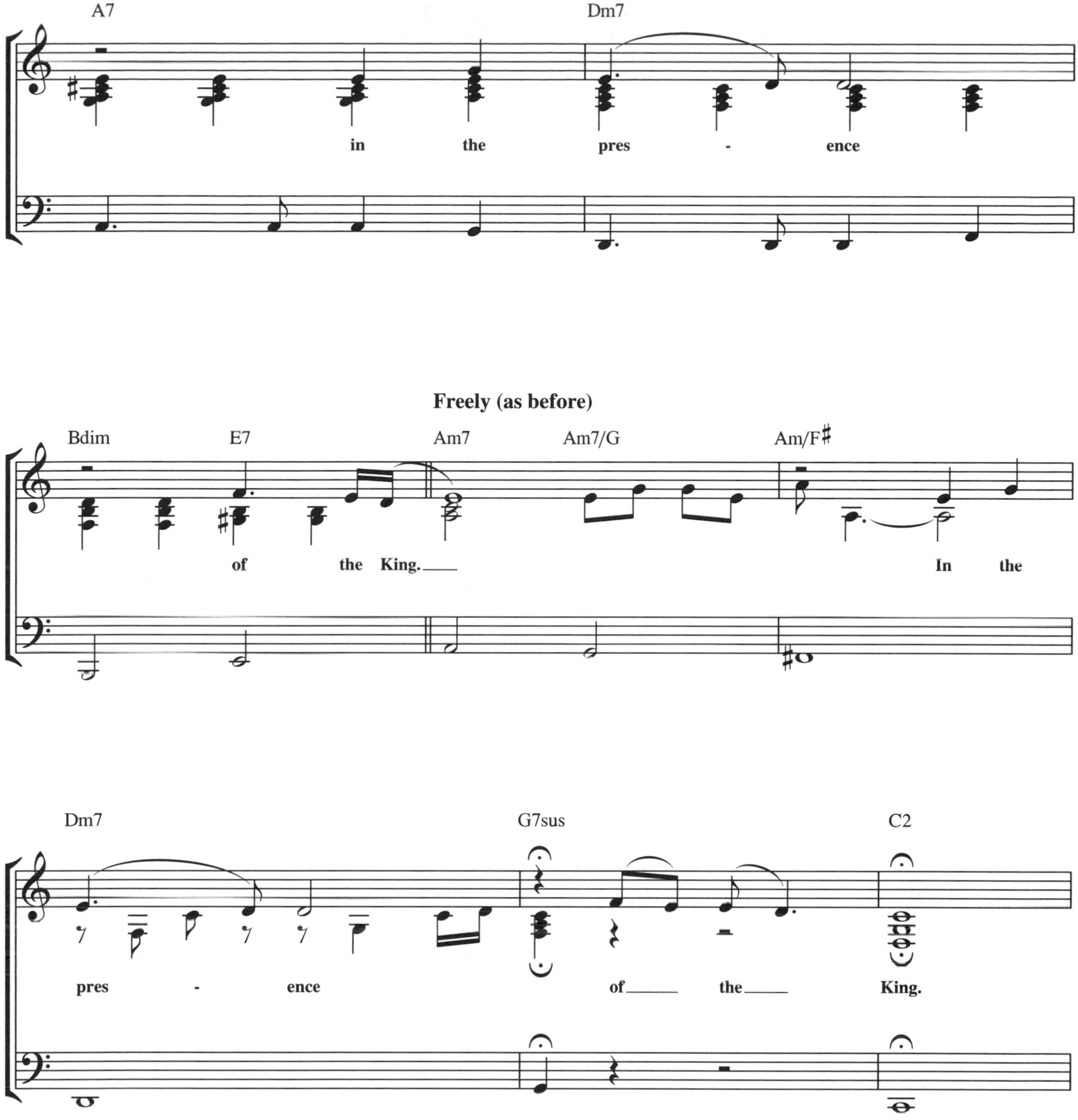

Chords Used in This Song

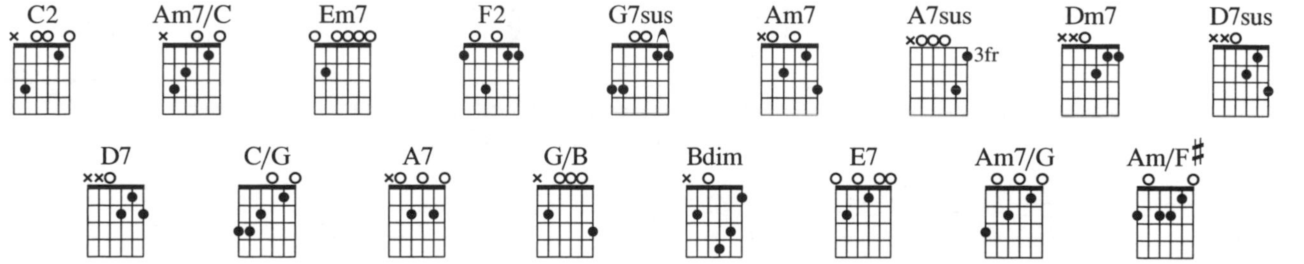

Indescribable

Words and Music by
LAURA STORY
Additional lyrics by JESSE REEVES

Capo 2 (A)
♩. = 60
Keyboard
(Guitar)
G♯m (F♯m)
F♯/A♯ (E/G♯)
1. From the high - est of heights to the depths of the sea,
2. Who has told ev - 'ry light - ning bolt where it should go
B (A)
F♯/A♯ B C♯m7 (E/G♯) (A) (Bm7)
cre - a - tions re - veal - ing Your maj - es - ty.
or seen heav - en - ly store - hous - es lad - en with snow?
B (A)
A (G)
A(♯4) (G(♯4))
G♯m (F♯m)
F♯/A♯ (E/G♯)
B (A)
From the col - ors of Fall to the fra - grance of Spring,
Who i - mag - ined the sun and gives source to its light

F♯/A♯ B C♯m7 E/B
(E/G♯) (A) (Bm7) (D/A)
ev - 'ry crea - ture u - nique in the song that it
yet con - ceals it to bring us the cool - ness of
A E/G♯ F♯/A♯ B
(G) (D/F♯) (E/G♯) (A)
sings. All ex - claim - ing: In - de - scrib - a - ble,
night? None can fath - om.
F♯ E2
(E) (D2)
un - con - tain - a - ble; You placed the stars in the sky, and You know them by
G♯m B/D♯ E
(F♯m) (A/C♯) (D)
name. You are a - maz - ing, God;
B F♯
(A) (E)
All pow - er - ful, un - tam - a - ble.

E
(D)
G♯m
(F♯m)
Awe - struck, we fall to our knees as we hum - bly pro - claim
B/D♯
(A/C♯)
E2
(D2)
3rd time to CODA
1.
You are a - maz - ing, God.
2.
C♯m7
(Bm7)
B
(A)
A
(G)
You are a - maz - ing, God.
D
(C)

Chords Used in This Song

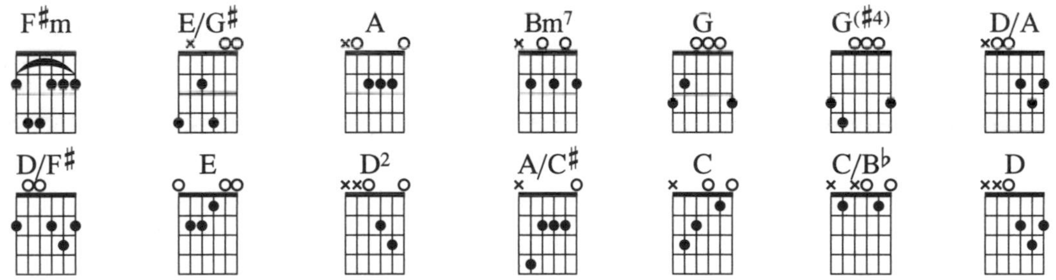

Jesus, Lover of My Soul

Words and Music by
PAUL OAKLEY

Capo 1 (A)
♩ = 60
Keyboard
(Guitar)
Gm (F♯m7) E♭ (D) B♭ (A)
It's all a - bout You, Je - sus,
F (E) Gm (F♯m7) E♭ (D) B♭ (A)
and all this is for You, for Your glo - ry and Your fame.
F (E) Gm (F♯m7) E♭ (D) B♭ (A)
It's not a - bout me, as if You should do things my
E♭ (D) B♭ (A) F (E) E♭ (D)
way; You a - lone are God, and I sur - ren - der

Fine
B♭ (A)
to Your ways. Je -
E♭ (D) F (E) B♭ (A) E♭ (D)
- sus, lov - er of my soul, all con - sum - ing fire
B♭ (A) Fsus (Esus) F (E) B♭ (A)
is in Your gaze. Je -
E♭ (D) F (E) B♭ (A) E♭ (D)
- sus, I want You to know I will fol - low You
B♭ (A) Fsus (Esus) F (E) B♭ (A)
all my days. For no one else in

Gm (F♯m7)
E♭ (D)
B♭ (A)
his - to - ry__ is like________ You,___ and his - to - ry___ it - self_
F (E)
E♭ (D)
B♭ (A)
— be - longs___ to You.____ Al - pha and__ O - me-
E♭ (D)
Gm (F♯m7)
E♭ (D)
B♭ (A)
- ga, You have loved________ me,____ and I will share_ e - ter-
D.S. (twice) al Fine 𝄋
E♭ (D)
Fsus (Esus)
F (E)
- ni - ty with__________ You.______ It's all a - bout

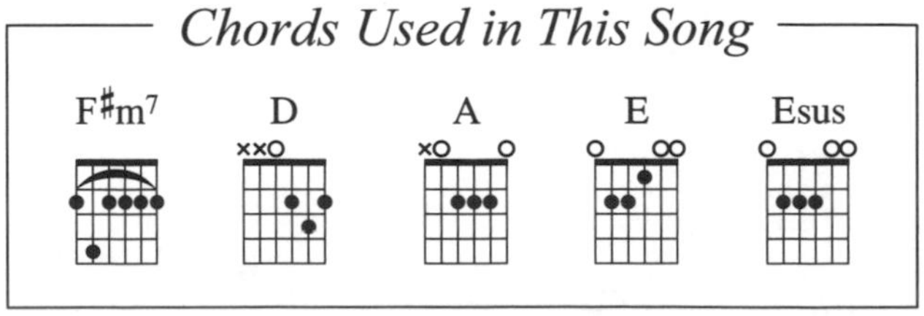
Chords Used in This Song
F♯m7
D
A
E
Esus

Jesus You Are Worthy

Words and Music by
BRENTON BROWN and DON WILLIAMS

♩ = 66
C
Je - sus You are mer - cy. Je - sus You are
C/B F G
jus - tice. Je - sus You are wor - thy. That is what You
C
are. You died a - lone to save me. You rose so You could raise
C/B F G
me. You did this all to make me a cho - sen child

C F G
of God. Wor - thy is the Lamb that once was slain.
C F G
To re - ceive all glo - ry, pow'r, and praise.
C F G
For with Your blood You pur - chased us for God
Am7 F G
Je - sus You are wor - thy. That is what You
C
are. Je - sus You are

C/B
— mer - cy. Je - sus You are justice. Je - sus You are
F G C
— wor - thy. That is what You are. You died a - lone to
C/B
— save me. You rose so You could raise me. You did this all to make
Am7 G C
— me a pre - cious child of God. Wor - thy is the
F G C
Lamb that once was slain. To re - ceive all

F G C
glo - ry, pow'r, and praise. For with Your blood You
F G Am7
2nd time to CODA
pur - chased us for God Je - sus You are
F G C
worthy. That is what You are. Per - fect sac - ri -
Dm7 Am7
- fice crushed by God for us. Bear - ing in Your
F G
hurt all that I de- serve. Mis - judged for my mis -

C/B
mer - cy. Je - sus You are jus - tice. Je - sus You are
F G C
wor - thy. That is what You are. You died a - lone to
C/B
save me. You rose so You could raise me. You did this all to make
Am7 G C
me a pre - cious child of God. Wor - thy is the
F G C
Lamb that once was slain. To re - ceive all

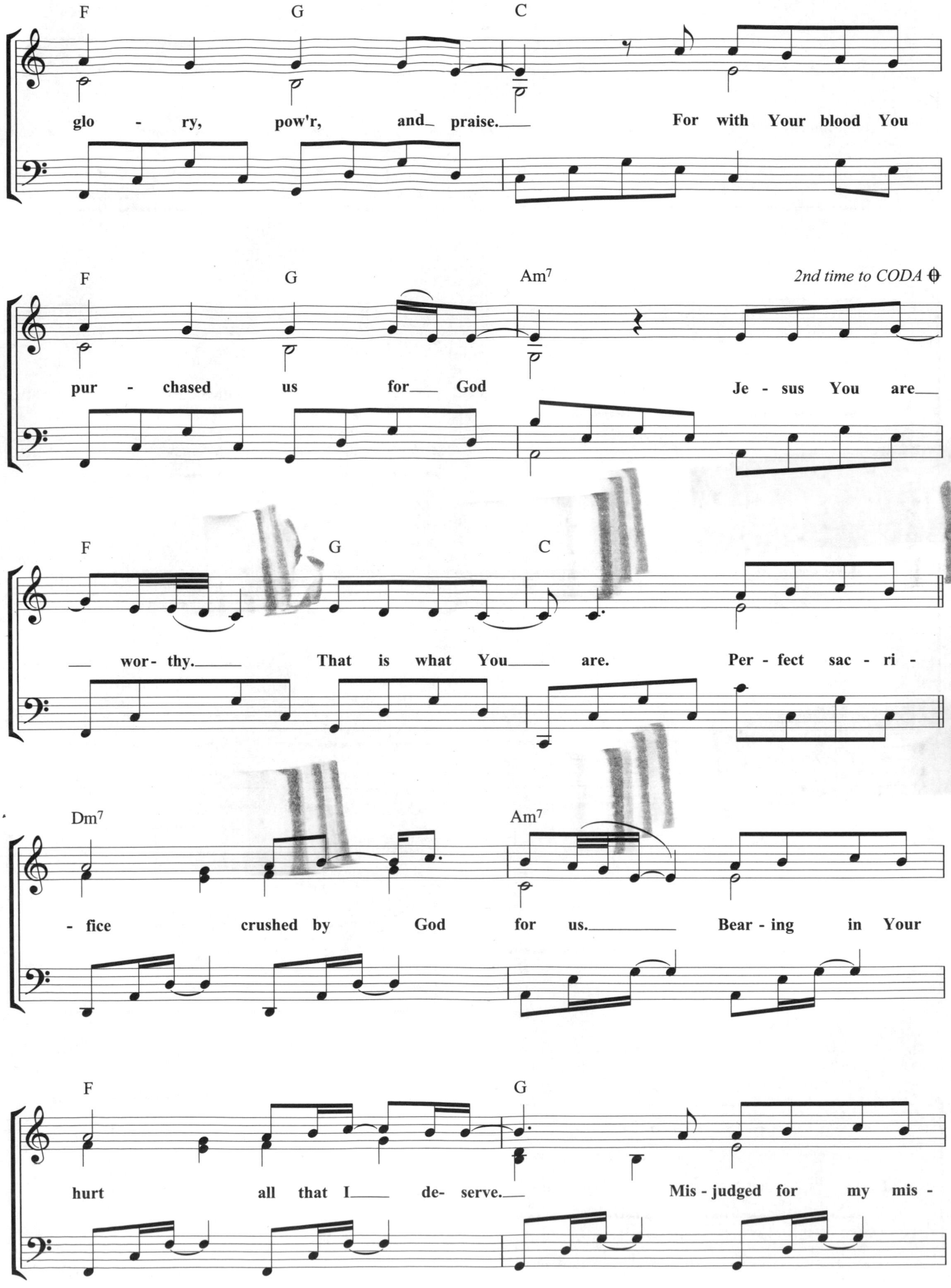
F G C
glo - ry, pow'r, and praise. For with Your blood You
F G Am7
2nd time to CODA
pur - chased us for God Je - sus You are
F G C
wor - thy. That is what You are. Per - fect sac - ri -
Dm7 Am7
- fice crushed by God for us. Bear - ing in Your
F G
hurt all that I de- serve. Mis - judged for my mis -

Dm7
Am7
deeds, You suf - fered si - lent - ly the on - ly guilt - less
F
G
D.S. al CODA
man in all of his - to - ry. How wor - thy is the
CODA
F
G
Am7
wor - thy. That is what You are. Je - sus You are
F
G
C
wor - thy. That is what You are.

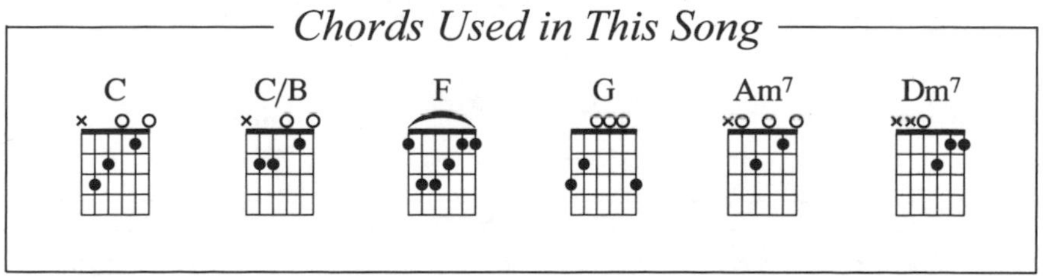
Chords Used in This Song
C
C/B
F
G
Am7
Dm7

Kindness

Words and Music by CHRIS TOMLIN,
JESSE REEVES and LOUIE GIGLIO

♩ = 74
Capo 1 (G)
Keyboard
(Guitar)
A♭ (G)
E♭/G (D/F♯)
Fm7 (Em7)
O - pen up the skies of mer - cy,
We can feel Your mer - cy fall - ing,
A♭/E♭ (G/D)
A♭ (G)
E♭/G (D/F♯)
You rain down the
You are turn - ing our
Fm7 (Em7)
E♭ (D)
A♭ (G)
cleans - ing flood. Heal - ing wa -
hearts back a - gain. And hear our prais -
E♭/G (D/F♯)
Fm7 (Em7)
A♭/E♭ (G/D)
- ters, rise a - round us,
- es rise to heav - en,

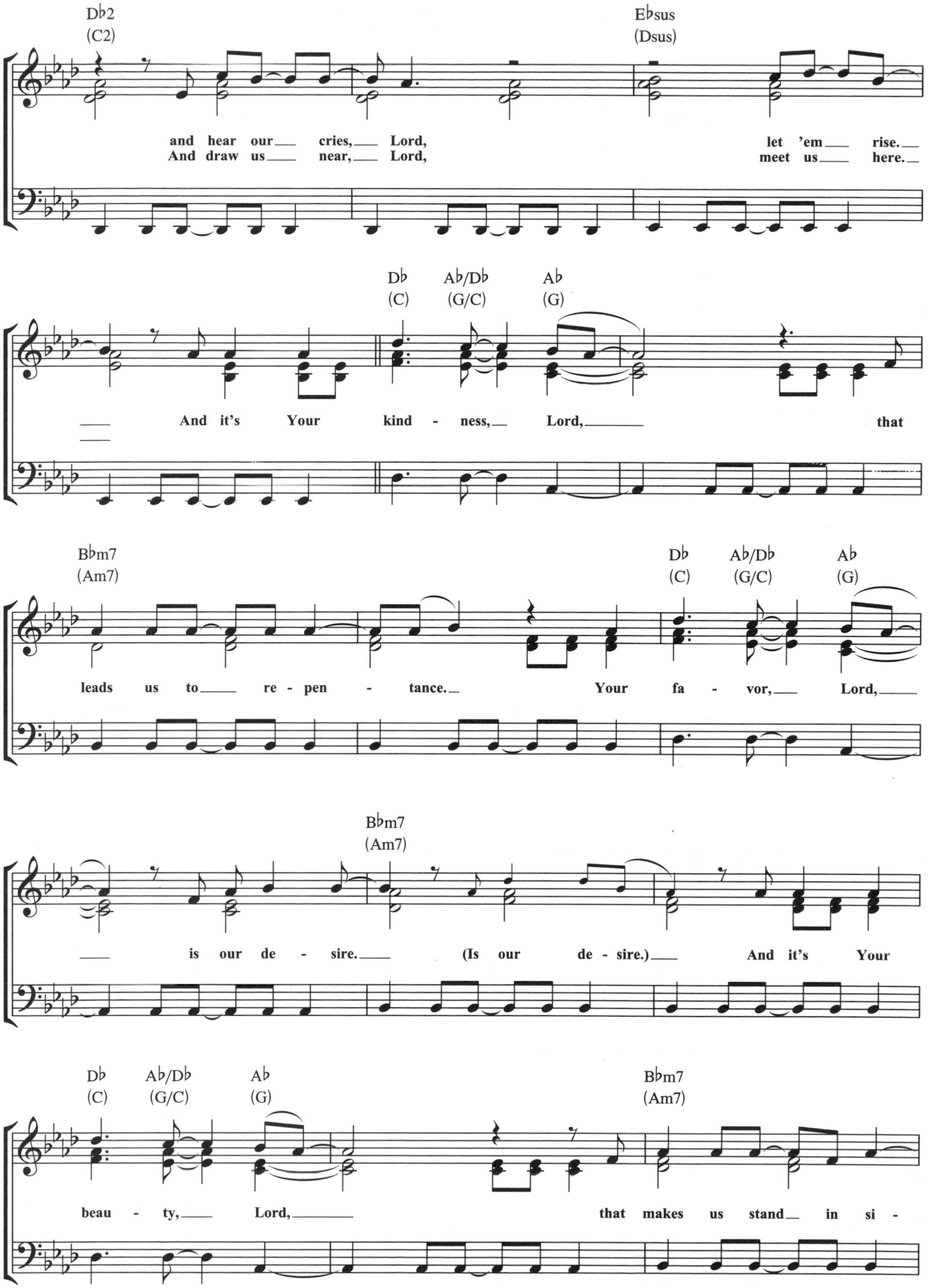

D♭2 (C2)
E♭sus (Dsus)
and hear our cries, Lord, let 'em rise.
And draw us near, Lord, meet us here.
D♭ (C) A♭/D♭ (G/C) A♭ (G)
And it's Your kindness, Lord, that
B♭m7 (Am7)
D♭ (C) A♭/D♭ (G/C) A♭ (G)
leads us to repentance. Your favor, Lord,
B♭m7 (Am7)
is our desire. (Is our desire.) And it's Your
D♭ (C) A♭/D♭ (G/C) A♭ (G)
B♭m7 (Am7)
beauty, Lord, that makes us stand in si-

D♭2
(C2)
- lence. and Your love, Your love,
A♭
(G)
is bet - ter than life.
B♭m7
(Am7)
D♭2
(C2)
A♭
(G)
B♭m7
(Am7)
D♭2
(C2)
1.
2.
A♭
(G)
You're bet - ter than all the rich - es of

Bbm7
(Am7)
Db2
(C2)
the world
bet - ter than all
(Bet - ter than all the rich - es of the world.
Ab
(G)
Bbm7
(Am7)
Db2
(C2)
the rich - es of the world.
Bet - ter than all the rich - es
Ab
(G)
Bbm7
(Am7)
You're bet - ter than all the rich - es of the world
of the world.
Bet - ter than all
Db2
(C2)
Ab
(G)
bet - ter than all the rich - es of
the rich - es of the world.
Bbm7
(Am7)
Db2
(C2)
the world
And it's Your
Lord, You're bet - ter than all the rich - es.)

D♭ (C) A♭/D♭ (G/C) A♭ (G) B♭m7 (Am7)
kind - ness, Lord, that leads us to re - pen -
D♭ (C) A♭/D♭ (G/C) A♭ (G)
- tance. Your fa - vor, Lord, is our de - sire.
B♭m7 (Am7) D♭ (C) A♭/D♭ (G/C) A♭ (G)
(Is our de - sire.) And it's Your beau - ty, Lord,
B♭m7 (Am7)
that makes us stand in si - lence. and Your
D♭2 (C2) 1.
love, Your love,

Chords Used in This Song

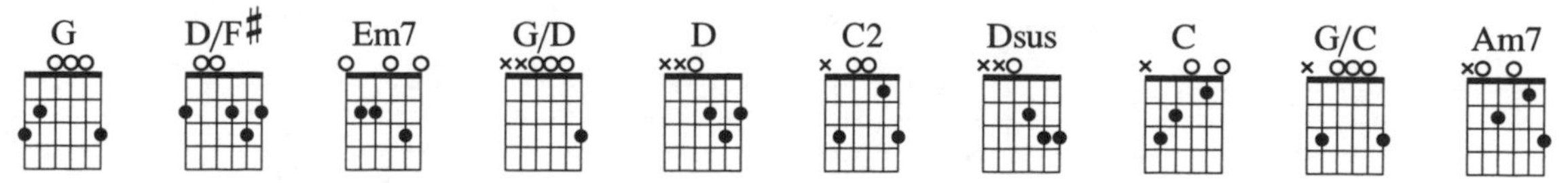

King of Glory

Words and Music by
CHRIS TOMLIN and JESSE REEVES

♩ = 100
G
1. Lift up your gaze, be lift - ed up, tell ev - 'ry -
(2. Lift up your) hands, be lift - ed up. Let the re -
C2
one how great the love,
deemed de - clare the love.
Em7
the love come down from heav - en's gate
And we bow down at heav - en's gate
C2
to kiss the earth with hope and grace.
to kiss the feet of hope and grace.
Sing:
G
Who is this King of Glo - ry?
C2
The Lord, strong

Em7
and might - y! Who is this King of Glo - ry?
C2 G
The Lord, strong and might - y!
1. 2. C2
2. Lift up your There is one God; He is
D Em7 G
Ho - ly. There is one Lord o - ver ev - 'ry - thing. There is
C2 D Em7
one King, He is Je - sus, King of glo - ry, strong

1. G
2. C2
G
and might - y! There is
and might - y!
You are the King
of Glo - ry,
C2
the Lord,
strong
and might - y!
Em7
You are the King
of Glo - ry,
C2
the Lord,
strong
1.
and might - y!
2.
and might - y!
G

Chords Used in This Song

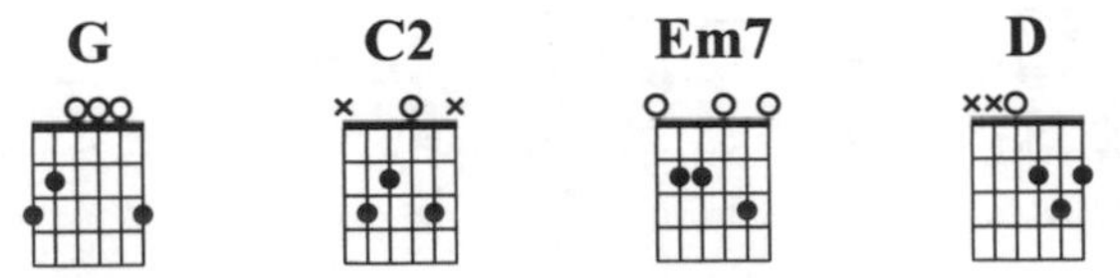
G
C2
Em7
D

Lamb of God

Words and Music by
REBECCA ST. JAMES
MATT BRONLEEWE
and JEREMY ASH

♩ = 92
Em C G D
1. I hear a voice of man - y peo - ple,
2. So let us be glad, let us re - joice,
Em C G D
I hear a voice like a might - y thun - der
— and let us give hon - or, glo - ry to the Lord.
Em C G D
sing - ing, Hal - le - lu - jah! For the Lord He reigns
And may ev - 'ry tribe and ev - 'ry tongue
C Bsus Em
Sing - ing, Hal - le - lu - jah! For the Lord He reigns
gath - er and sing prais - es to the ho - ly One.

Em C Am Bsus Em C
Lamb of God, ho - ly, Lord, You are
Am Bsus Em C Am Bsus
ho - ly. Lamb of God, ho - ly. You are
Em C Am Bsus Em
ho - ly.
1.
2.
Am/E
Em Am/E Em

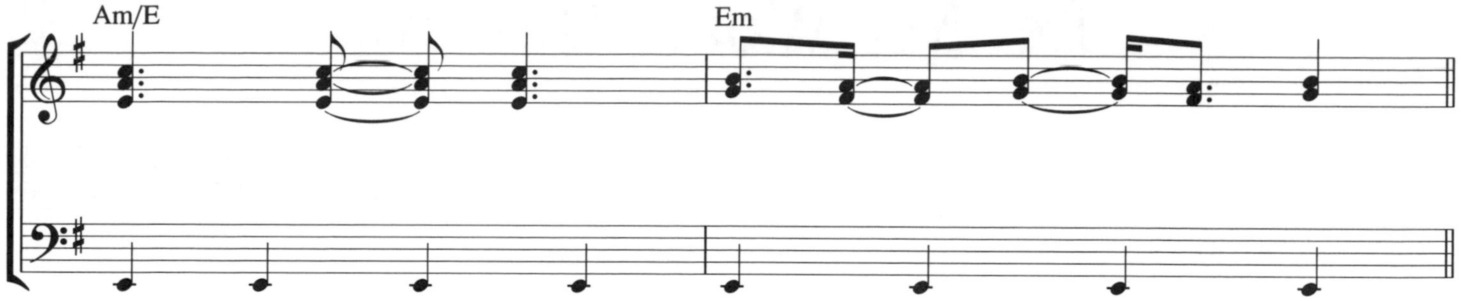

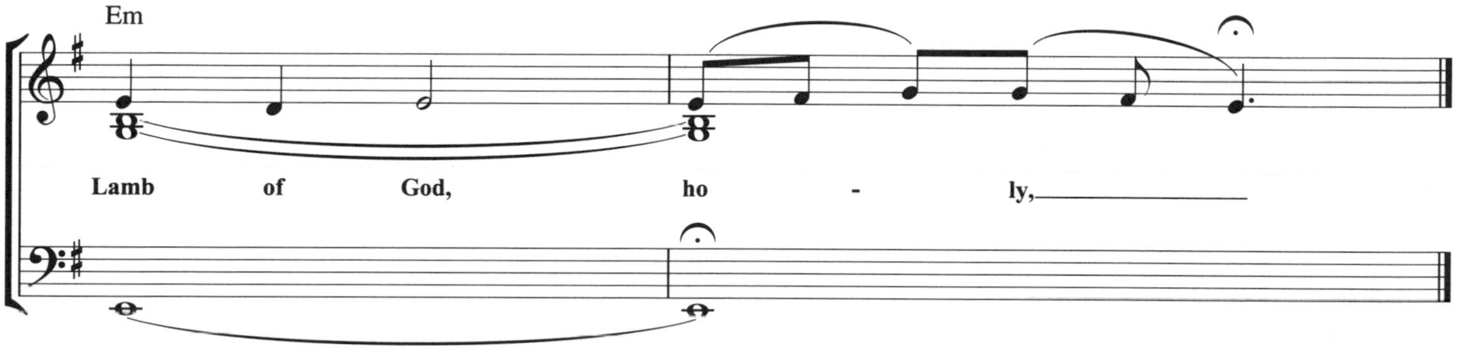

Chords Used in This Song

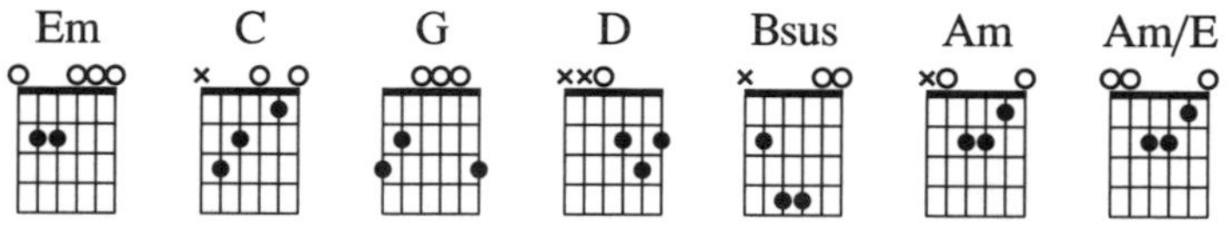

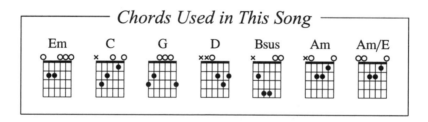

Let My Words Be Few

Words and Music by
MATT REDMAN and BETH REDMAN

♩ = 84
G
Gaug
1. You are God in heav - en, and here
2. The sim-plest of all love songs, I want
Em
Cmaj7
am I on earth,
to bring to You,
G
Gaug
so I'll let my words be few.
so I'll let my words be few.
Em
Cmaj7
C
Am7
G/B
Je - sus, I am so
Je - sus, I am so

C D G
— in love___ with You.___
— in love___ with You.___
F
And I'll stand in awe___ of You;___
Em Am7 G/B C G
yes, I'll stand in awe___
F Em C
of You.___ And I'll let___
Am7 G/B C Am7 G/B
my words___ be few,___ Je - sus, I___ am so___

C D G
1.
— in love — with You. —
2.
G F
And I'll stand in awe — of You; —
Em Am7 G/B C G
— yes, I'll stand in awe —
F Em
1.2.
C D
— of You. — And I'll
3.
C Am7 G/B C
And I'll let — my words — be few, — Je -

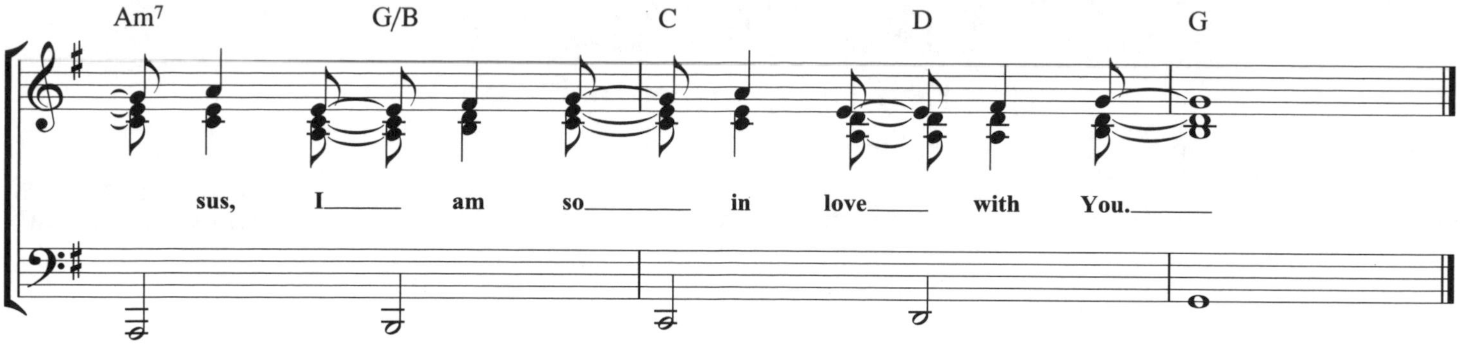
Am7
G/B
C
D
G
sus, I___ am so___ in love___ with You.___

Chords Used in This Song

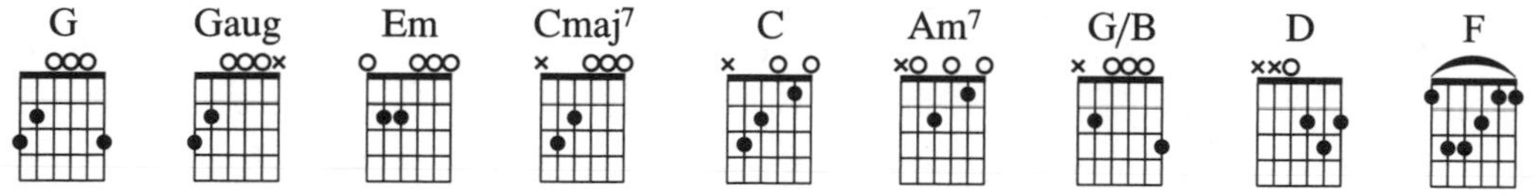

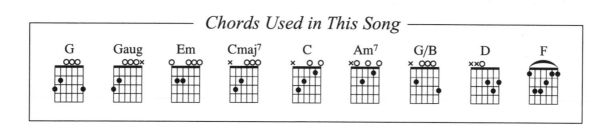

Like The Angels
(When I am Sinking Down)

Words and Music by
BRENTON BROWN

Capo 1 (C)
♩ = 75
Keyboard
(Guitar)
D♭ (C)
When I am sink - ing down, when I am lost at sea, no so - lace to be found,
(When I am all a) - lone, no land is in my sight. All oth - ers lost from view,
G♭2 (F2)
no ground be - neath my feet.
and comes the dark - 'ning night.
D♭ (C)
G♭2 (F2)
A♭sus (Gsus)
I turn to You as I go
I reach for You as I go

D♭ (C)
G♭2 (F2)
A♭sus (Gsus)
— down — I reach for You through roar - ing —
— down — I look to You through roar - ing —
D♭ (C)
G♭2 (F2)
A♭sus (Gsus)
— waves. — My on - ly hope is in Your —
— waves. —
B♭m7 (Am7)
G♭2 (F2)
A♭sus (Gsus)
— arms. — My on - ly prayer is that you'd —
D♭ (C)
G♭ (F)
— save me. — 'Cause You make me soar — like the
D♭ (C)
D♭/C (C/B)
an - gels. — You let me walk —

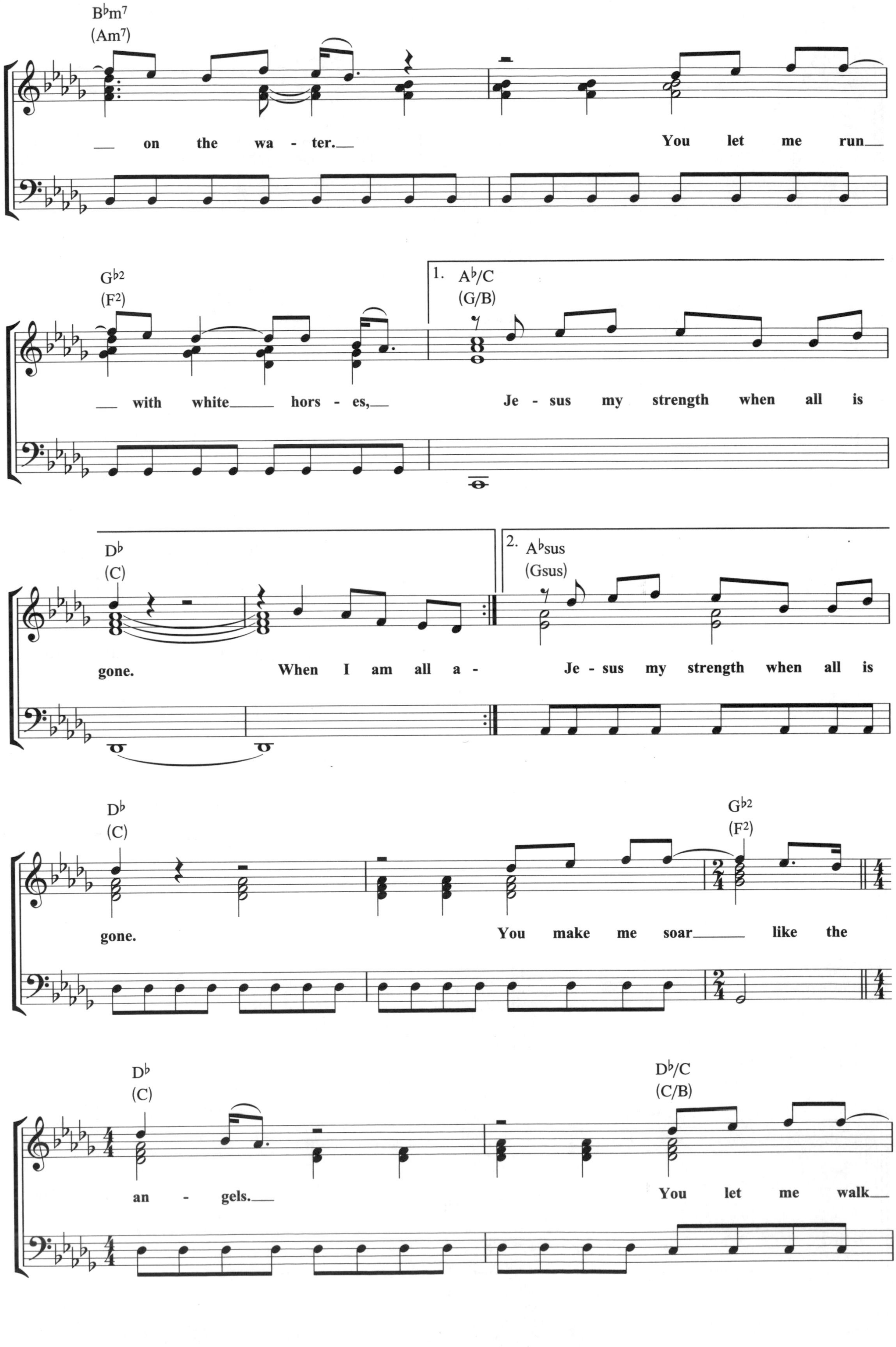
B♭m7
(Am7)
__ on the wa - ter.__
You let me run__
G♭2
(F2)
__ with white__ hors - es,__
1. A♭/C
(G/B)
Je - sus my strength when all is
D♭
(C)
gone.
When I am all a -
2. A♭sus
(Gsus)
Je - sus my strength when all is
D♭
(C)
gone.
You make me soar__
G♭2
(F2)
like the
D♭
(C)
an - gels.__
D♭/C
(C/B)
You let me walk__

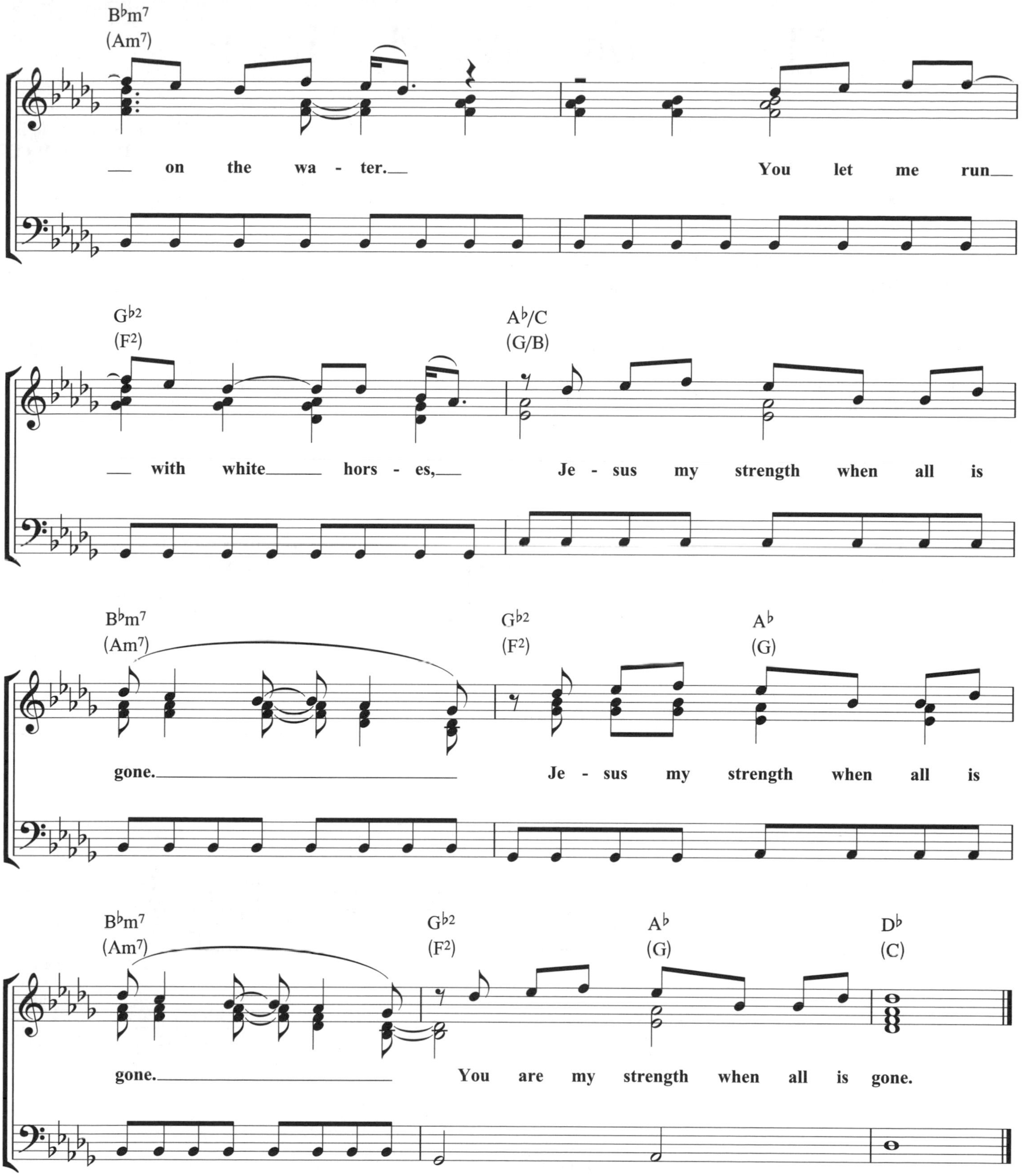
B♭m7
(Am7)
— on the wa - ter.— You let me run—
G♭2
(F2)
A♭/C
(G/B)
— with white— hors - es,— Je - sus my strength when all is
B♭m7
(Am7)
G♭2
(F2)
A♭
(G)
gone.— Je - sus my strength when all is
B♭m7
(Am7)
G♭2
(F2)
A♭
(G)
D♭
(C)
gone.— You are my strength when all is gone.

Chords Used in This Song

C
F2
Gsus
Am7
F
C/B
G/B
G

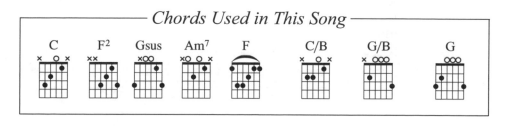

Lord You Have My Heart

Words and Music by
MARTIN SMITH

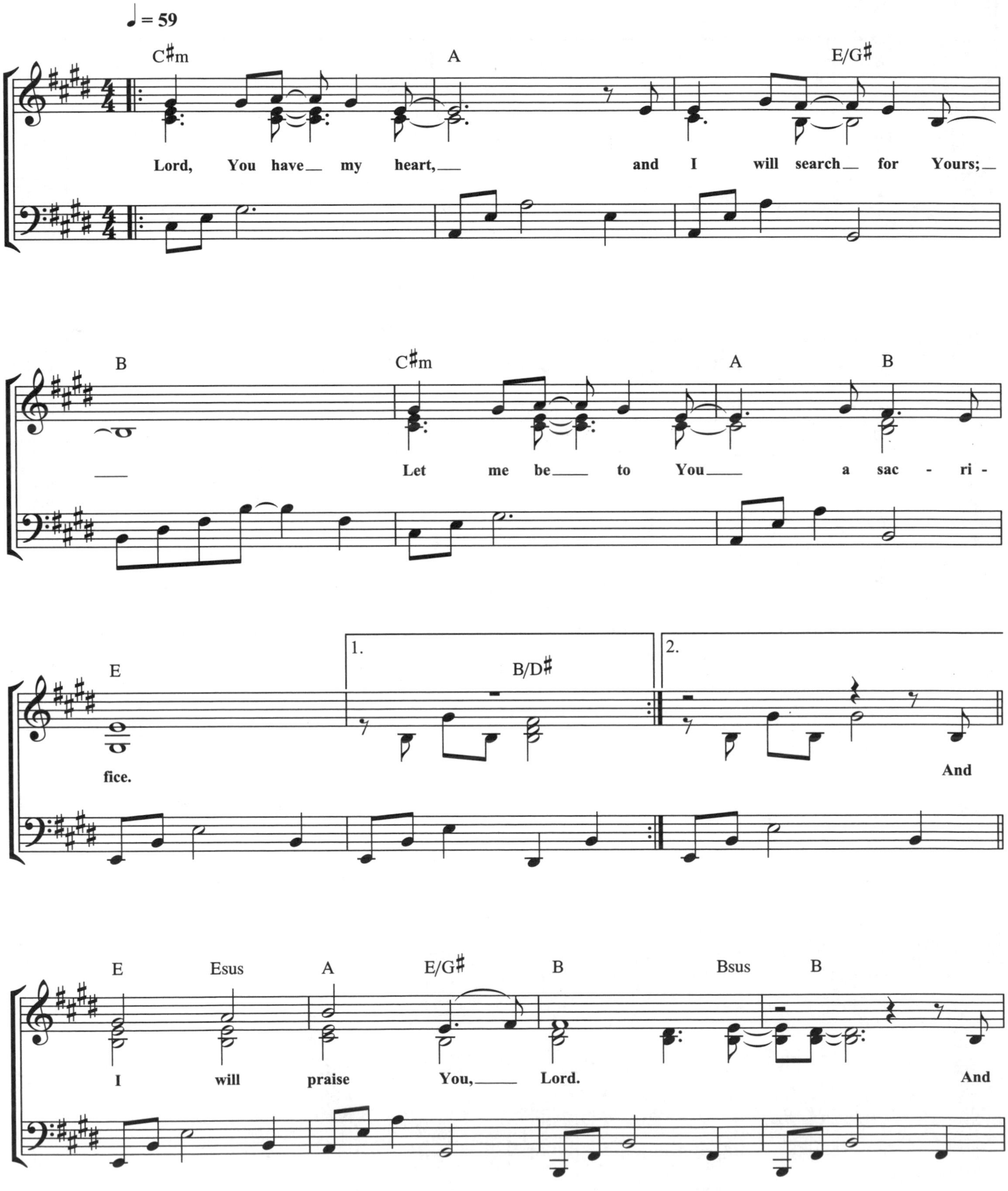
♩ = 59
C♯m
A
E/G♯
Lord, You have my heart, and I will search for Yours;
B
C♯m
A
B
Let me be to You a sac - ri -
E
1.
B/D♯
2.
fice.
And
E
Esus
A
E/G♯
B
Bsus
B
I will praise You, Lord.
And

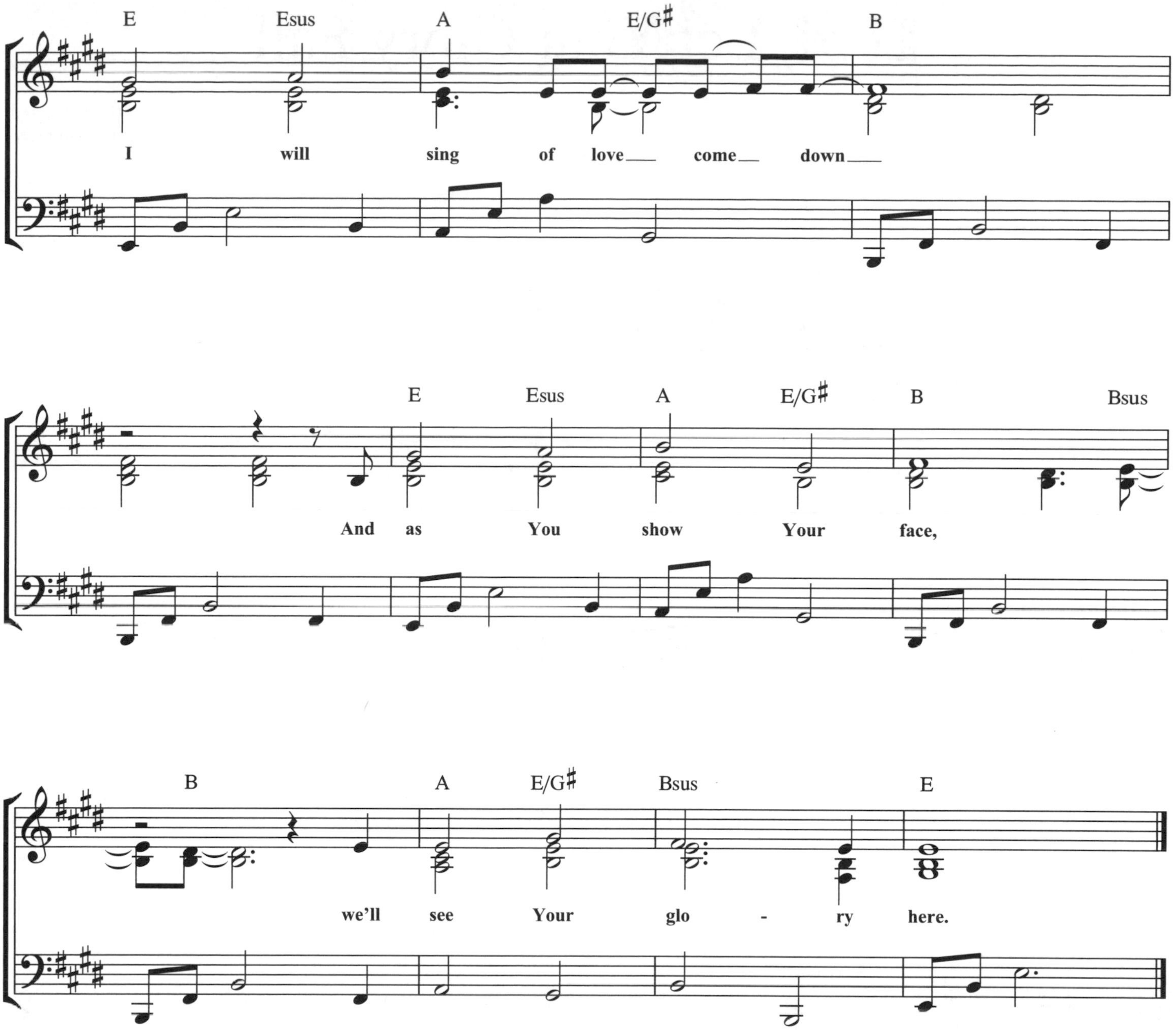
E Esus A E/G♯ B
I will sing of love come down
And as You show Your face,
E Esus A E/G♯ B Bsus
B A E/G♯ Bsus E
we'll see Your glo - ry here.

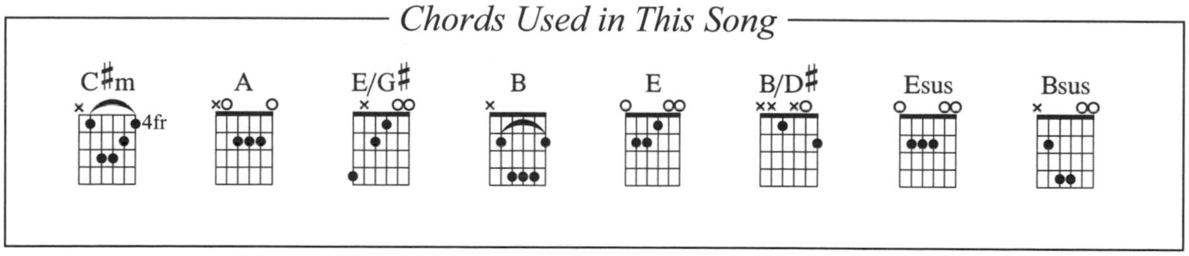
Chords Used in This Song
C♯m
4fr
A
E/G♯
B
E
B/D♯
Esus
Bsus

Lord, Let Your Glory Fall

Words and Music by
MATT REDMAN

Capo 1 (D)
♩ = 88
Keyboard
(Guitar)
E♭ (D)
A♭2 (G2)
1. Lord, let Your glo - ry fall
(2. Voic - es in u - ni) - son
E♭maj7/G (Dmaj7/F♯)
A♭2 (G2)
as on that an - cient day,
giv - ing You thanks and praise,
Cm (Bm)
B♭ (A)
A♭2 (G2)
songs of en - dur - ing love
joined by the in - stru - ments
Fm7 (Em7)
A♭ (G)
E♭ (D)
and then Your glo - ry came.
and then Your glo - ry came.

Eb/G
(D/F#)
Ab2
(G2)
And as a sign to You
Your pres - ence like a cloud
Ebmaj7/G
(Dmaj7/F#)
Ab2
(G2)
that we would love the same,
up - on that an - cient day,
Cm
(Bm)
Ab2
(G2)
our hearts will sing that song:
the priests were o - ver - whelmed
Fm7
(Em7)
Ab
(G)
Eb
(D)
God, let Your glo - ry come.
be - cause Your glo - ry came.
Eb/G
(D/F#)
You are good, You are good, and Your

A♭
(G)
E♭/G
(D/F♯)
love en - dures. You are good, You are good, and Your
A♭
(G)
Cm7
(Bm7)
E♭/G
(D/F♯)
3rd time to CODA
love en - dures. You are good, You are good, and Your
A♭
(G)
E♭
(D)
love en - dures to - day.
1.
2. A♭2
(G2)
2. Voic - es in u - ni -
Oh, Your
Cm
(Bm)
A♭
(G)
an - ger lasts a mo - ment, but your fa - vor lasts a life - time.

1.
2.
E♭ (D)
B♭ (A)
Yeah, yeah. Your
E♭ (D)
3. A sacrifice was
A♭2 (G2)
Ebmaj7/G (Dmaj7/F♯)
made, and then Your fi - re
A♭2 (G2)
Cm (Bm)
B♭ (A)
came; they knelt up - on the

A♭2 (G2) Fm7 (Em7) A♭ (G)
ground, and with one voice they
E♭ (D)
praised. They sang,
E♭/G (D/F♯) A♭2 (G2)
"Come, Lord.
E♭/G (D/F♯) A♭2 (G2)
Lord, let Your glo - ry fall,
E♭/G (D/F♯) A♭2 (G2)
let You glo - ry

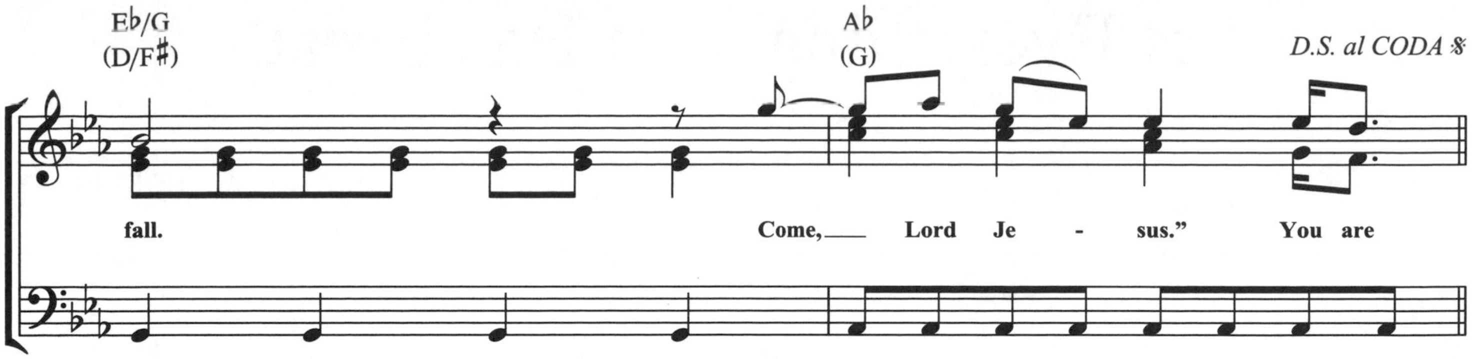

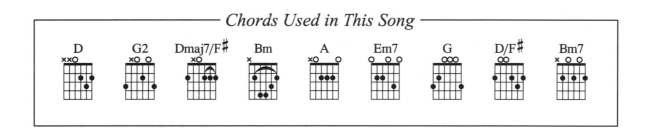

Chords Used in This Song

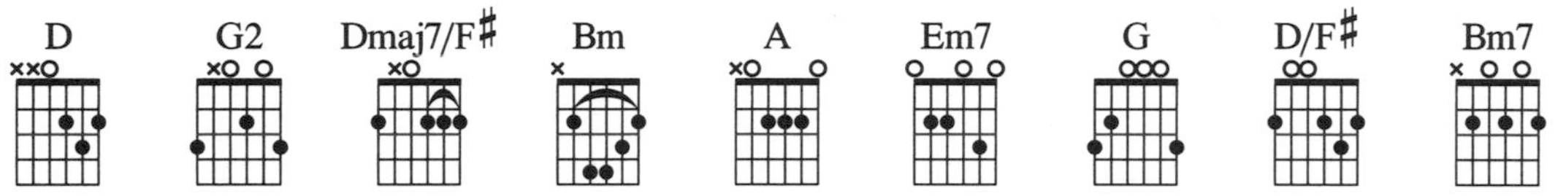

Let Everything That Has Breath

Words and Music by
MATT REDMAN

♩ = 120
E
E/D♯
Let ev - 'ry - thing that, ev - 'ry - thing that,
C♯m7
A
ev - 'ry - thing that has breath praise the Lord.
E
E/F♯
Let ev - 'ry - thing that, ev - 'ry - thing that,
3rd time to CODA
C♯m7
A
ev - 'ry - thing that has breath praise the Lord

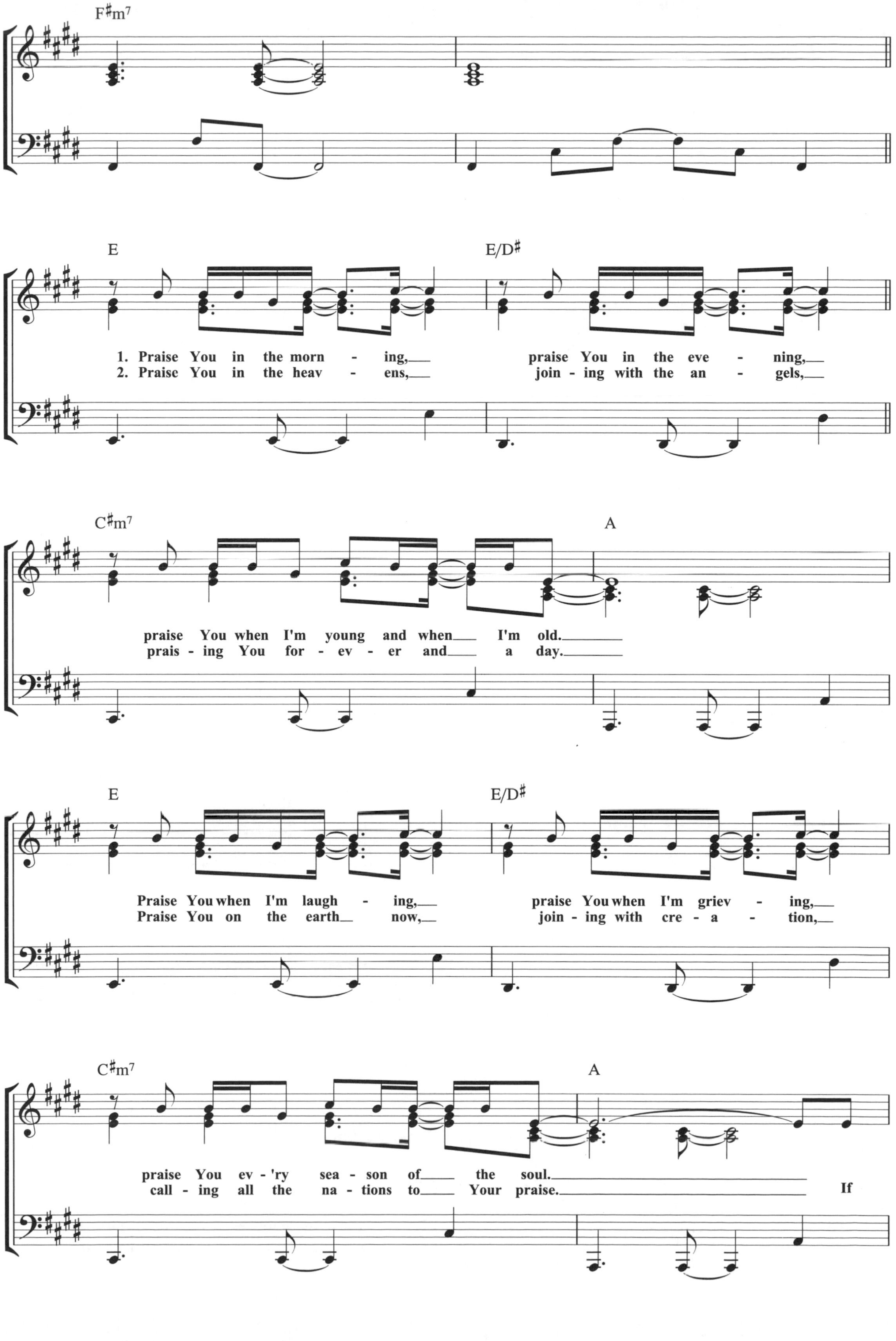
F♯m7
E
E/D♯
1. Praise You in the morn - ing, praise You in the eve - ning,
2. Praise You in the heav - ens, join - ing with the an - gels,
C♯m7
A
praise You when I'm young and when I'm old.
prais - ing You for - ev - er and a day.
E
E/D♯
Praise You when I'm laugh - ing, praise You when I'm griev - ing,
Praise You on the earth now, join - ing with cre - a - tion,
C♯m7
A
praise You ev - 'ry sea - son of the soul.
call - ing all the na - tions to Your praise. If

F♯m7
E2/G♯
we could see how much You're worth, Your
(they)
F♯m7
E2/G♯
pow'rs, Your might, Your end - less love, then
F♯m7
E2/G♯
sure - ly we would nev - er cease to
A
1.
2.
D.C. al CODA
praise.
CODA
A
E
has breath praise the Lord.

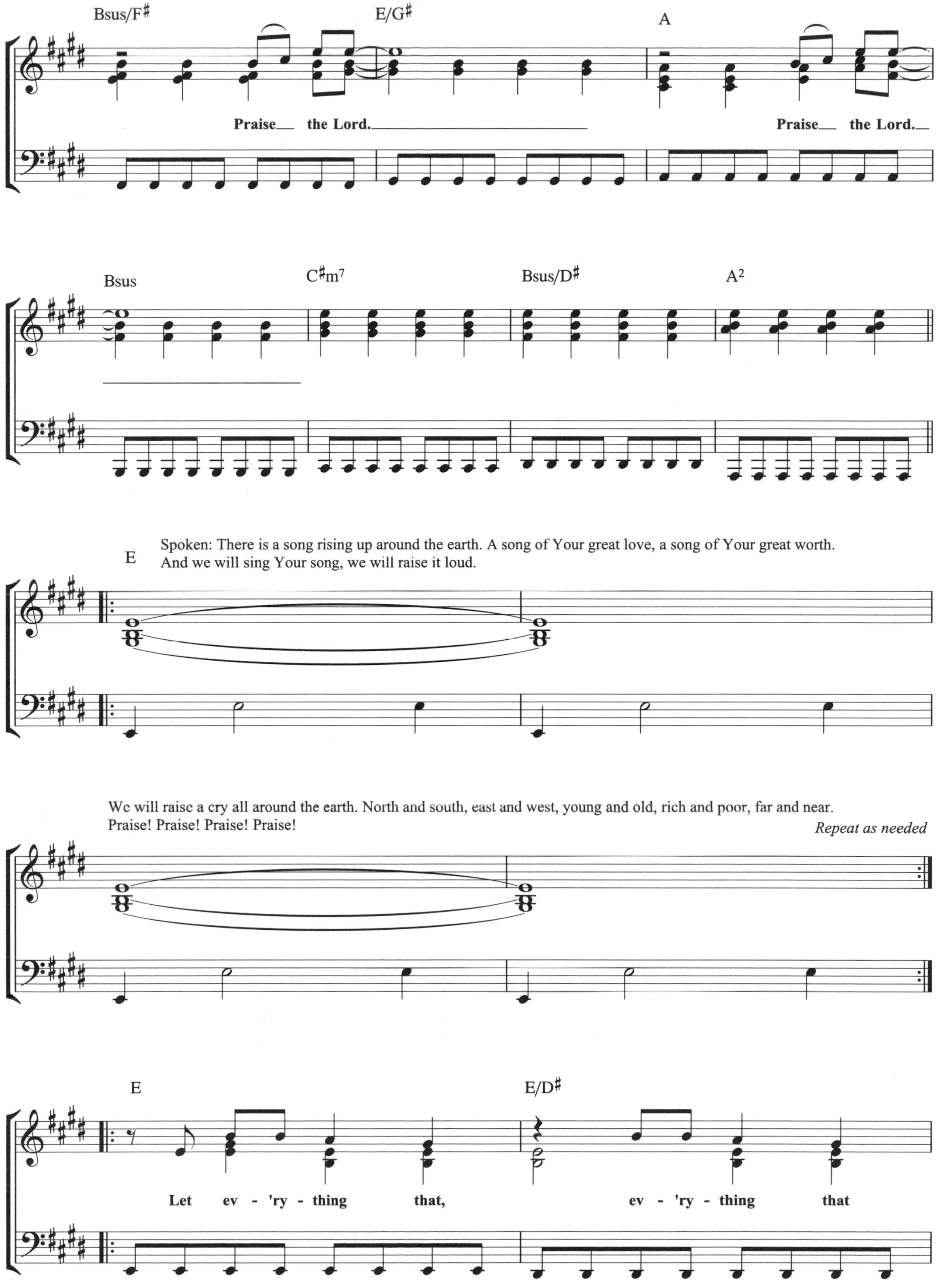
Bsus/F♯
E/G♯
A
Praise the Lord.
Praise the Lord.
Bsus
C♯m7
Bsus/D♯
A2
E
Spoken: There is a song rising up around the earth. A song of Your great love, a song of Your great worth.
And we will sing Your song, we will raise it loud.
We will raise a cry all around the earth. North and south, east and west, young and old, rich and poor, far and near.
Praise! Praise! Praise! Praise!
Repeat as needed
E
E/D♯
Let ev - 'ry - thing that, ev - 'ry - thing that

C#m7
A
ev - 'ry - thing that has breath praise the Lord.
E
E/F#
C#m7
Let ev - 'ry-thing that, ev - 'ry - thing that, ev - 'ry-thing that
1.
2.
A
A
E
has breath praise the Lord has breath praise the Lord.

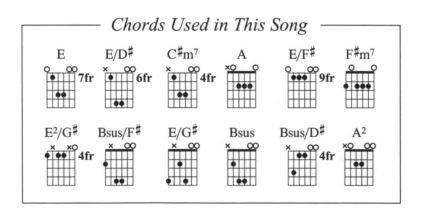

Chords Used in This Song

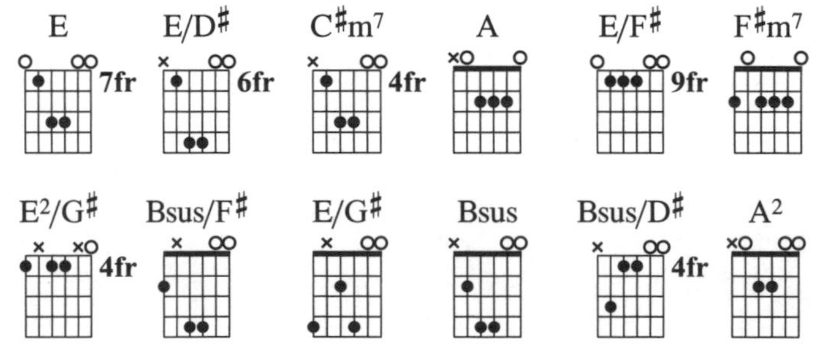

Lost in Wonder
(You Chose the Cross)

Words and Music by
MARTYN LAYZELL

Capo 3 (G) ♩ = 72

Keyboard
(Guitar)
B♭ (G)
1. You chose the cross with ev - 'ry breath; the
(2. You) loosed the cords of sin - ful - ness, and
Gm7 (Em7)
E♭2 (C2)
per - fect life, the per - fect death. You chose the cross.
broke the chains of my dis - grace; You chose the cross.
B♭ (G)
F/A (D/F♯)
B♭ (G)
A crown of thorns You wore for us, and
Up from the grave vic - to - ri - ous, You
Gm7 (Em7)
E♭2 (C2)
crowned us with e - ter - nal life; You chose the cross.
rose a - gain so glo - ri - ous; You chose the cross.

B♭ (G) F (D) Cm7 (Am7) B♭/D (G/B)
And though Your soul was o - ver - whelmed with pain,
The sor - row that sur - round - ed You was mine.
Fsus (Dsus) F (D) B♭/D (G/B) Cm7 (Am7) B♭/D (G/B)
o - be - di - ent to death, You o - ver -
Yet, "Not My will, but Yours be done," You
Fsus (Dsus) F (D) B♭ (G)
- came. I'm lost in won - der, I'm lost in
said.
Gm7 (Em7) E♭2 (C2)
love, I'm lost in praise for - ev - er - more.
F (D) B♭ (G)
Be - cause of Je - sus' un - fail - ing

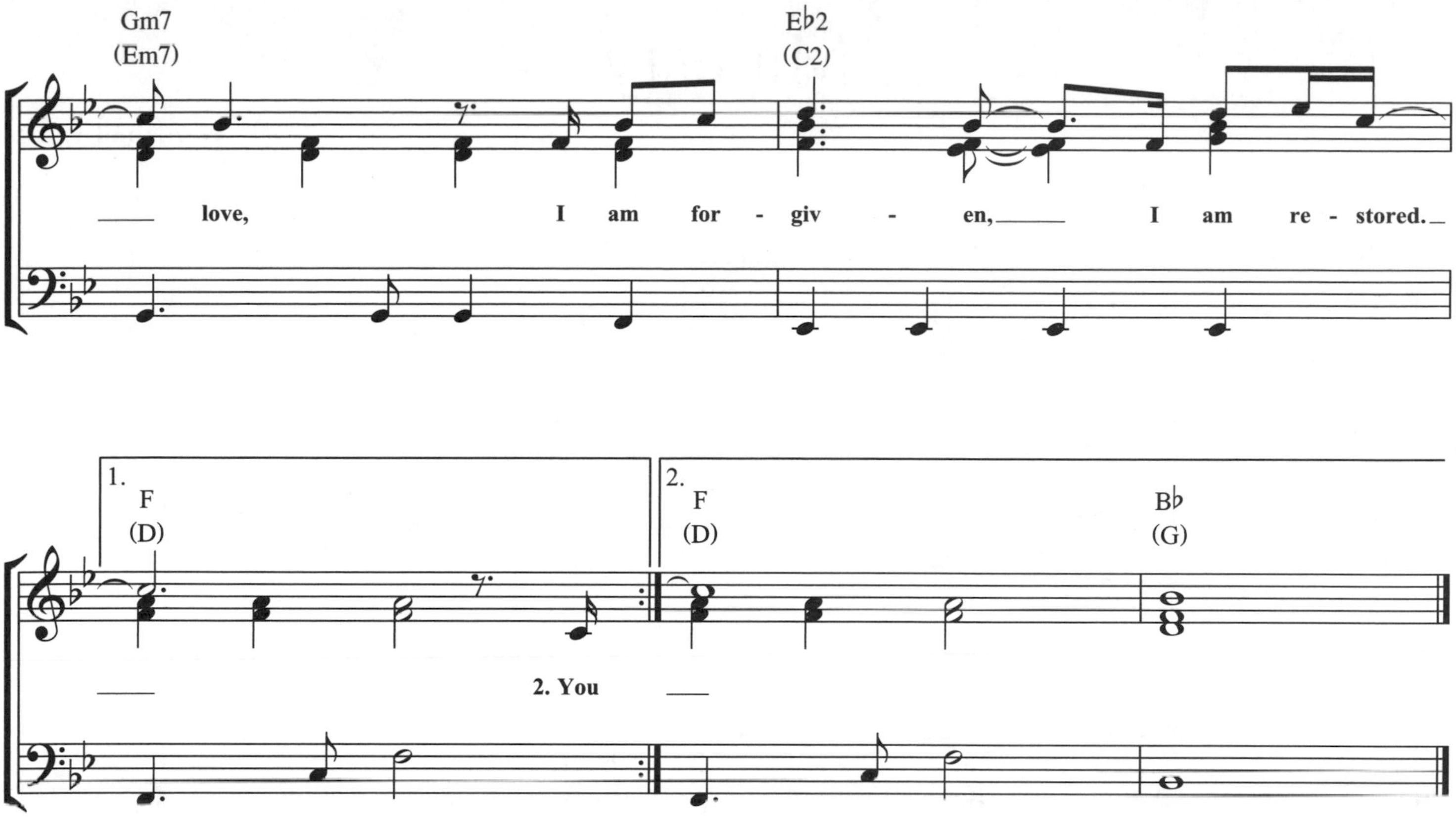

Chords Used in This Song

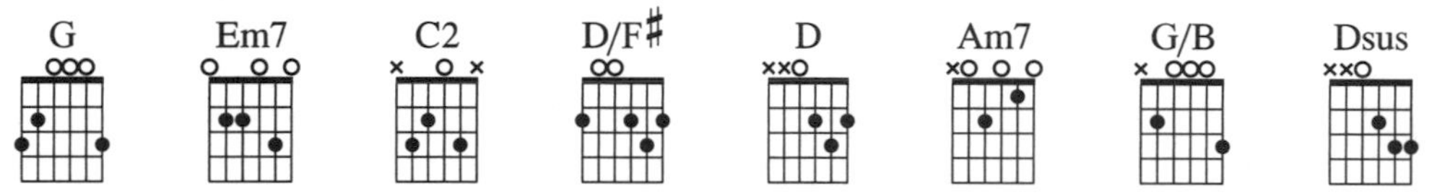

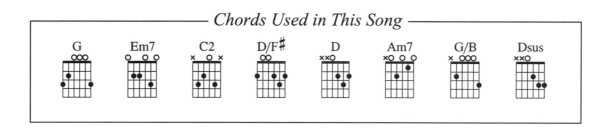

Majesty

Words and Music by
MARTIN SMITH and
STUART GARRARD

♩ = 76
Am
G
Fmaj7
1. Here I am,
2. Here I am,
C/E
Fmaj7
hum - bled by Your maj - es - ty,
hum - bled by the love that You give, for -
C/E
G/B
E7/G♯
cov - ered by Your grace so free.
giv - en so that I can for - give.
Am
G
Fmaj7
Here I am,
Here I stand,

C/E
Fmaj7
know - ing I'm a sin - ful man
know - ing I am Your de - sire,
C/E
G/B
E7/G♯
cov - ered by the blood of the Lamb.
sanc - ti - fied by glo - ry and fire.
Am
G/B
C
Now I've found the great - est love of all
Am
G/B
C
is mine since You laid down Your life,
D/F♯
F
the great - est sac - ri - fice.

C
1.2. Sing - in' maj - es - ty,
3. Maj - es - ty,
G
Am
maj - es - ty;
maj - es - ty;
F
C
Your grace has found me just as I
For - ev - er I am changed by Your
G
1. Am
emp - ty hand - ed, but a - live in Your hands.
in the
F
2. Am
hand - ed, but a - live in Your hands.

D.S.
3.
F
Am
Fmaj7
Sing - in' presence of Your maj - es - ty,
Am
G
F
Am
G
F
Sing - in'
C
G
Am
F
maj - es - ty,
maj - es - ty;
Your
C
G
grace has found me just as I am:
emp - ty

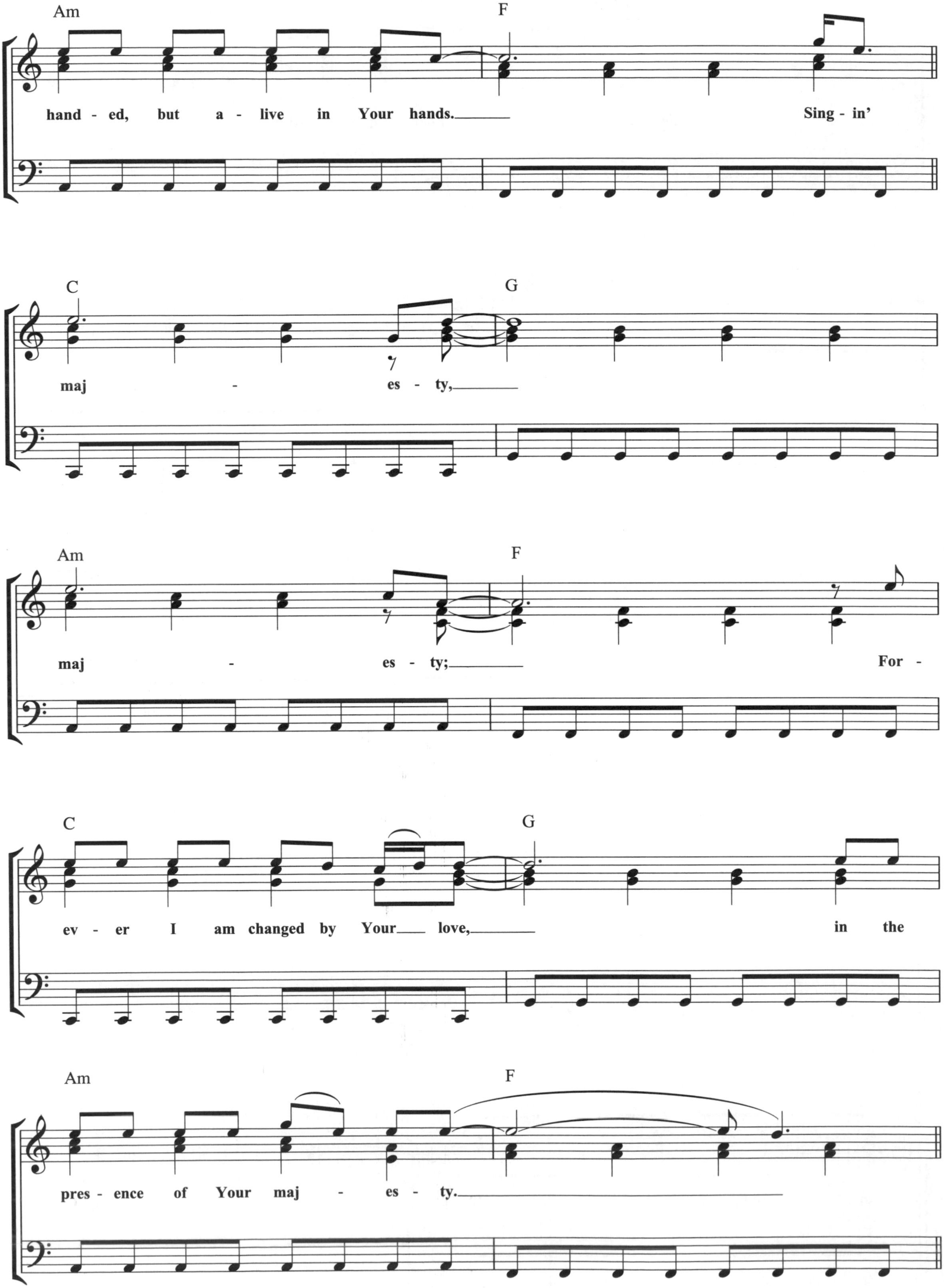
Am
F
hand - ed, but a - live in Your hands.
Sing - in'
C
G
maj - es - ty,
Am
F
maj - es - ty;
For -
C
G
ev - er I am changed by Your love,
in the
Am
F
pres - ence of Your maj - es - ty.

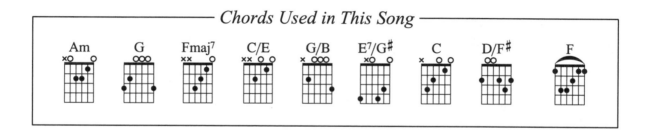

Chords Used in This Song

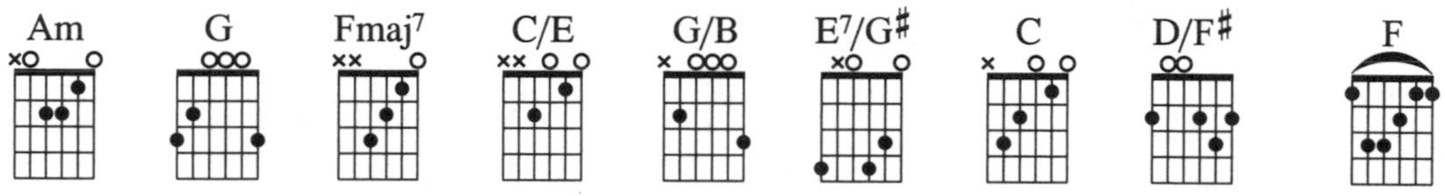

Marvelous Light

Words and Music by
CHARLIE HALL

Capo 2 (A)

♩ = 120

Keyboard
(Guitar)
B
(A)
E²
(D²)
Into marvelous light I'm running, out of darkness,
G♯m⁷
(F♯m⁷)
F♯
(E)
out of shame. Through the cross You are the truth, You
E²
(D²)
B
(A)
are the life, You are the way.
Bsus
(Asus)

B
(A)
E2
(D2)
1. I once was fa - ther - less, a strang - er
2. My dead heart now is beat - ing, my deep - est
B
(A)
with no hope. Your kind - ness wak - ened me,
stain's now clean. Your breath fills up my lungs;
E2
(D2)
B
(A)
wak - ened me from my sleep, now. Your love, it
Now I'm free, now I'm free. My dead heart
E2
(D2)
beck - ons deep - ly, a call to come and die.
now is beat - ing, my deep - est stain's now clean.
B
(A)
E2
(D2)
By grace now I will come and take this life,
Your breath fills up my lungs; Now I'm free,

G♯m7 (F♯m7) F♯ (E)
take Your life. Sin has lost its pow - er,
now I'm free.
E2 (D2) G♯m7 (F♯m7)
death has lost its sting. From the
F♯ (E) E (A)
grave You've ris - en vic - to - rious - ly.
B (A) E2 (D2)
In - to mar - vel - ous light I'm run - ning, out of dark - ness,
G♯m7 (F♯m7) F♯ (E)
out of shame. Through the cross You are the truth, You

E2 (D2)
B (A)
are the life, You are the way. In - to mar - vel - ous
E2 (D2)
light I'm run - ning, out of dark - ness, out of shame.
G#m7 (F#m7)
F# (E)
E2 (D2)
Through the cross You are the truth, You are the life, You
B (A)
arc the way.
1.
Bsus (Asus)
2.
E2 (D2)
Spoken: There's no more shame.

Bsus (Asus)
G♯m7 (F♯m7)
F♯sus (Esus)
No more shame.
E2 (D2)
And now we show the world Christ in you.
B (A)
Lift my
hands and spin a - round,
E2 (D2)
see the light that I have found.
F♯sus (Esus)
G♯m7 (F♯m7)
F♯sus (Esus)
Oh, the mar - vel - ous light, mar - vel - ous light. It's
1. E2 (D2)
Christ in You.
2. E2 (D2)
- vel - ous light.

B
(A)
E2
(D2)
In - to mar - vel - ous light I'm run - ning, out of dark - ness,
G♯m7
(F♯m7)
F♯
(E)
out of shame. Through the cross You are the truth, You
E2
(D2)
2nd time rit.
1.
2.
B
(A)
are the life, You are the way. are the way.

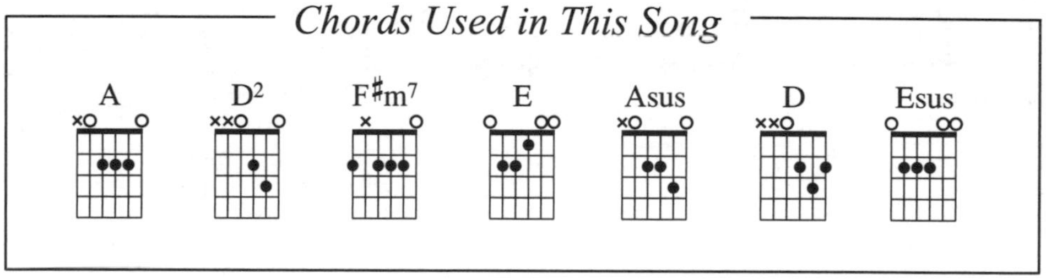
Chords Used in This Song
A
D2
F♯m7
E
Asus
D
Esus

Mighty Is the Power of the Cross

Words and Music by
CHRIS TOMLIN, SEAN CRAIG
and JESSE REEVES

Capo 2 (E) ♩ = 69
Keyboard
(Guitar)
G♭ (E)
E♭m (C♯m)
What can take a dy - ing man and raise him up to life a - gain?
What re - stores our faith in God, what re - veals the Fa - ther's love?
C♭ (A)
D♭/F (B/F♯)
What can heal a wound - ed soul, what can make us white as snow?
What can lead the way - ward home, what can melt a heart of stone?
G♭ (E)
E♭m (C♯m)
What can fill the emp - ti - ness, what can mend our brok - en - ness,
What can free the guilt - y ones, what can save and o - ver - come,
C♭ (A)
D♭ (B)
brok - en - ness?
o - ver - come?

C♭2 (A2) D♭ (B) G♭ (E) G♭/B♭ (E/G♯) C♭ (A) G♭/B♭ (E/G♯)
Might - y, awe - some, won - der - ful is the ho - ly cross
D♭ (B) D♭sus (Bsus) D♭ (B) C♭2 (A2) D♭ (B) G♭ (E) G♭/B♭ (E/G♯)
where the Lamb laid down His life to
3rd time to CODA
C♭ (A) G♭/B♭ (E/G♯) D♭ (B) C♭2 (A2) E♭m7 (C♯m7)
lift us from the fall. Might - y is the
1.
D♭/F (B/D♯) G♭ (E) C♭ (A)
pow - er of the cross.
2.
D♭/F (B/D♯) C♭ (A)
pow - er of the cross. Itís a mir - a - cle to me,

G♭/B♭ (E/G♯)
C♭ (A)
itís a mir - a - cle to me, and itís still a mys - ter - y,
G♭/B♭ (E/G♯)
C♭ (A)
and itís still a mys - ter - y. itís a mir - a - cle_ to me,
G♭/B♭ (E/G♯)
A♭m7 (F♯m7)
D♭/F (B/D♯)
D.S. al CODA 𝄋
the pow - er of God, for those who be - lieve.
CODA
D♭/F (B/D♯)
G♭ (E)
pow - er of the cross._

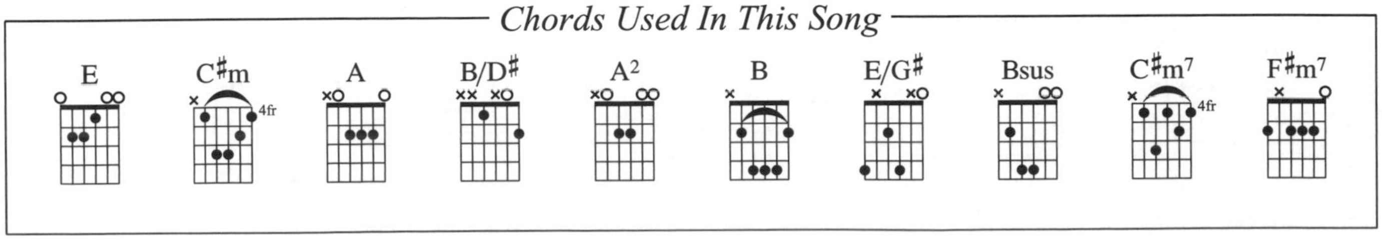
Chords Used In This Song
E
C♯m
4fr
A
B/D♯
A2
B
E/G♯
Bsus
C♯m7
4fr
F♯m7

My Drink
(I Remember You)

Words and Music by
CHARLIE HALL and
TODD CROMWELL

♩ = 88
F♯m
See the blaze that burns in me when I
E
see You; and You look at me, O Lord.
D2
F♯m
On You I med - i - tate, and as

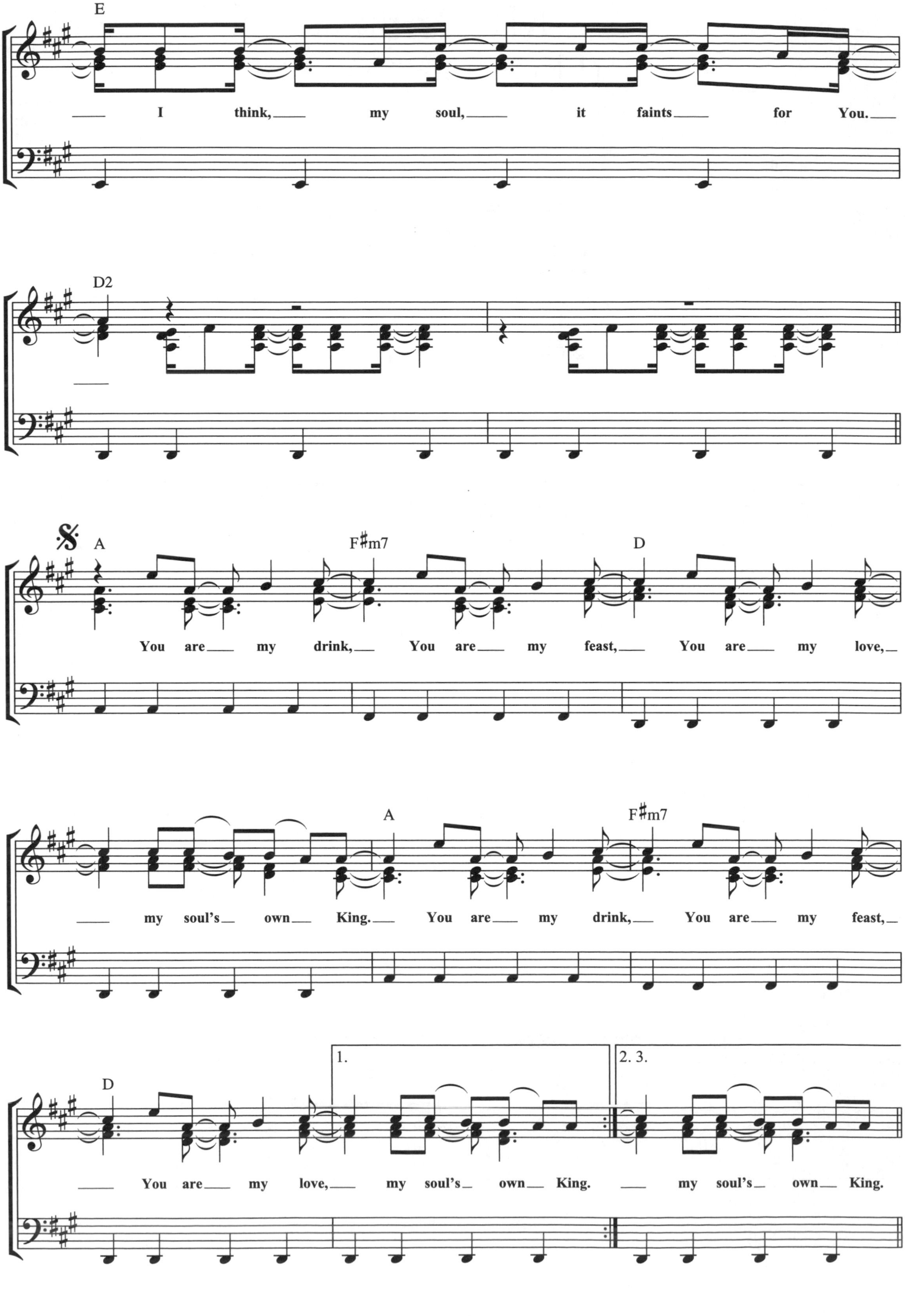

E
I think, my soul, it faints for You.
D2
A
F♯m7
D
You are my drink, You are my feast, You are my love,
my soul's own King.
A
F♯m7
You are my drink, You are my feast,
D
You are my love,
1.
my soul's own King.
2. 3.
my soul's own King.

D/F♯ E/G♯ F♯m7 E D/F♯ E/G♯
F♯m7 E 2nd time: FINE D/F♯ E/G♯
Your bod - y and Your blood, and I
F♯m7 E D/F♯ E/G♯
re-mem - ber You.
Up - on the cross You hung, and I
1. F♯m7 E
re-mem - ber You.
2. F♯m7
D.S. al FINE
re-mem - ber You.

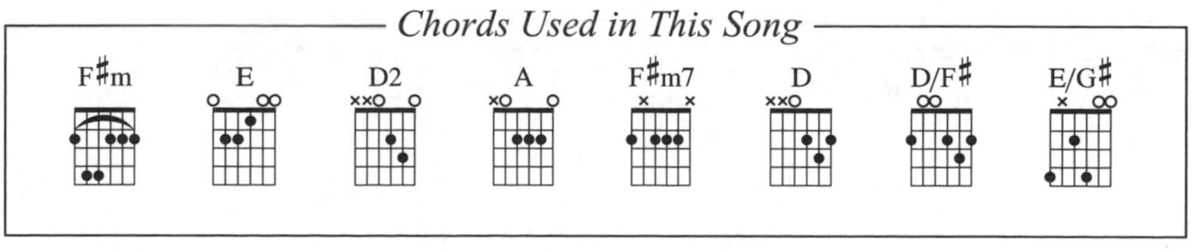
Chords Used in This Song
F♯m E D2 A F♯m7 D D/F♯ E/G♯

My Glorious

Words and Music by
STUART GARRARD
and MARTIN SMITH

♩ = 80
F♯m7
1. The world's shak - ing with the love of
2. Clouds are break - ing, heav - en's come to
D
God.
earth.
Bm
F♯m7
Great and glo - rious, let the whole earth
Hearts a - wak - 'ning, let the church bells
D
sing.
ring.
Bm
And all

D
A/C♯
you ev - er do is change the old for new.
Bsus
Peo - ple we be - lieve that
A
E/G♯
God is big - ger than the air I
F♯m7
E
breathe, the world we'll leave.
A
E/G♯
God will save the day, and all will

F♯m7
1.
E
say ___ my glo - ri - ous!
F♯m7
Bm7
C♯m7
2.
E
ous! ___ My glo - ri - ous, ___ my glo - ri -
D
E
ous, ___ my glo - ri - ous, ___ my glo - ri -
D/F♯

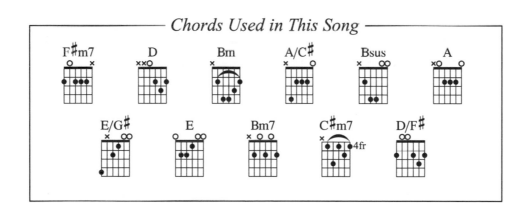

Chords Used in This Song

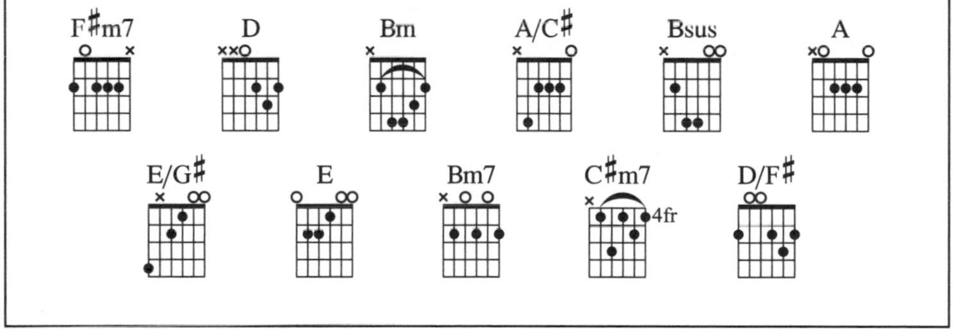

My Tribute

Words and Music by
ANDRAE CROUCH

Moderately slow 𝅗𝅥 = 60
C 7
C 7/B
How ___ can I say thanks ___
C7/B♭
for all the ___ things _
Asus
A7
Dm7
that You've done ___ for me? _
Dm7/A
Dm(maj7)
Dm7/A
Things ___ so un - de - served, ___

Dm7
Dm7/A
Fm/D
and yet You gave
to prove Your love for me.
C/G
And the voic - es
Am7
Am7/G
Am/F♯
of a mill - ion an - gels
could not
Fm/D
ex - press
my grat - i - tude.
C/E
C/D
C♯dim7
All that I am
and ev - er hope to be

Dm7 Em7 F2 G7sus
I owe it all
Cmaj7
to Thee.
G7sus G7 C
To God be the
Em7 A7 Dm7
glo - ry, to God be the
Fm/D G E7sus E7
glo - ry, to God be the

Am7
Am7/G
Am/F♯
glo - ry, for the things He has
G7sus
G
C
done. For with His blood,
(His
(2nd & 3rd times, Lead Vocal ad lib.)
Em7
A7
He has saved me. and
blood, He has saved me.
Dm7
Fm/D
with His pow'r, He has raised
His pow'r, He has
G
E7sus
E7
me. To God. be the
raised me. To God,

3rd time, to CODA 2
Am7
D7
C/G
glo - ry, for the things
glo - ry.)
2nd time, to CODA 1
G7sus
G
Csus
C
He has done. Just
Dm/B
E7
let me live my life,
Am
Am(maj7)
and let it be pleas - ing Lord, to
Am7
Am6
Fmaj7
Thee. And should I gain

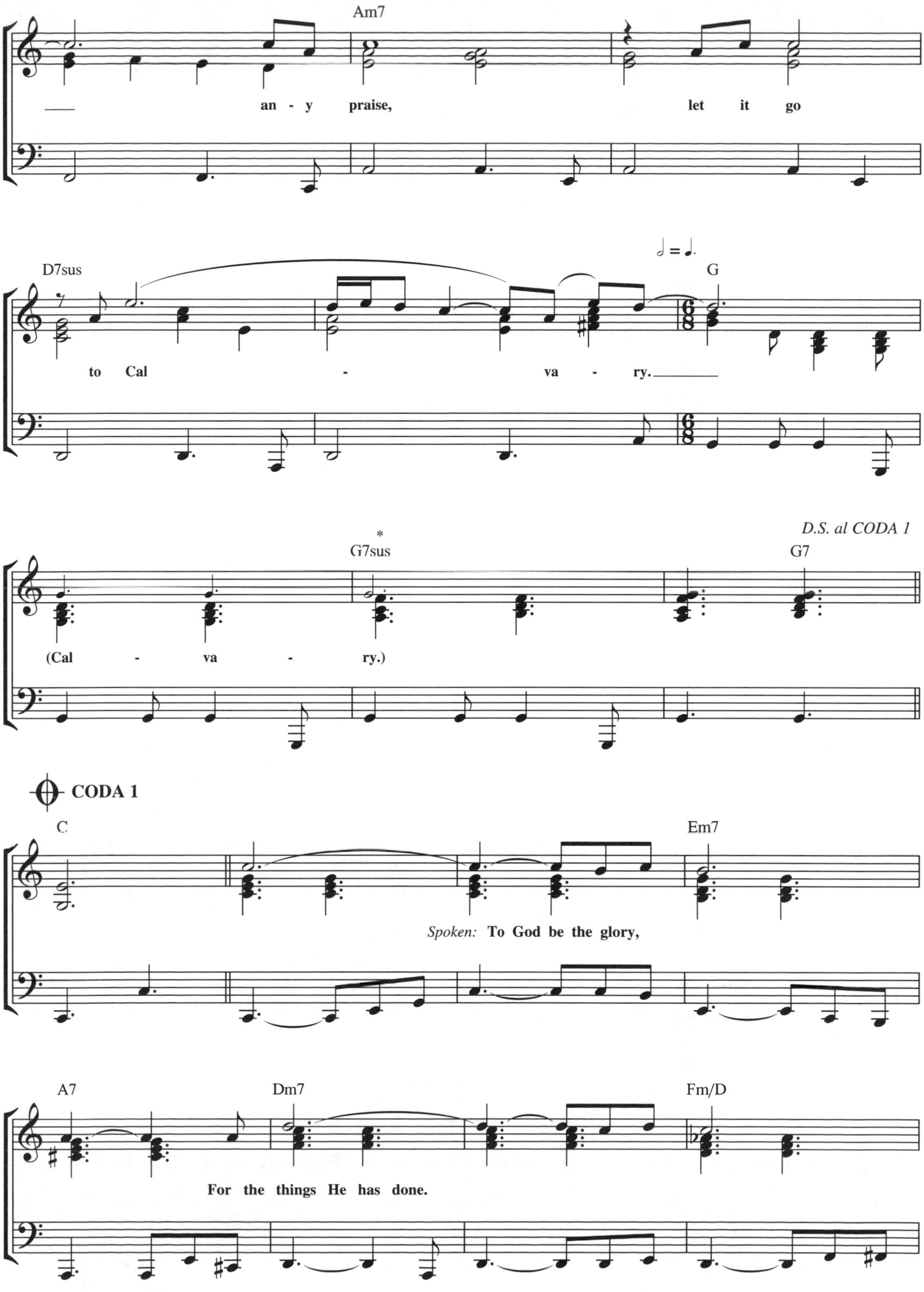
Am7
any - y praise, let it go
D7sus
G
to Cal - va - ry.
D.S. al CODA 1
G7sus
G7
(Cal - va - ry.)
CODA 1
C
Em7
Spoken: To God be the glory,
A7
Dm7
Fm/D
For the things He has done.

*At this point the recorded version modulates up ½-step to D♭.

G
E7sus
E7
Am7
Wherever you are, give Him praise.
The Bible says,
D7/A
Am/F♯
G7sus
"Let everything that has breath praise the Lord." He is worthy.
CODA 2
D.S. al CODA 2
G7
Sung: Oh, for with His
C/G
G♯aug
things He has
Am7
D7sus
C/G
done. For the things, oh, He is
Lead Vocal ad lib. to end
E7
E7/G♯
Am7
Lord. For the things He has

Chords Used in This Song

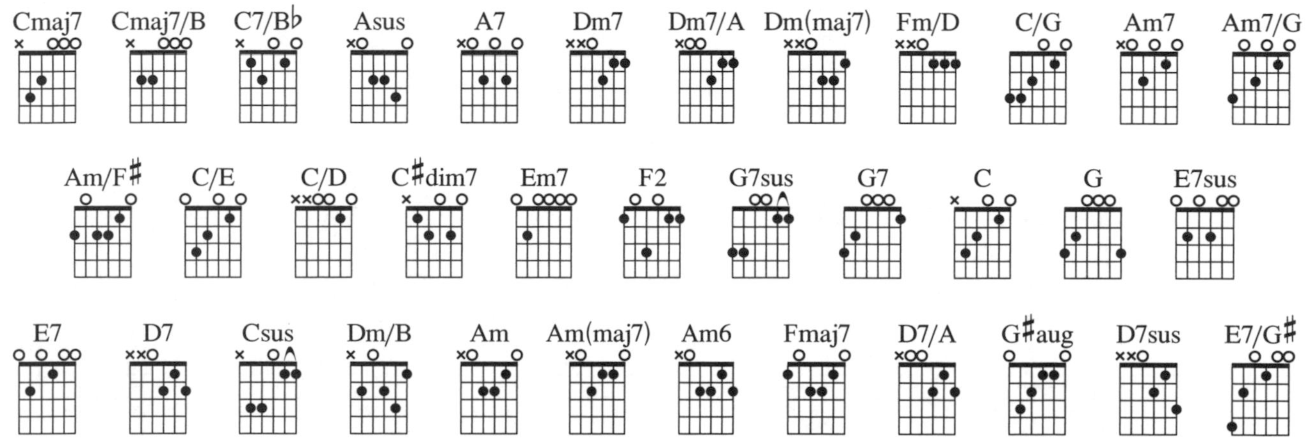

Name Above All Names

Words and Music by
TIM HUGHES

♩ = 120
A
Your name is high - ly ex - alt - ed;
Rul - ers will one day be si - lent,
F♯m
Je - sus for - ev - er be glo - ri - fied,
lost in the won - der and awe of Your name,
E/G♯
For - ev - er be glo - - ri - fied.
the won - der and awe of Your name.
D2
A
Your name has
E - ter - nal,

F#m
pow - er to con - quer, Your fame re -
none is Your e - qual. We cry,
B/D#
sounds through - out heav - en and earth, re -
"No oth - er God but You,
Dmaj7
sounds through - out heav - en and earth.
no oth - er God but You."
A
Name a - bove all names,
F#m
You are glo - ri - ous.

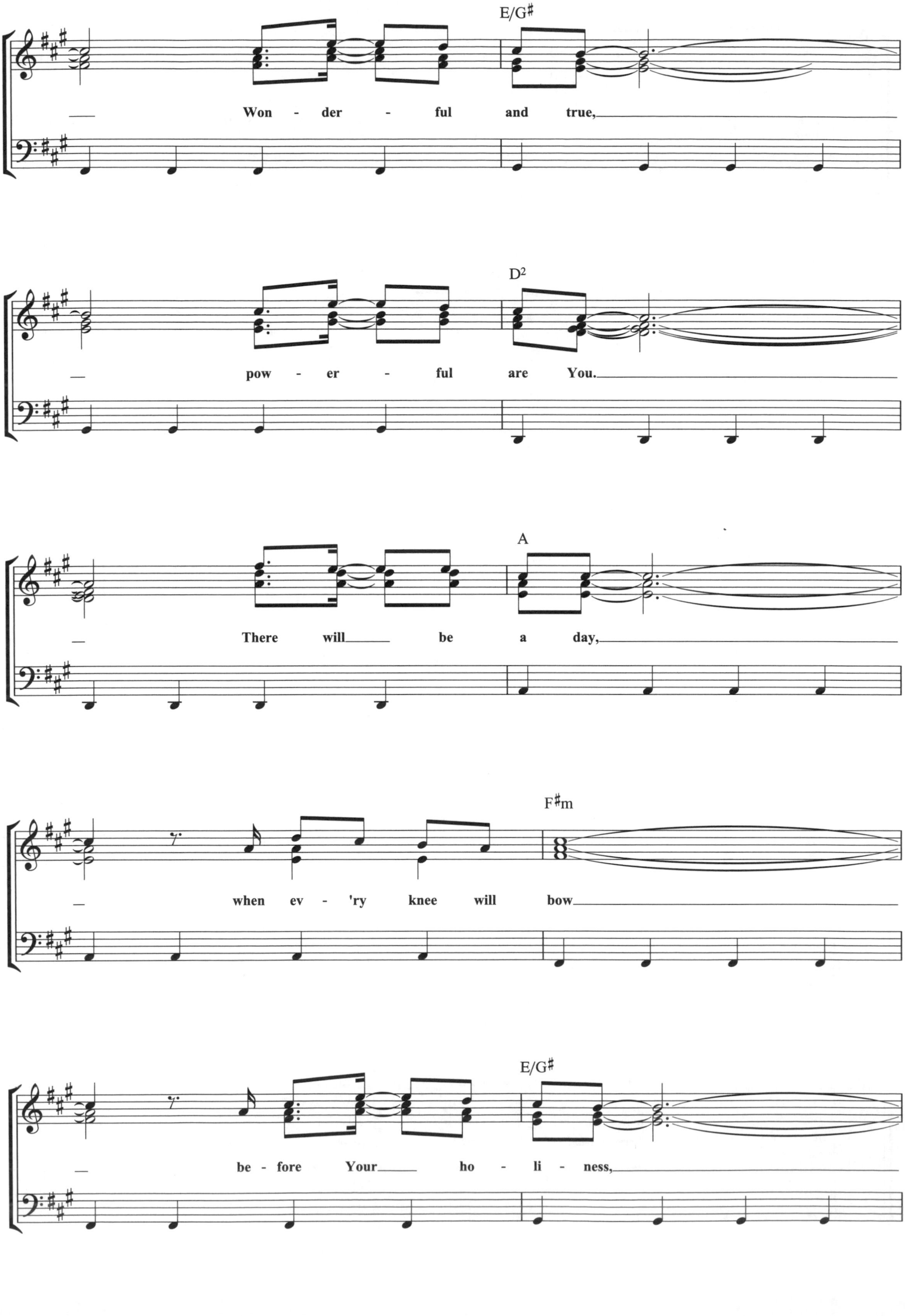
E/G♯
Won - der - ful and true,
D²
pow - er - ful are You.
A
There will be a day,
F♯m
when ev - 'ry knee will bow
E/G♯
be - fore Your ho - li - ness,

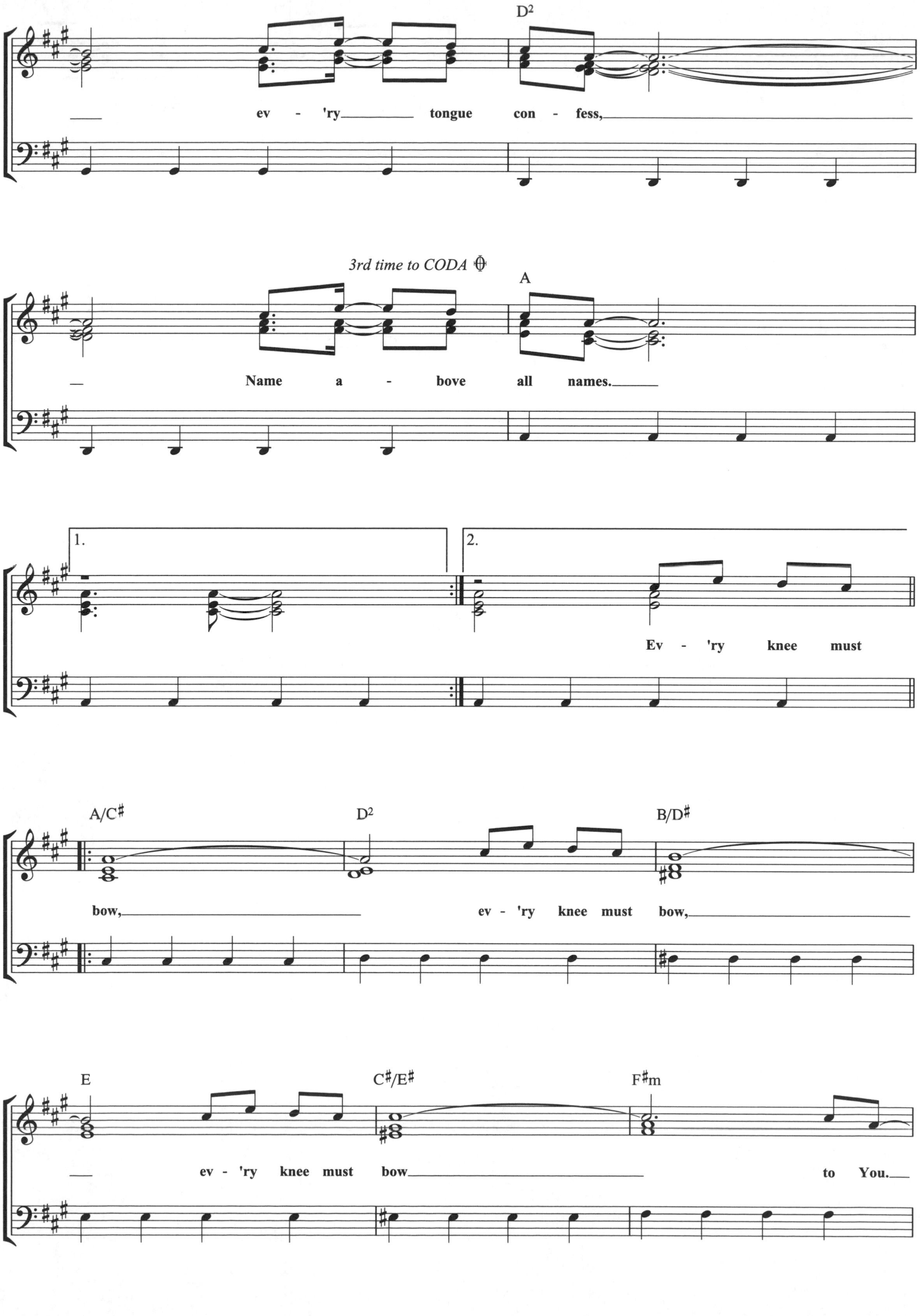
D2
ev - 'ry tongue con - fess,
3rd time to CODA
A
Name a - bove all names.
1.
2.
Ev - 'ry knee must
A/C♯
D2
B/D♯
bow, ev - 'ry knee must bow,
E
C♯/E♯
F♯m
ev - 'ry knee must bow to You.

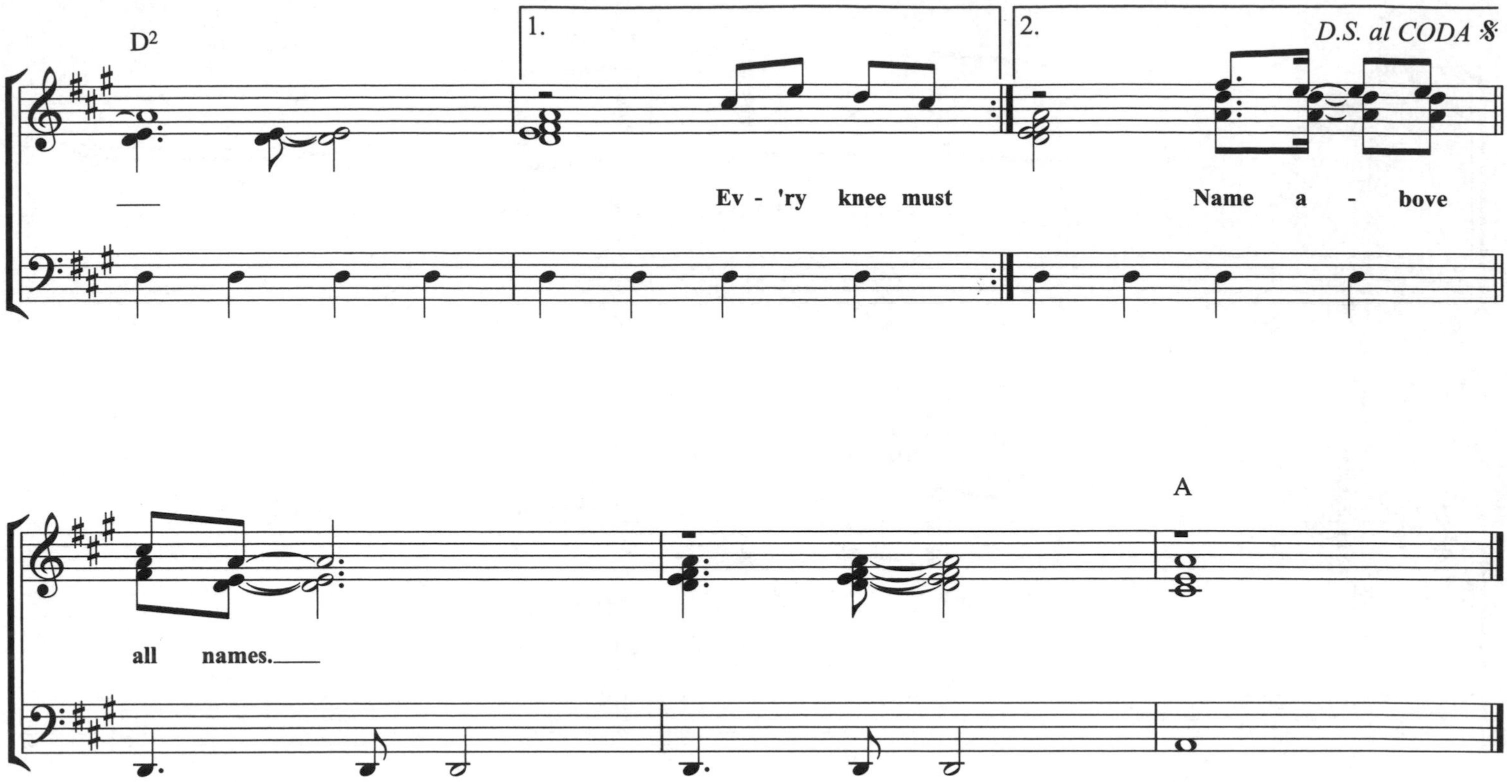
D2
1.
2.
D.S. al CODA
Ev - 'ry knee must
Name a - bove
all names.
A

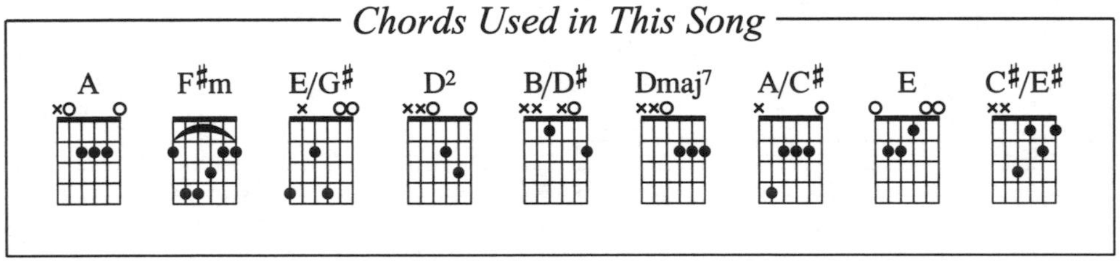
Chords Used in This Song
A
F#m
E/G#
D2
B/D#
Dmaj7
A/C#
E
C#/E#

No One Like You

Words and Music by
DAVID CROWDER, JACK PARKER,
MIKE DODSON, JASON SOLLEY,
MIKE HOGAN and JEREMY BUSH

Capo 2 (E)

♩ = 88

F♯ (E) D♯m7 (C♯m7) F♯/C♯ (E/B) B2 (A2)
2. You are more, beau-ti-ful than an-y-one ev-er.
3. Ev-'ry-where, You are there, Earth or air, sur-round-ing.
Ev-'ry day, You're the same; You nev-er change, no nev-er.
I'm not a-lone, the heav-ens sing a-long. My God You're so a-stound-ing.
2nd time go to CHORUS
And how could I ev-er de-ny the love of my Sav-ior.
How could You be so good to me? E-ter-nal-ly, I be-lieve.
These 4 measures 1st time only
You are to me, ev-'ry-thing; all I need, for-ev-er.
Go on to CHORUS
C♯ (B) B/D♯ (A/C♯) C♯/E♯ (B/D♯)
How could You be so good?

CHORUS
F♯ (E) C♯ (B) D♯m7 (C♯m7) B2 (A2)
There is no one like You.
F♯ (E) C♯ (B)
There has nev - er
1. D♯m7 (C♯m7) B2 (A2)
ev - er been an - y - one like You.
2. D♯m7 (C♯m7) B2 (A2)
ev - er been an - y - one like You,
F♯ (E) F♯/C♯ (E/B)
You, You, You, You,
D♯m7 (C♯m7) B2 (A2)
You, You.
F♯ (E) F♯/C♯ (E/B)
D♯m7 (C♯m7) B2 (A2)
C♯sus (Bsus)
How could You

B2
(A2)
C#sus
(Bsus)
be so good to me?
B2
(A2)
C#sus
(Bsus)
We're not a - lone,
B2
(A2)
C#sus
(Bsus)
so sing a - long.
We're not a - lone,
B2
(A2)
so sing a - long,
sing a - long,
sing a - long.
F#
(E)
C#
(B)
There is

D#m7
(C#m7)
B2
(A2)
F#
(E)
C#
(B)
no one like You. There has nev - er,
1.
D#m7
(C#m7)
B2
(A2)
ev - er been an - y - one like You.
2.
D#m7
(C#m7)
B2
(A2)
ev - er been. There is
no one like our
F#
(E)
God.

Chords Used in This Song

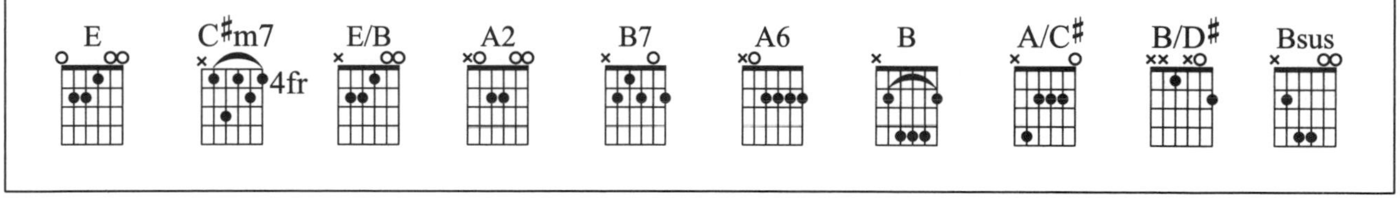
E
C#m7
4fr
E/B
A2
B7
A6
B
A/C#
B/D#
Bsus

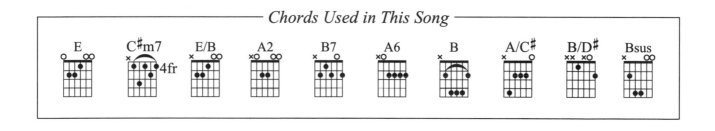

Not To Us

Words and Music by
CHRIS TOMLIN
and JESSE REEVES

Capo 2 (A)

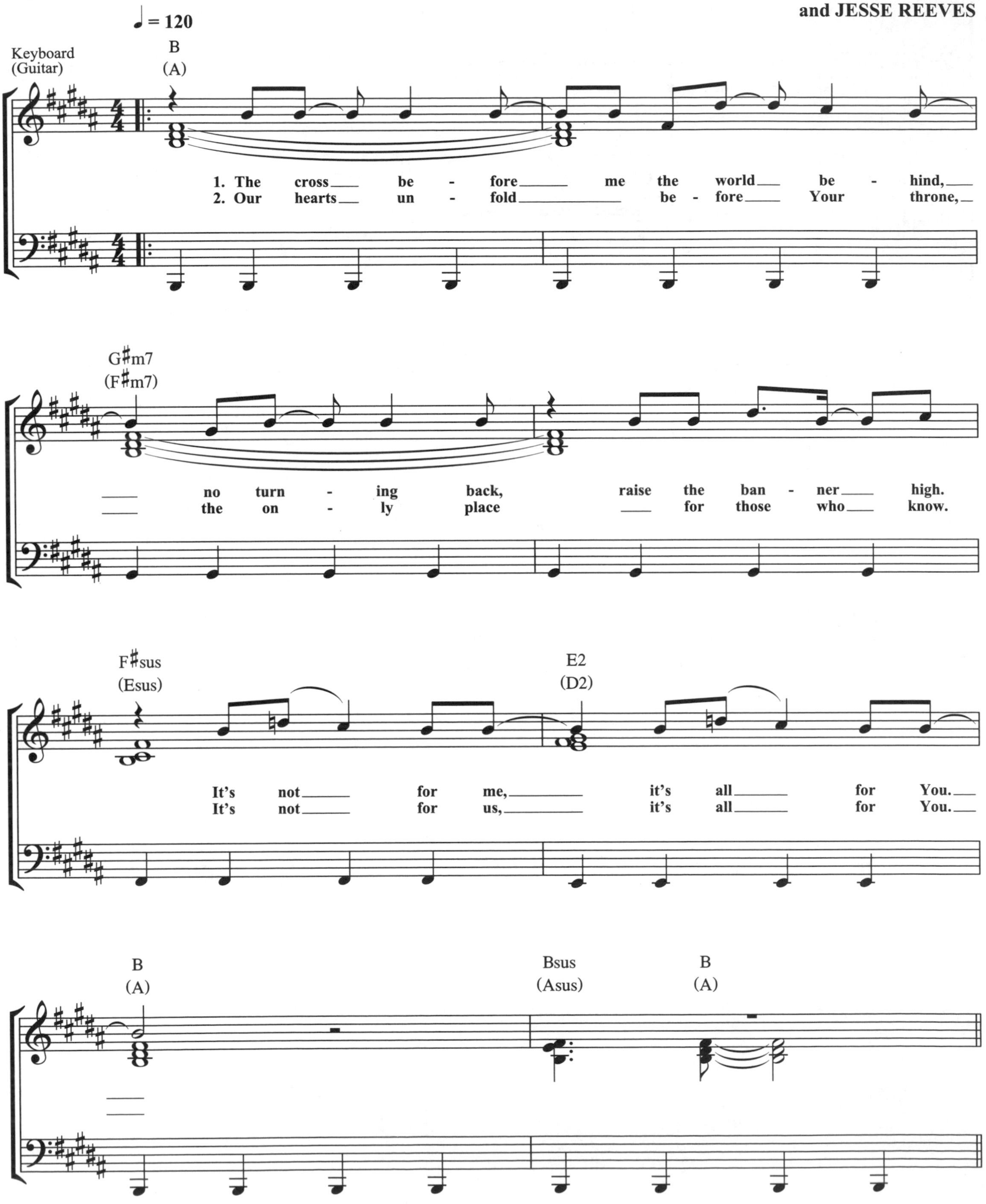
♩ = 120
Keyboard
(Guitar)
B
(A)
1. The cross be - fore me the world be - hind,
2. Our hearts un - fold be - fore Your throne,
G♯m7
(F♯m7)
no turn - ing back, raise the ban - ner high.
the on - ly place for those who know.
F♯sus
(Esus)
E2
(D2)
It's not for me, it's all for You.
It's not for us, it's all for You.
B
(A)
Bsus
(Asus)
B
(A)

Let the heav - ens shake and split the sky,
Send Your ho - ly fire on this of - fer - ing,
G♯m7
(F♯m7)
let the peo - ple clap their hands and cry.
let our wor - ship burn for the world to see.
F♯sus
(Esus)
E2
(D2)
It's not for us, it's all for You.
It's not for us, it's all for You.
B
(A)
Bsus
(Asus)
B
(A)
Not to us,
but to Your name
A/E
(G/D)
E
(D)
be the glo -

A/E (G/D) E (D) B (A)
- ry. Not to us, but to Your name
A/E (G/D) E (D) 1. A/E (G/D) E (D) B (A)
be the glo - ry.
B2 (A2) Emaj7 (Dmaj7) E (D) A/E (G/D) E (D)
2. A/E (G/D) E (D) B (A)
- ry. The earth is shak - ing, the
E6 (D6) E (D)
moun - tains shout - ing, it's all for You.

E6 (D6) E (D) G♯m7 (F♯m7)
The waves are crash - ing, the
F♯sus (Esus) E (D)
sun is rag - ing, it's all for You.
B (A)
The u - ni - verse spin - ning and sing - ing,
E6 (D6) E (D) E6 (D6) E (D)
it's all for You. Your
G♯m7 (F♯m7) F♯sus (Esus)
chil - dren danc - ing, danc - ing, danc - ing,

E (D)
Bsus (Asus)
B (A)
it's all for You, it's all for You,
Bsus (Asus)
B (A)
E2 (D2)
E (D)
Emaj7 (Dmaj7)
E (D)
All glo-
B (A)
-ry and hon-or and praise, all glo-
Emaj7 (Dmaj7)
-ry and hon-or and praise, all glo-
G♯m7 (F♯m7)
F♯ (E)
-ry and hon-or and praise, all glo-

Emaj7
(Dmaj7)
1.
2.
- ry and hon - or and praise.
All glo -
B
(A)
A/E
(G/D)
E
(D)
Not to us,
but to Your name
be the glo -
A/E
(G/D)
E
(D)
G♯m7
(F♯m7)
F♯
(E)
- ry.
Not to us,
but to Your name
E
(D)
B
(A)

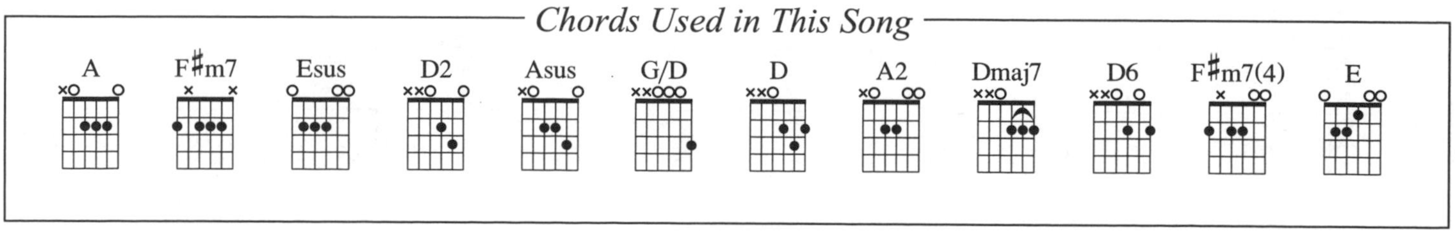
Chords Used in This Song
A
F♯m7
Esus
D2
Asus
G/D
D
A2
Dmaj7
D6
F♯m7(4)
E

Nothing But the Blood

Capo 2 (A)

Words and Music by
MATT REDMAN

Keyboard
(Guitar)
♩ = 80
B
(A)
G♯m7
(F♯m)
1.2. Your blood speaks a bet - ter word than all the emp - ty claims
(3. Your) cross tes - ti - fies in grace, tells of the Fa - ther's heart
B
(A)
G♯m7
(F♯m)
I've heard up - on this earth, speaks right - eous - ness for me,
to make a way for us. Now bold - ly we ap - proach;
F♯
(E)
E
(D)
and stands in my de - fense; Je - sus, it's Your blood.
not earth - ly con - fi - dence, it's on - ly by Your blood.
B
(A)
1.
G♯m7
(F♯m7)
F♯
(E)
2. Your blood
2.,3.
G♯m7
(F♯m7)
F♯
(E)

B (A) G♯m7 (F♯m7)
What can wash away our sins? What can make us whole again?
F♯ (E) E (D)
Nothing but the blood, nothing but the blood of
B (A) F♯ (E) E (D) B (A)
Jesus. What can wash us pure as snow,
G♯m7 (F♯m7)
welcomed as the friends of God?
F♯ (E) 3rd time to CODA E (D) B (A) 2nd time to CODA
Nothing but Your blood, nothing but Your blood, King Jesus.

F♯ (E) E (D) B (A) F♯ (E) E (D)
D.S. al CODA
King Je - sus.
3. Your cross
CODA
F♯ (E) E (D) B2 (A2) F♯ (E) E (D)
Vocals ad lib.
B2 (A2)
1. F♯ (E) E (D)
2. F♯ (E) E (D)
B2 (A2) F♯ (E) E (D)
It's the blood, it's the blood. It's the blood, it's the blood.
D.S. al CODA
B2 (A2) F♯ (E) E (D)
It's the blood, it's the blood. Yeah, what can wash us?

CODA
E
(D)
B
(A)
Noth - ing but Your blood, King Je - sus.
F♯
(E)
E
(D)
B
(A)
F♯7/C♯
(E7/B)
E2
(D2)
Vocals ad lib.
Oh, King Je - sus.
B
(A)
F♯7/C♯
(E7/B)
E2
(D2)
B
(A)
1.
F♯7/C♯
(E7/B)
E2
(D2)
2.
F♯
(E)
E
(D)
B
(A)

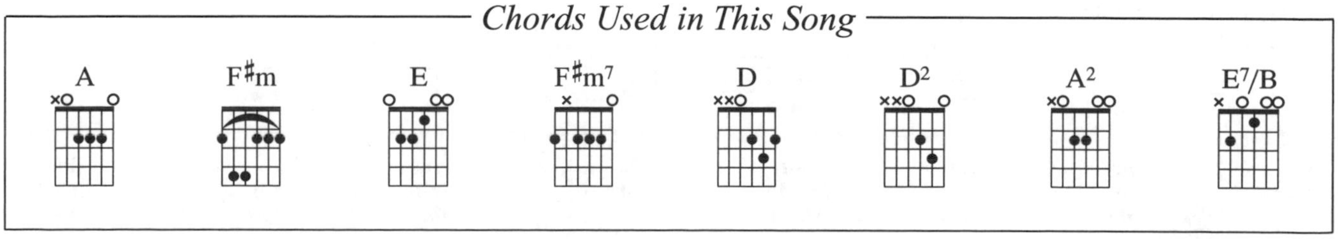
Chords Used in This Song
A
F♯m
E
F♯m7
D
D2
A2
E7/B

O Come, Be Born Again

Words and Music by
JENNIFER MARTIN

Capo 1 (A) ♩ = 100

Keyboard
(Guitar)
B♭ (A)
Cm/B♭ (Bm/A)
F7/A (E7/G♯)
B♭sus (Asus)
B♭ (A)
1. Ba - by born in Beth - le - hem,
2. Chos - en One who chose to be
3. All who strug - gle, all who sin,
Come be born in me a - gain.
Suf - f'ring Sav - ior, Ser - vant King.
Come and be - come born a - gain.
B♭2 (A2)
E♭maj7 (Dmaj7)
Cm7 (Bm7)
Since You don't mind dir - ty sta - bles,
Since You don't des - pise the bro - ken,
Come and lay your heav - y bur - dens
Gm7 (F♯m7)
B♭/A (A/G♯)
B♭/D (A/C♯)
E♭ (D)
D7 (C♯7)
Here's my heart not fit or a - ble
Here's my life laid bare and o - pen
At the cross where all's for - giv - en.

Gm (F♯m) F/A (E/G♯) B♭ (A) B♭sus (Asus) B♭ (A)
To re - ceive such maj - es - ty.
To re - ceive Your mer - - cy
At His feet new life be - gins,
B♭sus (Asus) B♭ (A) Gm (F♯m) Cm/E♭ (Bm/D) F7 (E7) B♭sus (Asus) B♭ (A)
Still, You hum - bly come to me. O
As Your Spir - it calls to me: O
Come, O sin - ner in - to Him. And
F/A (E/G♯) B♭/D (A/C♯) E♭2 (D2) B♭/D (A/C♯)
come, O
come, O
come, O
D7 (C♯7) Gm (F♯m) B♭ (A)
come. O
come. O
come. O
last time rit.
3rd time to CODA
F/C (E/B) B♭/D (A/C♯) E♭2 (D2) B♭/D (A/C♯) E♭ (D) B♭/F (A/E) F7sus (E7sus)
come, O come, be born a -
come, O come, be born a
come, O come, be born a

1.2.
B♭
(A)
E♭/B♭
(D/A)
B♭
(A)
gain.
gain.
E♭/B♭
(D/A)
3.
B♭
(A)
D.S. al CODA 𝄋
gain.
And
CODA
B♭
(A)
E♭/B♭
(D/A)
B♭
(A)
gain.

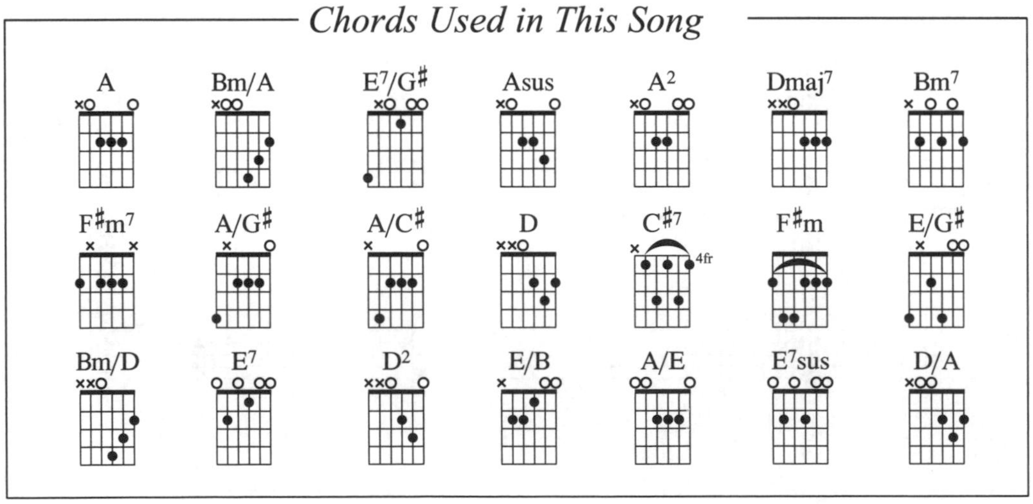
Chords Used in This Song
A
Bm/A
E7/G#
Asus
A2
Dmaj7
Bm7
F#m7
A/G#
A/C#
D
C#7
4fr
F#m
E/G#
Bm/D
E7
D2
E/B
A/E
E7sus
D/A

O Come Let Us Adore Him

Arranged by Terl Bryant and Matt Redman

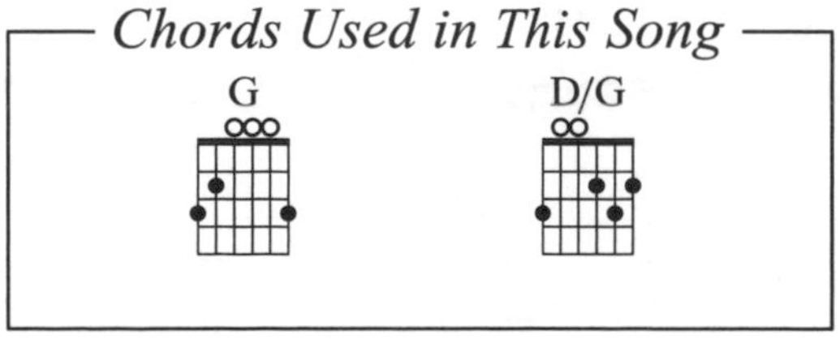
Chords Used in This Song
G
D/G

Oh, Lord You're Beautiful

Words and Music by
KEITH GREEN

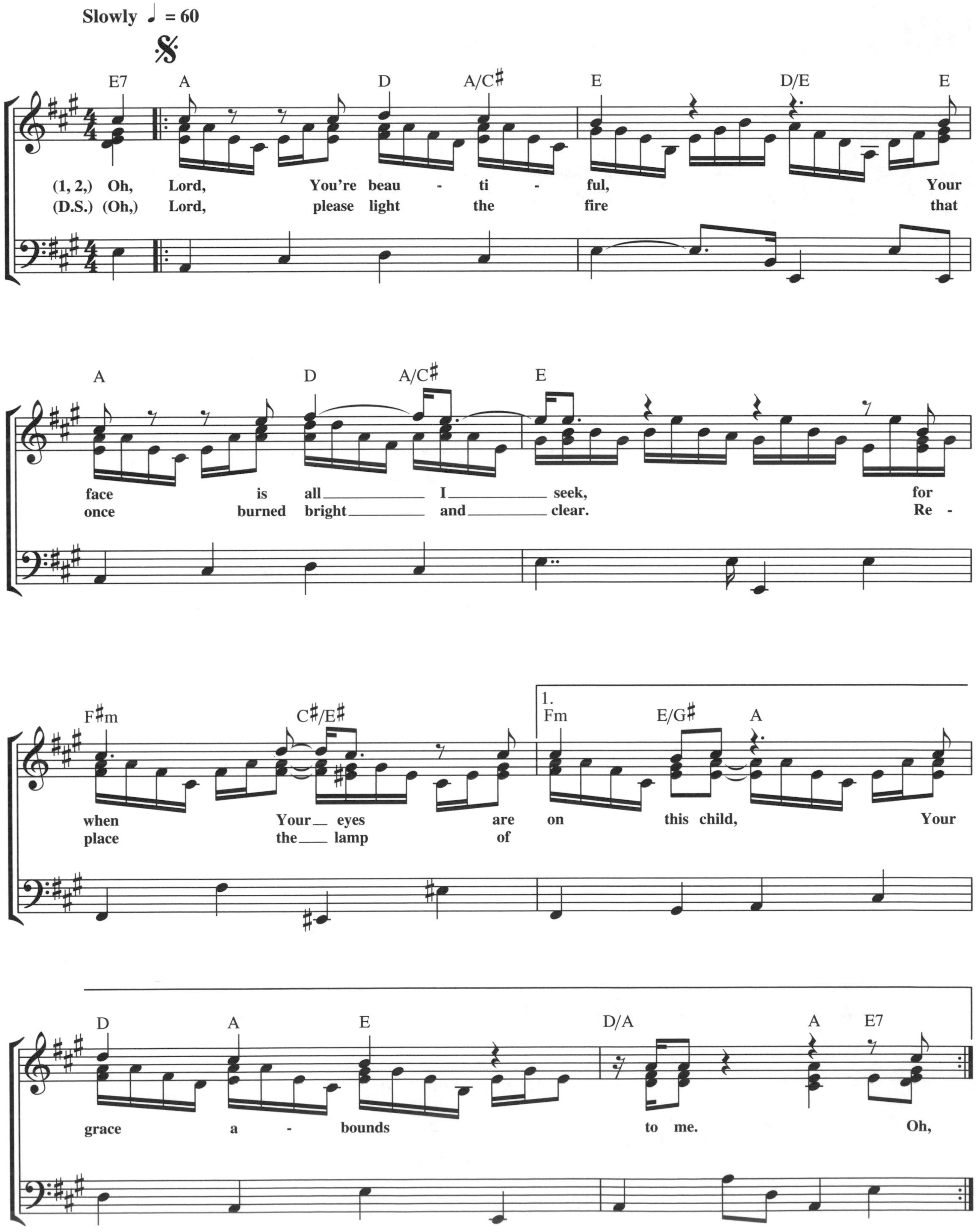
Slowly ♩ = 60
E7 A D A/C♯ E D/E E
(1, 2,) Oh, Lord, You're beau - ti - ful, Your
(D.S.) (Oh,) Lord, please light the fire that
A D A/C♯ E
face is all I seek, for
once burned bright and clear. Re -
F♯m C♯/E♯ 1. Fm E/G♯ A
when Your eyes are on this child, Your
place the lamp of
D A E D/A A E7
grace a - bounds to me. Oh,

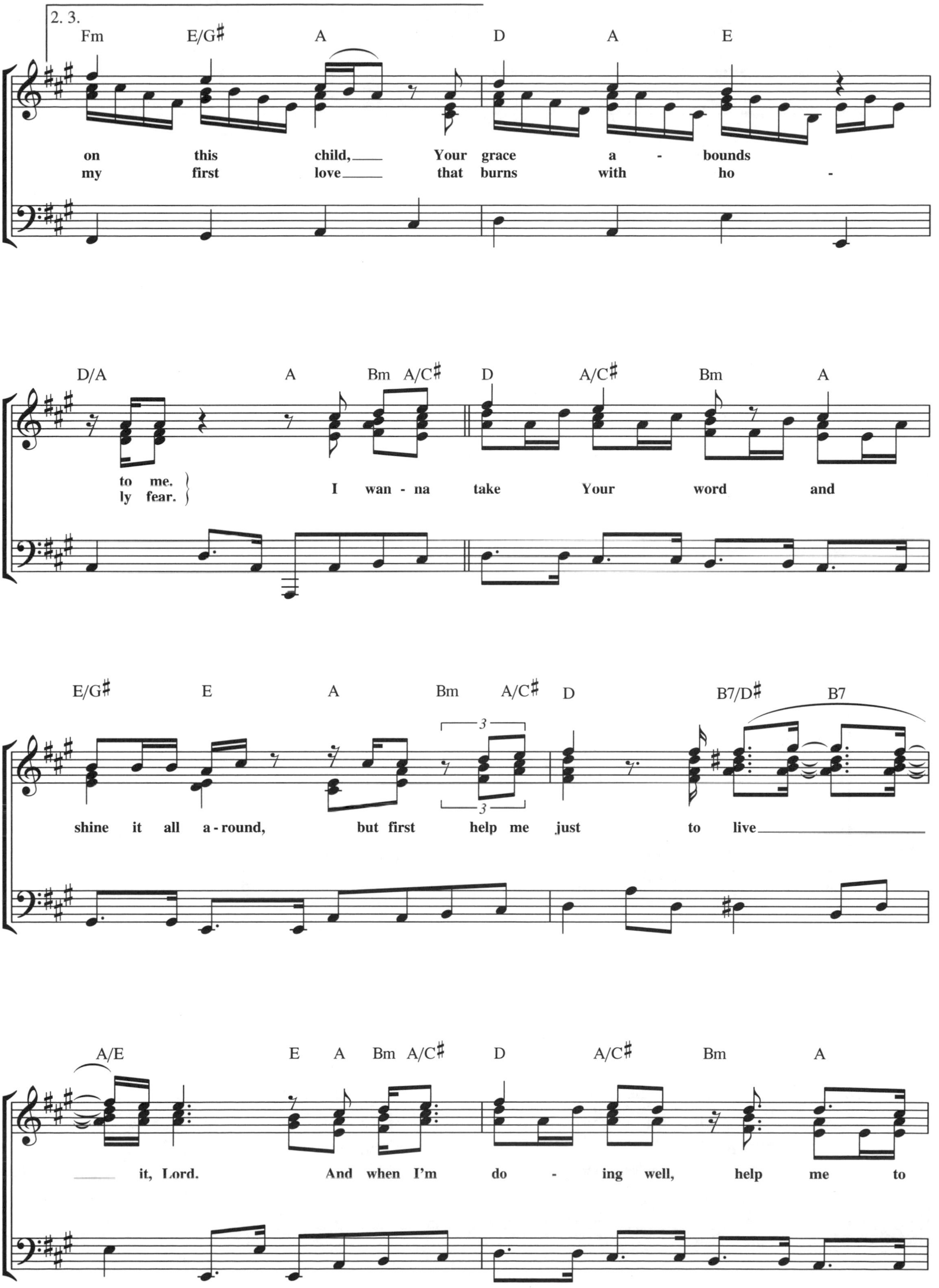
2. 3.
Fm E/G♯ A D A E
on this child, Your grace a - bounds
my first love that burns with ho -
D/A A Bm A/C♯ D A/C♯ Bm A
to me.
ly fear.
I wan - na take Your word and
E/G♯ E A Bm A/C♯ D B7/D♯ B7
shine it all a - round, but first help me just to live
A/E E A Bm A/C♯ D A/C♯ Bm A
it, Lord. And when I'm do - ing well, help me to

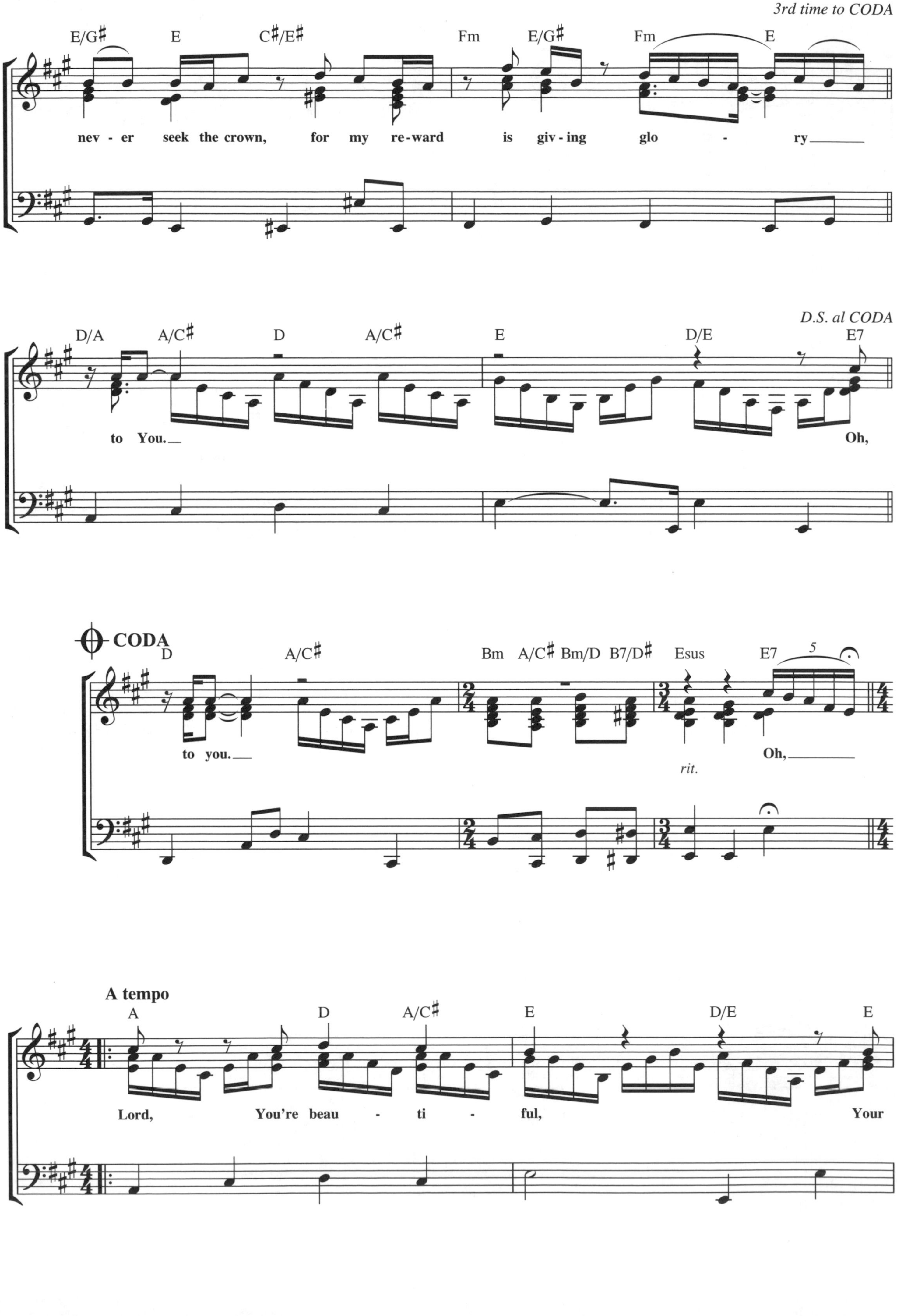
3rd time to CODA
E/G♯ E C♯/E♯ Fm E/G♯ Fm E
nev - er seek the crown, for my re-ward is giv - ing glo - ry
D.S. al CODA
D/A A/C♯ D A/C♯ E D/E E7
to You. Oh,
CODA
D A/C♯ Bm A/C♯ Bm/D B7/D♯ Esus E7
5
to you. Oh,
rit.
A tempo
A D A/C♯ E D/E E
Lord, You're beau - ti - ful, Your

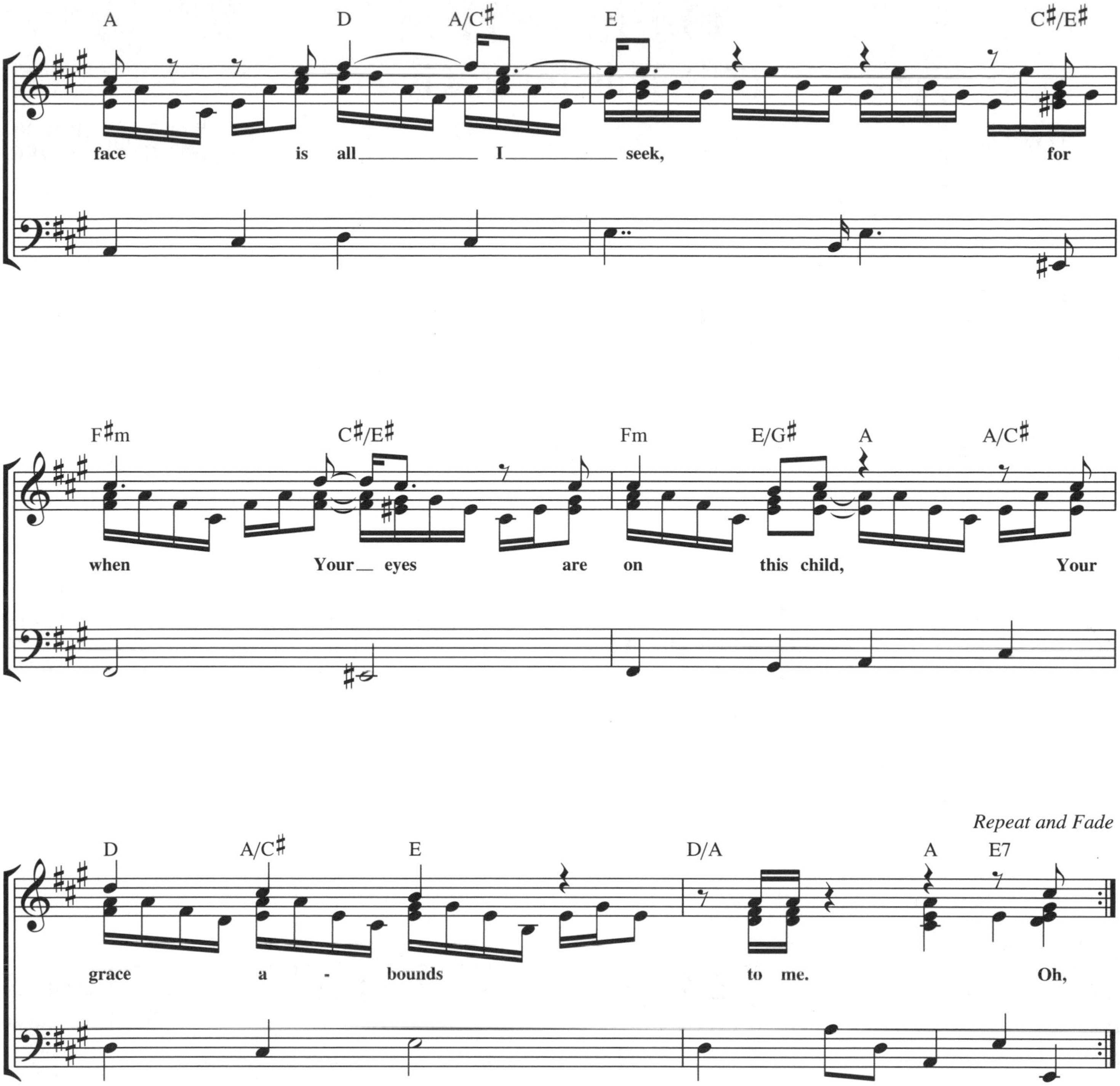
A D A/C♯ E C♯/E♯
face is all I seek, for
F♯m C♯/E♯ Fm E/G♯ A A/C♯
when Your eyes are on this child, Your
Repeat and Fade
D A/C♯ E D/A A E7
grace a - bounds to me. Oh,

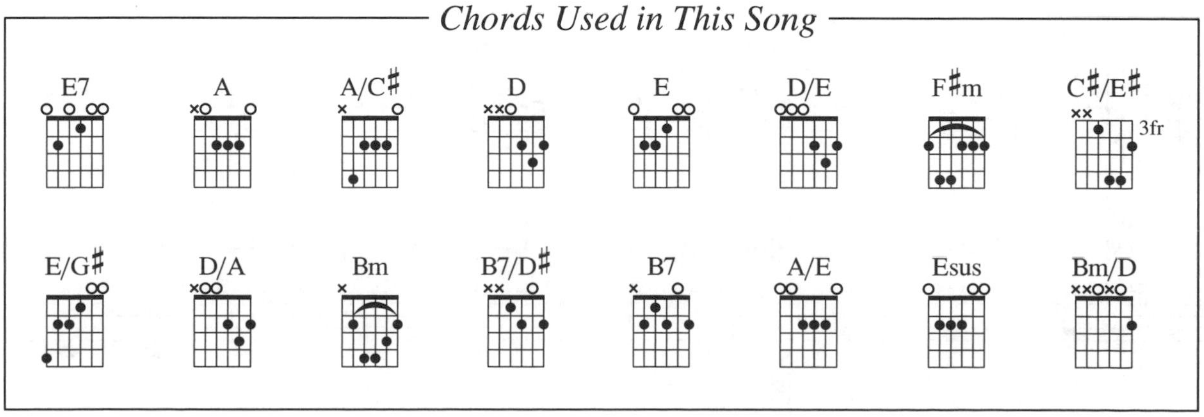
Chords Used in This Song
E7 A A/C♯ D E D/E F♯m C♯/E♯
3fr
E/G♯ D/A Bm B7/D♯ B7 A/E Esus Bm/D

O Praise Him
(All This for a King)

Capo 1 (A)

Words and Music by
DAVID CROWDER

♩ = 116
Keyboard
(Guitar)
B♭2
(A2)
F/A
(E/G♯)
E♭
(D)
1. Turn your ear to heav - en, and hear the noise in - side, the sound of an - gel's awe, the sound of an - gel's songs, and all this for a King. We
2. Turn your gaze to heav - en and raise a joy - ous noise. The sound of sal - va - tion come, the sound of res - cued ones, and all this for a King. An -

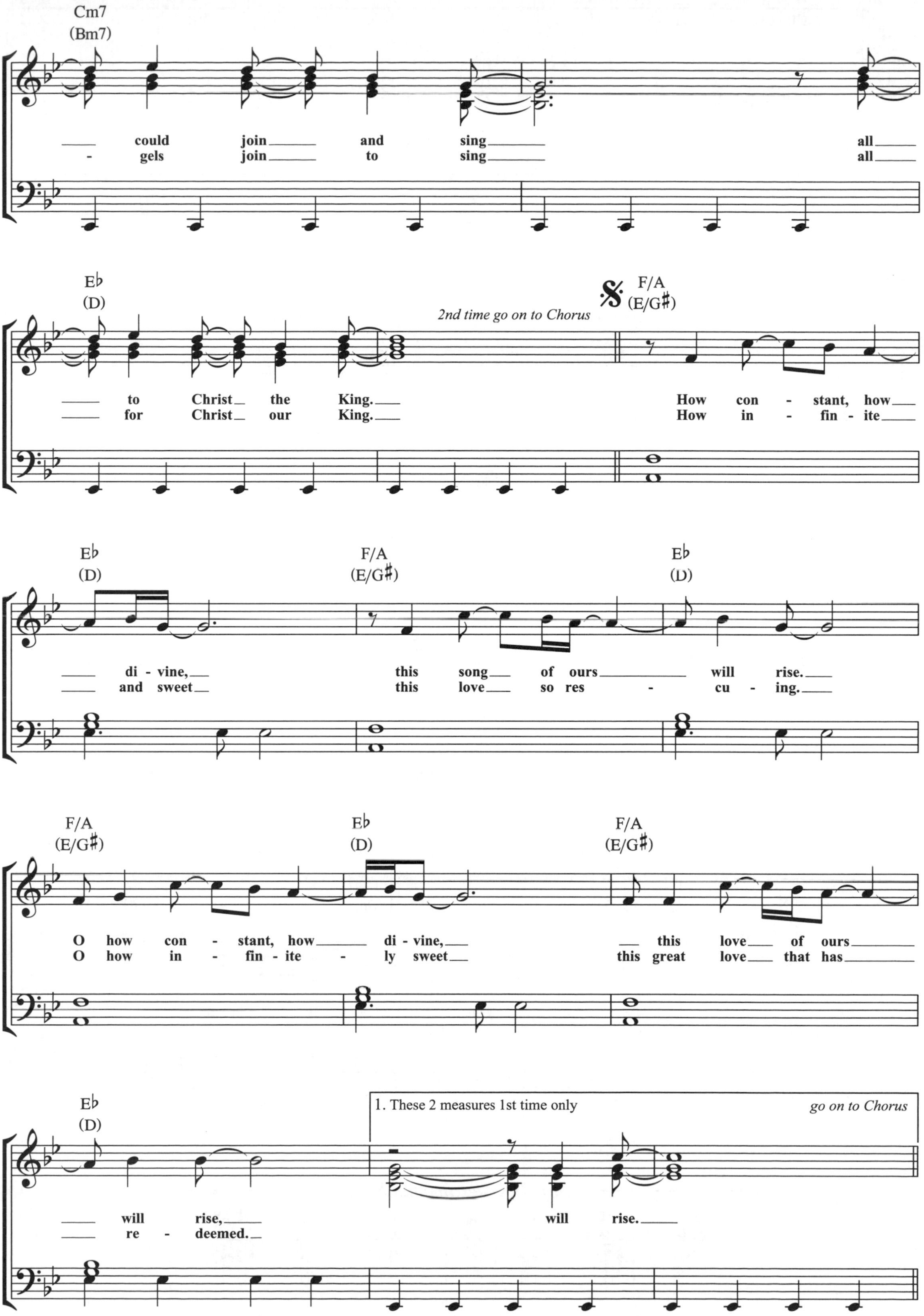
Cm7
(Bm7)
could join and sing all
gels join to sing all
E♭
(D)
2nd time go on to Chorus
F/A
(E/G♯)
to Christ the King. How con - stant, how
for Christ our King. How in - fin - ite
E♭
(D)
F/A
(E/G♯)
E♭
(D)
di - vine, this song of ours will rise.
and sweet this love so res - cu - ing.
F/A
(E/G♯)
E♭
(D)
F/A
(E/G♯)
O how con - stant, how di - vine, this love of ours
O how in - fin - ite - ly sweet this great love that has
E♭
(D)
1. These 2 measures 1st time only
go on to Chorus
will rise, will rise.
re - deemed.

2. These 4 measures 2nd time only
As one we sing.
CHORUS
B♭
(A)
B♭/A
(A/G♯)
O praise Him, O praise Him;
Al - le - lu - ia, A - le - lu - ia.
Gm7
(F♯m7)
He is ho - ly,
He is ho - ly,
E♭
(D)
1. 2.
Cm7
(Bm7)
2nd time D.S.
3.
Cm7
(Bm7)
B♭
(A)
He is ho - ly, yeah. - ly, yeah.
He is ho

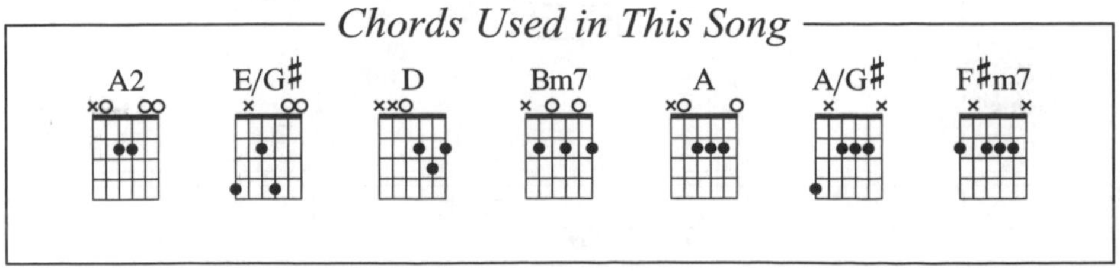
Chords Used in This Song
A2
E/G♯
D
Bm7
A
A/G♯
F♯m7

O Worship the King

Traditional
Arrangement and additional chorus by Chris Tomlin

Capo 1 (G)
♩. = 52
Keyboard
(Guitar)
A♭ (G)
D♭ (C)
E♭ (D)
E♭7 (D7)
1.O wor - ship the King, all glo - rious a - bove, O grate - ful - ly sing His won - der - ful love; Our Shield and De - fend - er, the An - cient of Days, Pa -
(2.O) tell of His might, O sing of His grace, Whose robe is the light and can - o - py space! His cha - riots of wrath the deep thun - der - clouds form, And
(3.O) mea - sure - less might, in - ef - fa - ble love; While an - gels de - light to wor - ship a - bove. Thy mer - cies how ten - der, how firm to the end, Our

A♭ (G)
E♭7 (D7)
vil - ioned in splen - dor, and gird - ed with
dark is His path on the wings of the
Mak - er, De - fend - er, Re - deem - er, and
A♭ (G)
4th time to CODA
praise.
storm.
Friend.
1.
2.3.
2. O
D♭2 (C2)
Fm7 (Em7)
You a - lone are the match - less

B♭m7
(Am7)
King, To You a - - lone be all
A♭/C
(G/B)
D♭2
(C2)
maj - es - ty. Your glo - ries and
Fm7
(Em7)
won - ders, what tongue can re - cite? You
B♭m7
(Am7)
A♭/C
(G/B)
breathe in the air, You
1. D♭2
(C2)
shine in the light.

2. D♭2
(C2)
3. O
A♭/C
(G/B)
Shine in the light.
B♭m7
(Am7)
A♭/C
(G/B)
You
D♭2
(C2)
shine in the light.
D.S. al CODA 𝄋
1. O

CODA

Chords Used in This Song

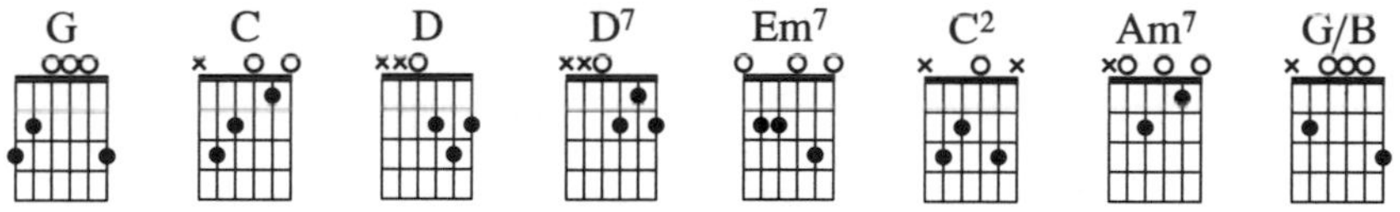

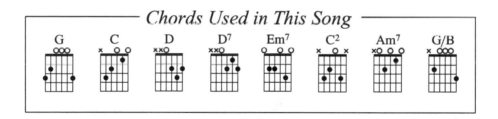

On The Third Day

Words and Music by
MATT MAHER and MARC BYRD

Moderately ♩ = 92

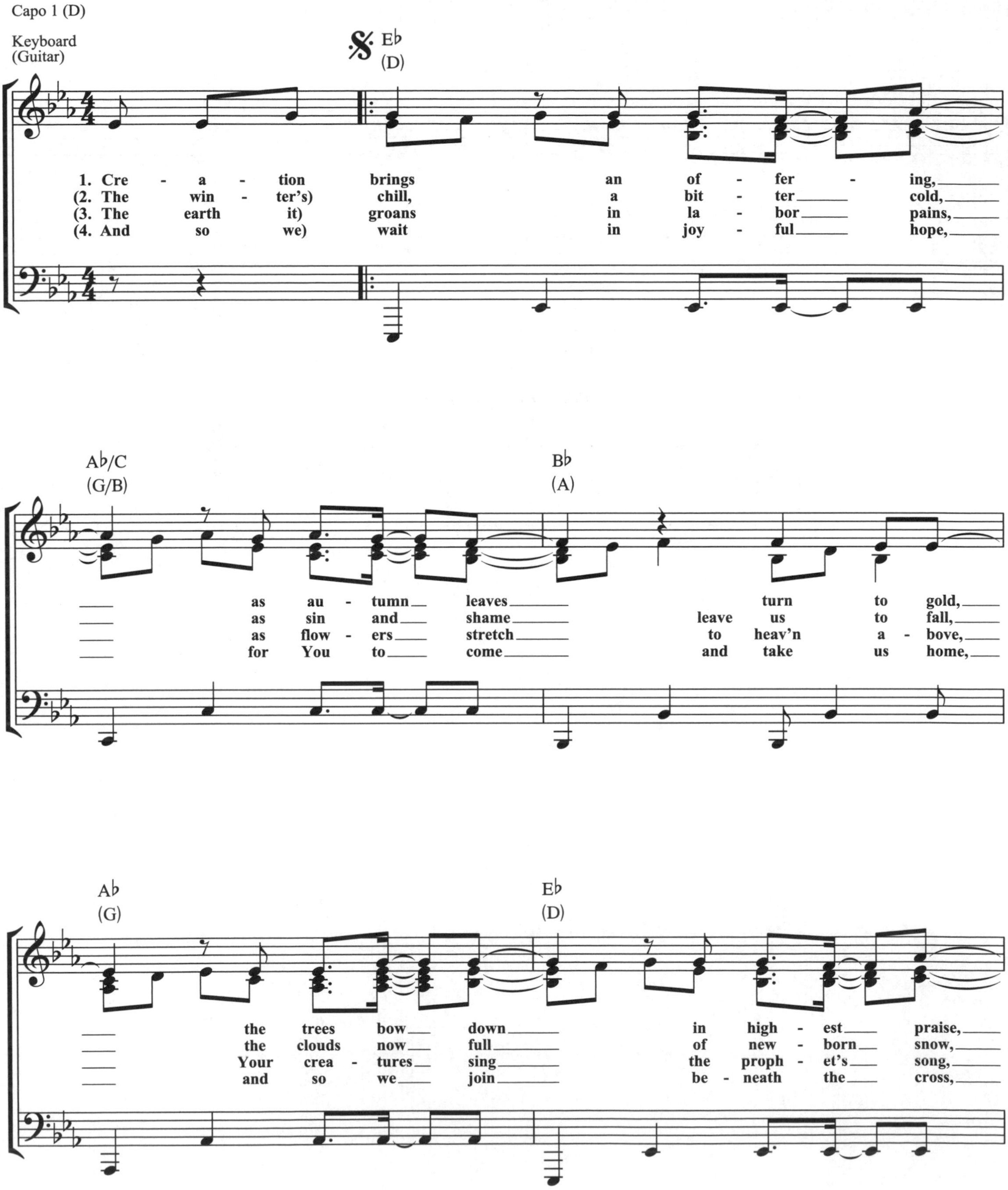
Capo 1 (D)
Keyboard
(Guitar)
E♭ (D)
1. Cre - a - tion brings an of - fer - ing,
(2. The win - ter's) chill, a bit - ter cold,
(3. The earth it) groans in la - bor pains,
(4. And so we) wait in joy - ful hope,
A♭/C (G/B)
B♭ (A)
as au - tumn leaves turn to gold,
as sin and shame leave us to fall,
as flow - ers stretch to heav'n a - bove,
for You to come and take us home,
A♭ (G)
E♭ (D)
the trees bow down in high - est praise,
the clouds now full of new - born snow,
Your crea - tures sing the proph - et's song,
and so we join be - neath the cross,

A♭/C
(G/B)
B♭
(A)
now made bare before Your throne.
for grace to come and save us all,
to be a gift of self - less love.
in suf - fer - ing from whence we go.
A♭
(G)
E♭/G
(D/F♯)
The west - ern sky an am - ber blaze,
with - in the dark - est night of man,
The sun is ris - ing in the east,
The great - est act of sov - □reign grace,
A♭
(G)
E♭/B♭
(D/A)
at the end of the day,
was found Your sav - ing hand,
and your spir - it is un - leashed,
in the un - i - verse dis - played,
A♭/C
(G/B)
E♭/B♭
(D/A)
For ev - □ry - thing must die

B♭ (A)
E♭ (D)
4th time to CODA
1., 3.
to rise a - gain.
2. The win - ter’s
4. And so we
2.
A♭ (G)
E♭ (D)
E♭/B♭ (D/A)
On the third day, be - hold the King, on the
A♭ (G)
Cm (Bm)
B♭ (A)
A♭ (G)
third day, death has no sting, on the third day, we’re for -
Cm (Bm)
B♭ (A)
E♭ (D)
D.S. al CODA (with repeat)
giv - en and rec - on - ciled.
3. The earth it
CODA
A♭ (G)
E♭ (D)
E♭/B♭ (D/A)
On the third day, be - hold the King, on the
the saints re - joice,

A♭ (G)
Cm (Bm)
B♭ (A)
third day, { death has no sting, / we lift our voice, } on the
A♭ (G)
Cm (Bm)
B♭ (A)
1., 3.
E♭ (D)
third day, { we□re for - giv - en and rec - on - ciled. / we□re u - nit - ed and glo - ri - fied. }
2.
E♭ (D)
On the
4.
E♭ (D)
A♭/E♭ (G/D)
E♭ (D)

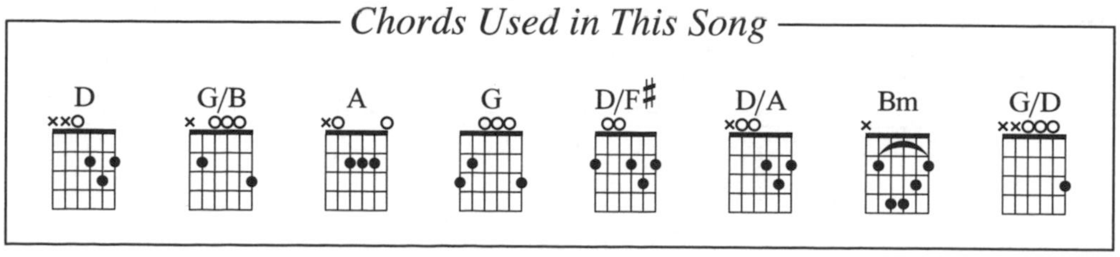

Chords Used in This Song
D
G/B
A
G
D/F♯
D/A
Bm
G/D

Once Again

Capo 1 (D)

♩ = 78

Words and Music by
MATT REDMAN

Keyboard
(Guitar)
E♭ (D)
B♭/E♭ (A/D)
A♭/E♭ (G/D)
E♭ (D)
1.2. Je - sus Christ, I think up - on Your sac - ri - fice;
3. Now You are ex - alt - ed to the high - est place,
A♭ (G)
E♭/G (D/F♯)
A♭ (G)
B♭sus (Asus)
B♭ (A)
You be - came noth - ing, poured out to death.
King of the heav - ens, where one day I'll bow.
E♭ (D)
B♭/E♭ (A/D)
A♭/E♭ (G/D)
E♭ (D)
Man - y times I've won - dered at Your gift of life, and
But, for now, I mar - vel at this sav - ing grace, and
A♭ (G)
B♭sus (Asus)
B♭ (A)
E♭ (D)
I'm in that place once a - gain.
I'm full of praise once a - gain.
A♭ (G)
B♭sus (Asus)
B♭ (A)
E♭ (D)
I'm in that place once a - gain.
I'm full of praise once a - gain.

Eb/G (D/F#) Ab (G) Eb/G (D/F#) Bbsus (Asus) Bb (A)
Once a - gain I look up - on the cross where You died. I'm
Eb/G (D/F#) Ab (G) Eb/G (D/F#) Bbsus (Asus) Bb (A)
hum - bled by Your mer - cy and I'm bro - ken in - side.
Cm7 (Bm7) Ab (G) Eb/G (D/F#) Bb (A) Ab/C (G) Bbsus (Asus) Bb (A)
Once a - gain I thank You, once a - gain I pour out my life.
Eb (D) FINE (repeat twice) Ab (G) Bbsus (Asus) Bb (A) Eb/G (D/F#)
Thank You for the cross. Thank You for the cross.
Ab (G) Bbsus (Asus) Bb (A) 1. Eb (D) 2. Eb (D) D.S. al FINE
Thank You for the cross, my Friend. Friend.
Chords Used in This Song
D A/D G/D D/F# G Asus A Bm7

Our Comforter

Words and Music by
CASEY McGINTY

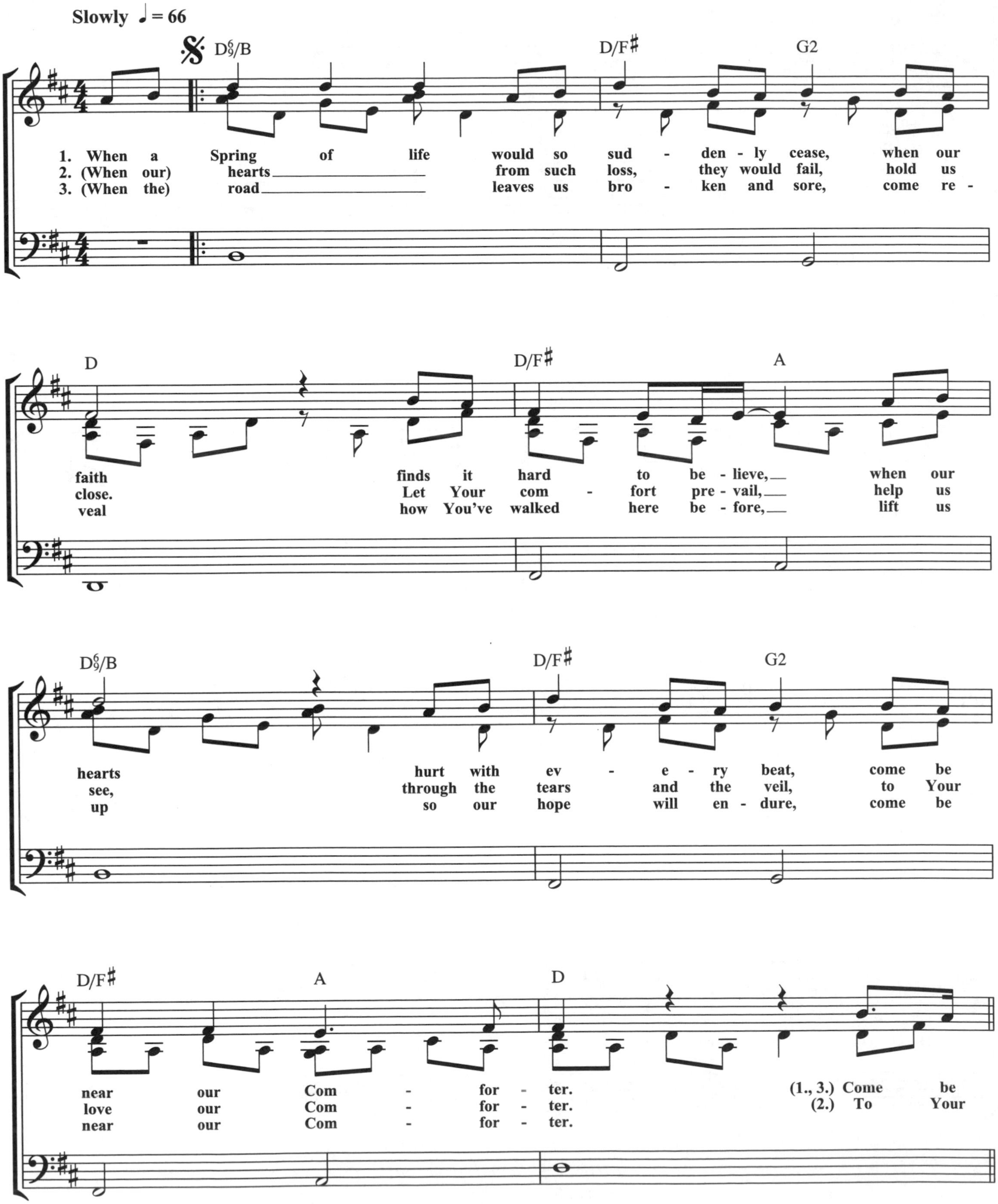
Slowly ♩ = 66
D6/9/B
D/F♯
G2
1. When a Spring of life would so sud - den - ly cease, when our
2. (When our) hearts from such loss, they would fail, hold us
3. (When the) road leaves us bro - ken and sore, come re -
D
D/F♯
A
faith finds it hard to be - lieve, when our
close. Let Your com - fort pre - vail, help us
veal how You've walked here be - fore, lift us
D6/9/B
D/F♯
G2
hearts hurt with ev - e - ry beat, come be
see, through the tears and the veil, to Your
up so our hope will en - dure, come be
D/F♯
A
D
near our Com - for - ter.
love our Com - for - ter.
near our Com - for - ter.
(1., 3.) Come be
(2.) To Your

In memory of Emily Mynster

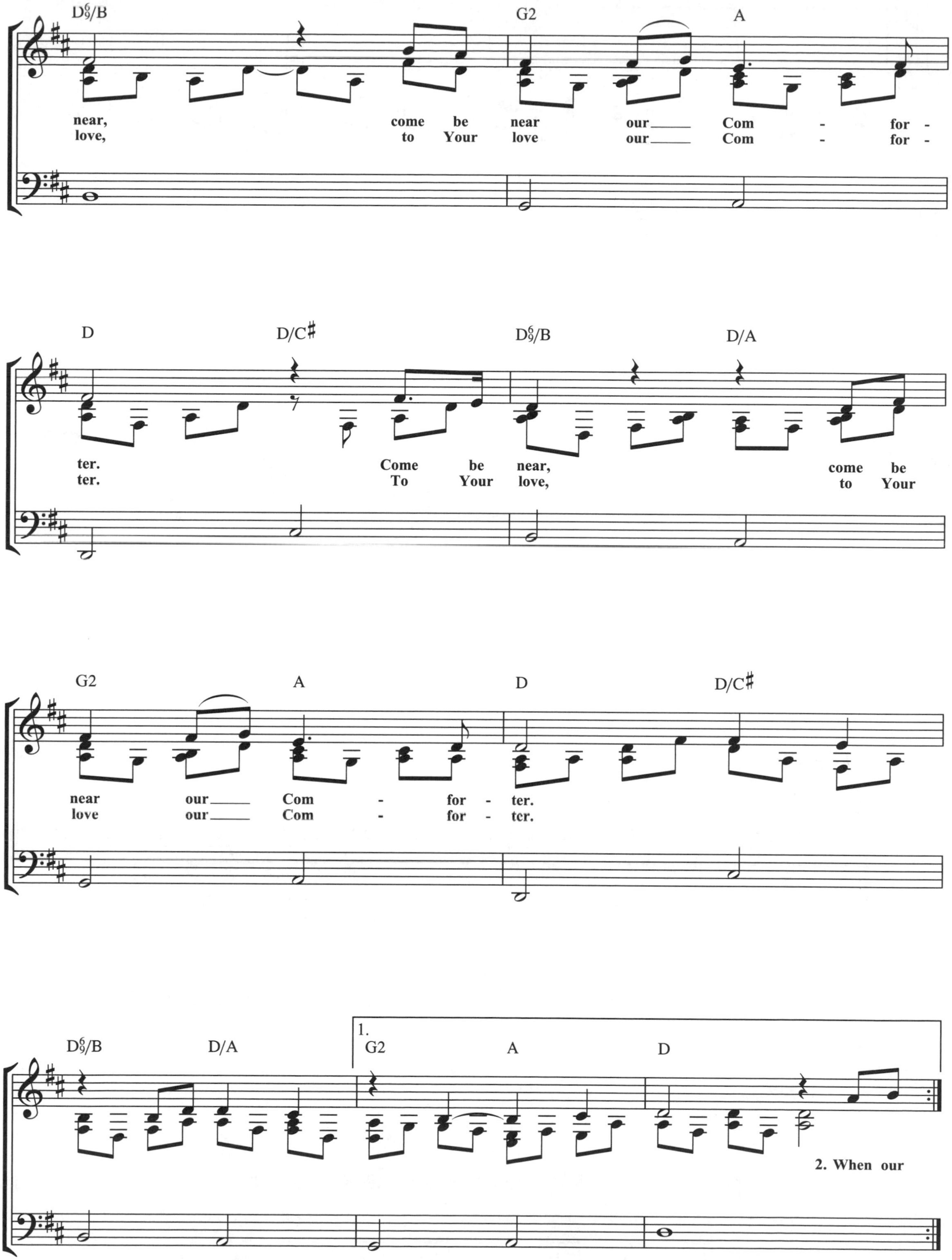
D6/9/B
G2
A
near, come be near our Com - for -
love, to Your love our Com - for -
D
D/C♯
D6/9/B
D/A
ter. Come be near, come be
ter. To Your love, to Your
G2
A
D
D/C♯
near our Com - for - ter.
love our Com - for - ter.
D6/9/B
D/A
1.
G2
A
D
2. When our

2., 3.
G2 D/F♯ Em7 A D D/C♯
To CODA
D.S. al CODA
(take 2nd ending)
D6/9/B D/A G2 A D
3. When the
CODA
D6/9/B D/A G2 A D
Come be near our Com - for - ter.

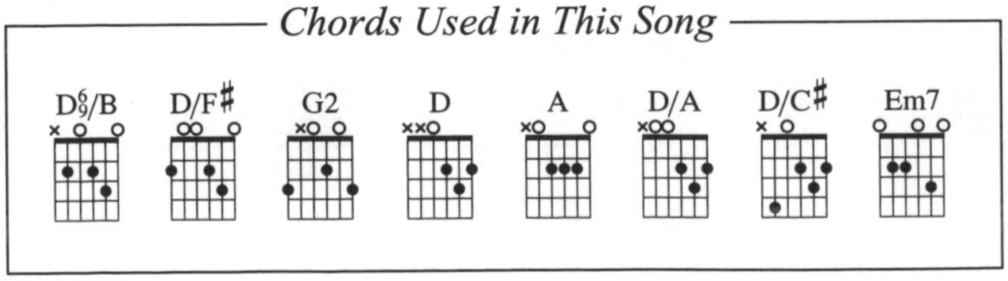
Chords Used in This Song
D6/9/B D/F♯ G2 D A D/A D/C♯ Em7

Praise The Name Of Jesus

Words and Music by
ROY HICKS Jr.

Slowly
D
G/D
D
G/D
D
Praise the name of Je - sus, praise the name of___ Je - sus.
G/D
D
G/D
D
G
D/F♯
He's my Rock, He's my For - tress, He's my De - liv - er - er. In
E
A2
A
D
G/B
A7
D
Him shall I___ trust.___ Praise the___ name of___ Je - sus.
Moderate Rock
D
G/D
D
D/F♯
Praise the name of Je - sus,___ praise the name of___

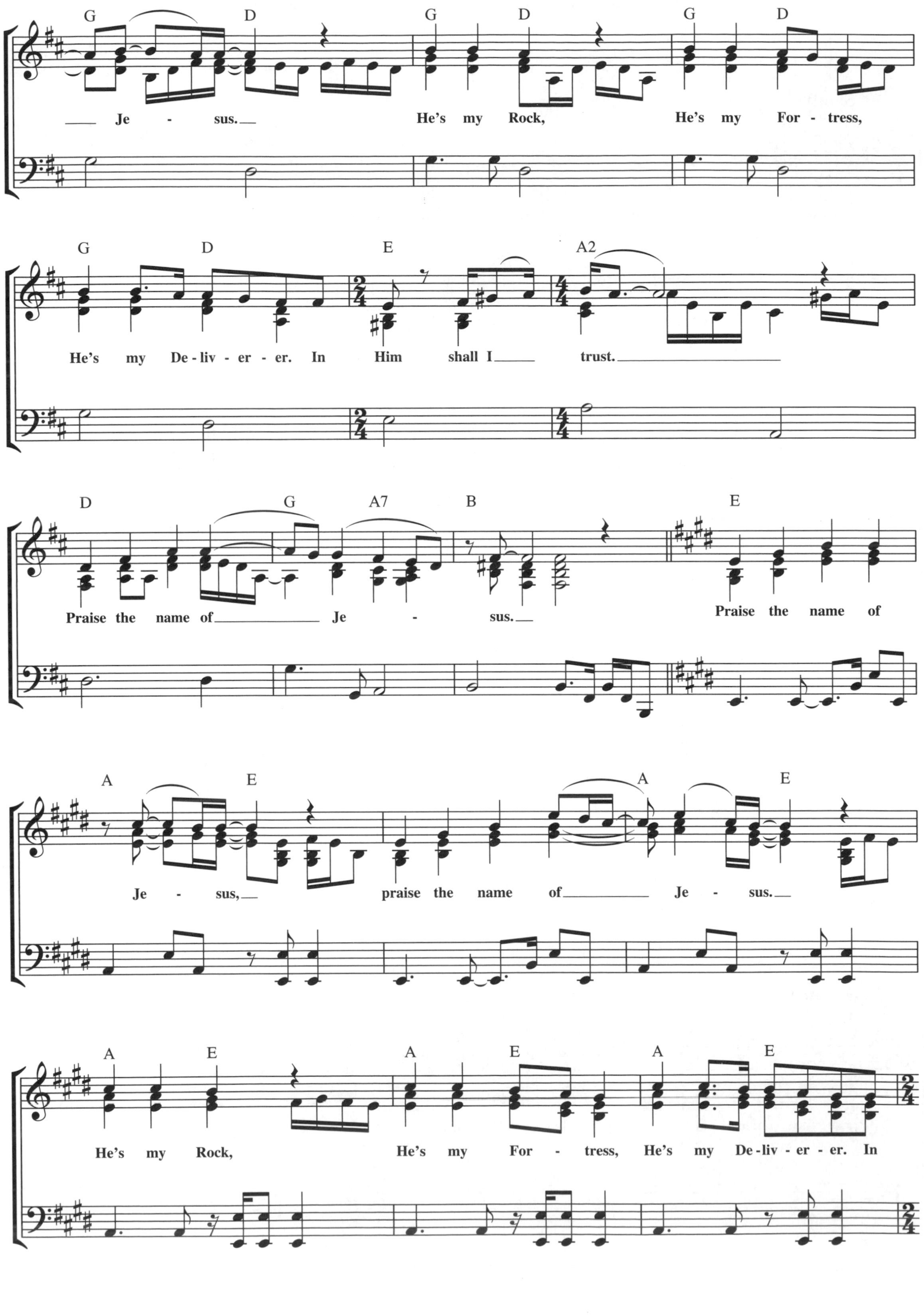
G D G D G D
Je - sus. He's my Rock, He's my For - tress,
G D E A2
He's my De - liv - er - er. In Him shall I trust.
D G A7 B E
Praise the name of Je - sus. Praise the name of
A E A E
Je - sus, praise the name of Je - sus.
A E A E A E
He's my Rock, He's my For - tress, He's my De - liv - er - er. In

F♯
B
E
Him shall I trust. Praise the name of
A
A/B
B
A
E
A
E
Je - sus. He's my Rock, He's my for - tress,
A
E
F♯
A/B
He's my de - li - ver - er. In Him shall I trust.
Slower, ♩=ca.60
B
E
A
B
E
rit.
Praise the name of Je - sus.

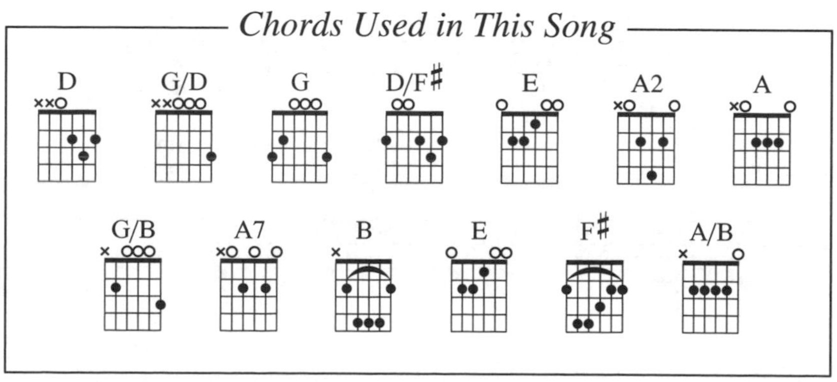
Chords Used in This Song
D
G/D
G
D/F♯
E
A2
A
G/B
A7
B
E
F♯
A/B

Our Love Is Loud

Words and Music by
DAVID CROWDER

A2 E F♯m7
When we lift our voic - es loud - er still, can
C♯m7 A2 E
You hear us? Can You feel? We love You, Lord, we love
E/D♯ C♯m7 A2
You, we love You. We love
E E/D♯
You, Lord, we love You, we love You.
3rd time to CODA
1.
C♯m7 A2 E

F♯m7
C♯m7
A2
2. When we sing
2.
A2
E
And our love is big, our love
F♯m7
E/G♯
is loud. Fill this place with this
A2
E
love, now. And our love is big, our love
F♯m7
E/G♯
is loud. Fill this place with this
2nd time: Fill our lungs to sing

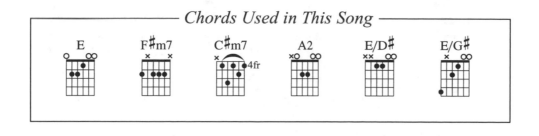

Chords Used in This Song

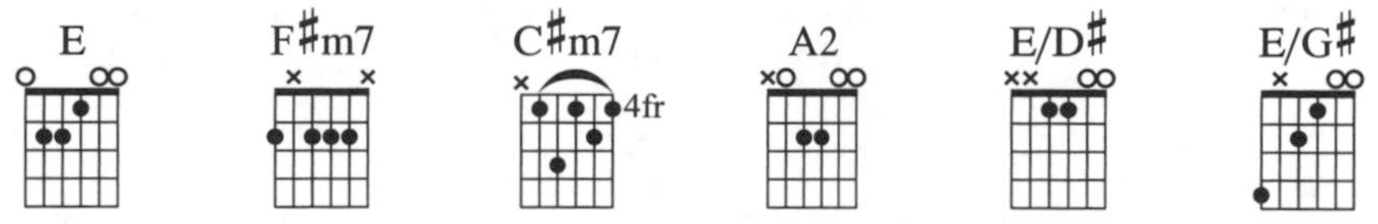

Overflow

Words and Music by
MATT MAHER

Capo 1 (E)

♩ = 100

Keyboard
(Guitar)
F (E)
B♭2 (A2)
Gm7(11) (F♯m(11))
C7sus (B7sus)
Your grace is pow - er. Your will
for - ev - er. Your love is a riv - er.
O - ver-flow in me.
Your Word; true pres - ence. Your bod - y; our re - com - pense.
Your wor - ship of You, it's Your gift from us to You.

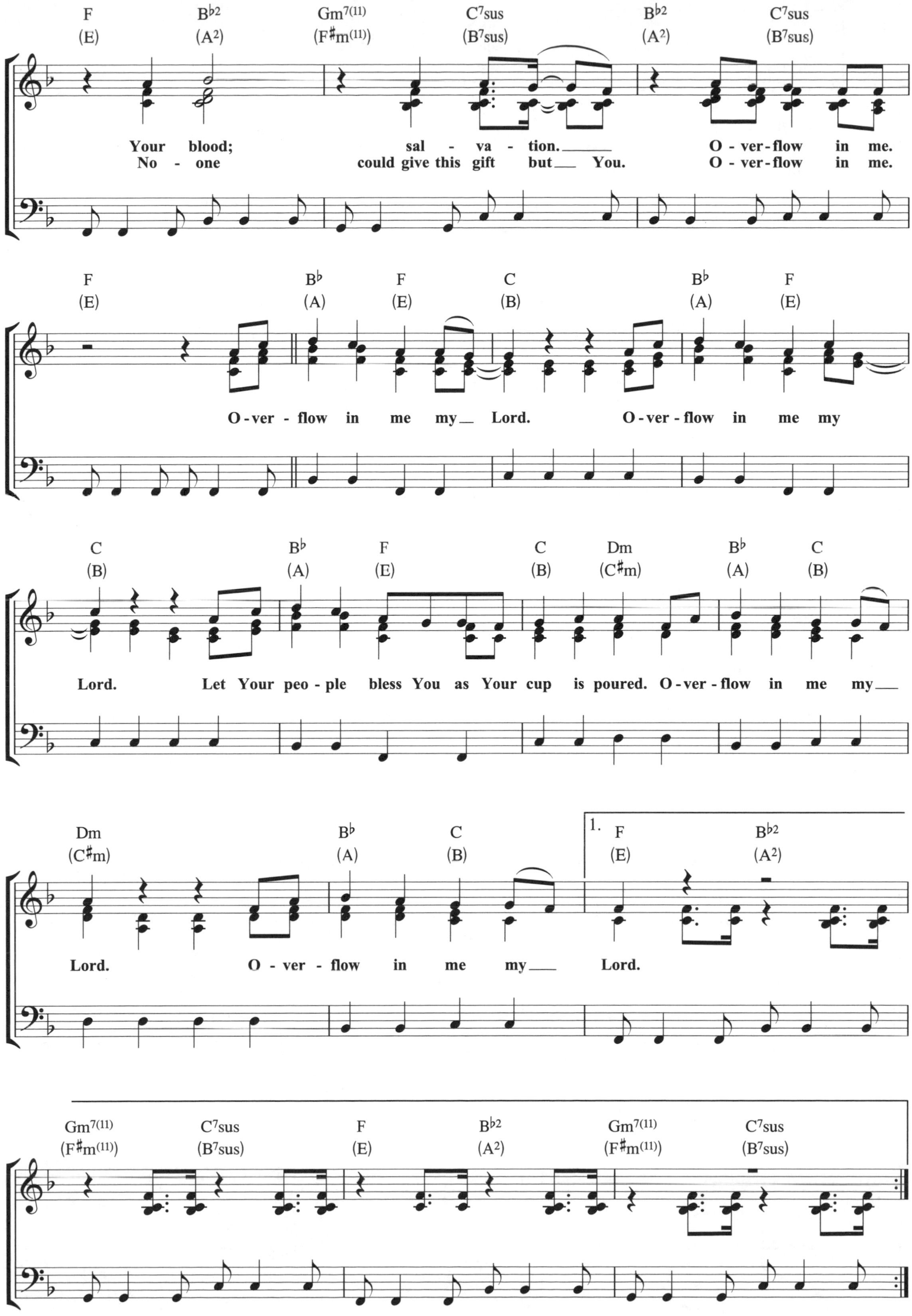
F (E) B♭2 (A2) Gm7(11) (F♯m(11)) C7sus (B7sus) B♭2 (A2) C7sus (B7sus)
Your blood; sal - va - tion. O - ver-flow in me.
No - one could give this gift but You. O - ver-flow in me.
F (E) B♭ (A) F (E) C (B) B♭ (A) F (E)
O-ver - flow in me my Lord. O-ver - flow in me my
C (B) B♭ (A) F (E) C (B) Dm (C♯m) B♭ (A) C (B)
Lord. Let Your peo - ple bless You as Your cup is poured. O-ver - flow in me my
Dm (C♯m) B♭ (A) C (B) 1. F (E) B♭2 (A2)
Lord. O - ver - flow in me my Lord.
Gm7(11) (F♯m(11)) C7sus (B7sus) F (E) B♭2 (A2) Gm7(11) (F♯m(11)) C7sus (B7sus)

2.
F (E) B♭ (A) F (E) C (B)
Lord. We lift up our hearts. We
B♭ (A) Dm (C♯m) C (B) B♭ (A) F (E)
lift up our souls. We lift up our
C (B) Dm (C♯m) Gm7(11) (F♯m(11)) C (B)
minds. And ev-'ry good thing is Yours. Yeah ev-'ry good thing
Gm7(11) (F♯m(11)) C (B) F (E) B♭2 (A2)
is Yours. So o - ver - flow.
Gm7(11) (F♯m(11)) C7sus (B7sus) F (E) B♭2 (A2) Gm7(11) (F♯m(11)) C7sus (B7sus) C (B)

F (E) B♭2 (A2) Gm7(11) (F♯m(11)) C7sus (B7sus) F (E) B♭2 (A2)
Gm7(11) (F♯m(11)) C7sus (B7sus) B♭ (A) F (E) C (B)
Oh, o - ver - flow in me my Lord. O - ver -
B♭ (A) F (E) C (B) B♭ (A) F (E)
- flow in me my Lord. Let Your peo - ple bless You as Your
C (B) Dm (C♯m) B♭ (A) C (B) F (E)
cup is poured. O - ver - flow in me my Lord. O - ver -
B♭ (A) F (E) C (B) B♭ (A) F (E)
- flow in me my Lord. O - ver - flow in me my

C (B) B♭ (A) F (E) C (B) Dm (C♯m)
Lord. Let Your peo - ple bless You as Your cup is poured. O - ver -
B♭ (A) C (B) Dm (C♯m) B♭ (A) C (B)
flow in me my Lord. O - ver - flow in me my
Dm (C♯m) B♭ (A) C (B) F (E) B♭2 (A2)
Lord. O - ver - flow in me my Lord.
Gm7(11) (F♯m(11)) C7sus (B7sus) F (E) B♭2 (A2) Gm7(11) (F♯m(11)) C7sus (B7sus)
O - ver - flow,
F (E) B♭2 (A2) Gm7(11) (F♯m(11)) C7sus (B7sus) F (E) B♭2 (A2)
Oh,

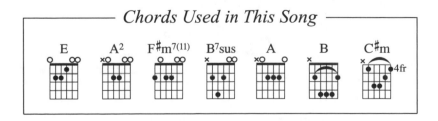

Chords Used in This Song

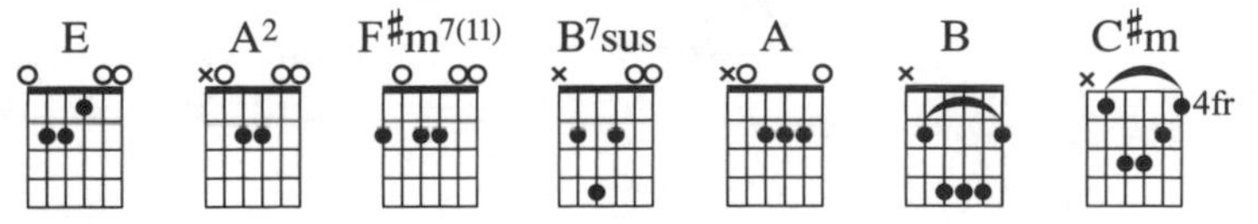

People Need The Lord

Words and Music by
GREG NELSON
and PHIL McHUGH

Moderate ♩=72
D
A/D
G/D
Ev - ery - day they pass me by,
We are called to take His light,
D
A/D
G/D
I can see it in their eyes,
to a world where wrong seems right.
F♯m7
Bm
emp - ty peo - ple filled with care,
What could be too great a cost for
Em
A7sus
rit.
A7
head - ed who knows where.
shar - ing life with one who's lost.

A tempo
D A/D G/D
On they go through pri - vate pain,
Through His love our hearts can feel
C D/F♯ G
liv - ing fear to fear,
all the grief they bear.
Em7♭5 D/F♯ G
laugh - ter hides their si - lent cries on - ly Je - sus hears.
They must hear the words of life on - ly we can share.
A tempo
A7sus rit. D Em7
Peo - ple need the Lord,
D/F♯ G A A/G
peo - ple need the Lord, at the end of

D/F♯ G Em7 A7sus
rit.
broken dreams He's the open door.
A tempo
D Em7 D/F♯
People need the Lord, people need the Lord,
To CODA
G A A/G D/F♯ G
when will we realize,
A tempo
Em7 A7 D A/D G/D
rit.
people need the Lord.
D/F♯ D/G A7 D.C. al CODA
rit.
CODA
A G
when will we

D/F♯ G A G D/F♯ G
re - al - ize, that we must give our lives for
Em7 A Bm
rit.
peo - ple need the Lord.
A tempo
E7 G A D
Peo - ple need the Lord.
A/D G/D D/F♯ D/G A7 D
rit.

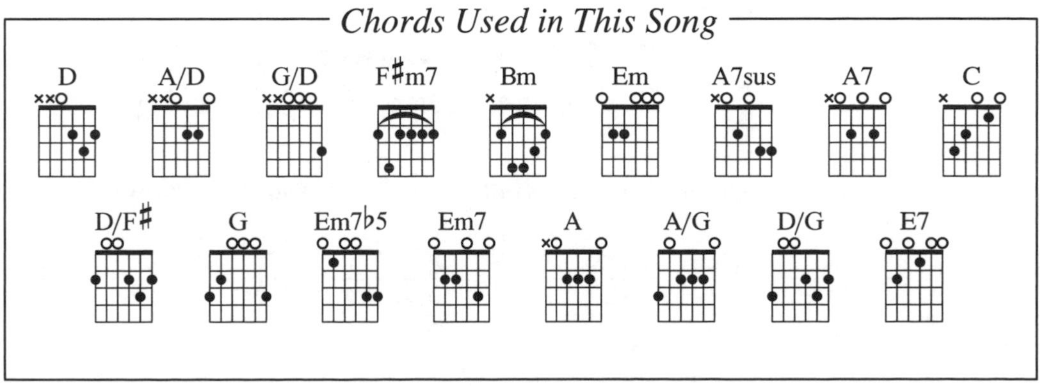
Chords Used in This Song
D A/D G/D F♯m7 Bm Em A7sus A7 C
D/F♯ G Em7♭5 Em7 A A/G D/G E7

Redeeming King

Words and Music by
JADON LAVIK

♩. = 60
D
C
You are the Lord exalted above the most
G
D/F♯
D
high, the Ruler of all,
C
G
worthy of all my praise. You are the Lord
D
C
G
mighty in all of Your ways,

D/F♯
D
C
for - ev - er the same,
so wor - thy of all my
G
praise.
And I lift my
G
C
G
hands in ho - ly de - vo - tion to You.
D/F♯
Em7
C
My life is my sac - ri - fice,
Am
G/B
C
D
dai - ly sur - ren - dered. And I lift my

voice un - a - shamed of my love for
G D/F♯ Em7
You. For You are the Lord
3rd time to CODA
4th time to CODA
C Am G/B 1. C
my re - deem - ing King.
G C G/B
2. C D Em7
C
You are the Lord King.

D
C
G
D/F♯
Em7
D
C
D
D.S. al CODA 𝄋
And I lift my
𝄌 CODA
C
D
Am
G/B
C
D
D.S. al CODA 𝄋
King, my re - deem - ing King. And I lift my
𝄌 𝄌 CODA
C
Am
G/B
C
King, my re - deem - ing King.

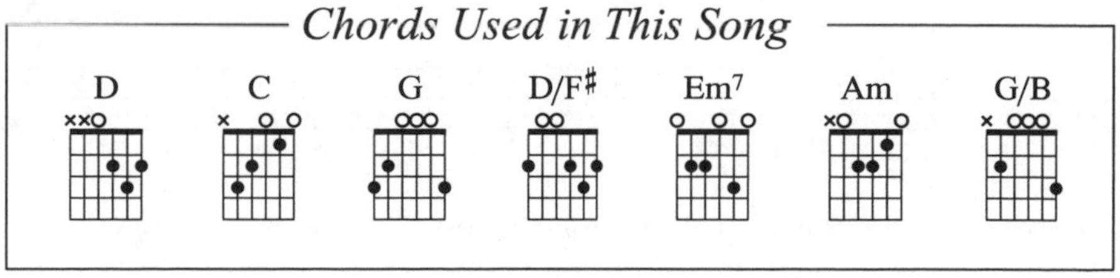
Chords Used in This Song
D
C
G
D/F♯
Em7
Am
G/B

Soon And Very Soon

Words and Music by
ANDRAE CROUCH

Moderate Gospel, ♩ = 82

1., 2., 5. Soon and ver - y soon,___
3. No more cry - ing there,___
4. No more dy - ing there,___
4th and 5th times, lead vocal ad lib.
we are go - ing to see the King,___

soon and ver - y soon,___
No more cry - ing there,___
No more dy - ing there,___
we are go - ing to see the King.___

Soon and ver - y soon,___
No more cry - ing there,___
No more dy - ing there,___
we are go - ing to see the King,___
Hal - le -

4th time, to CODA 1
5th time, to CODA 2

lu - jah, hal - le - lu - jah, we are go - ing to see the King.___

3.
G A7 D7 G A7 D7
Hal - le - lu - jah. Ooh, ooh, ooh, ooh, ooh,
G
ah. 4. No more dy - in' there.
CODA 1
G A7 D7
Hal - le - lu - jah.
G A7 D7 G G7 C
Ooh, ooh, ooh, ooh, ooh, ah. Should there be
D7 G G/B Cmaj7 Am7
an - y riv - ers we must cross, should there be an - y
D7 G7 C
moun - tains we must climb, God will sup -

D7 G G/B Cmaj7 Am7
ply all the strength that we need, give us grace 'til we reach
D7 G7 C
the oth - er side. We have come from
D7 G G/B Cmaj7 Am7
ev - 'ry na - tion, God knows each of us by name. Je - sus took His
D7 G7
blood and He washed our sins, and He washed them all a - way.
C D7 G G/B Cmaj7
Yes, there are some of us, who have laid down our lives, but we

D.C. al CODA 2
Am7 D7 G
all shall live a - gain on the oth - er side.
CODA 2
G A7 D7 G A7 D7
Hal - le - lu - jah, Ooh, ooh, ooh, ooh, ooh,
G A7 D7 G A7 D7 G
ah. Hal - le - lu - jah, Ooh, ooh, ooh, ooh, ooh. Hal - le -
A7 D7 G A7 D7 Gsus G
lu.... Ooh, ooh, ooh, ooh, ooh, ah.

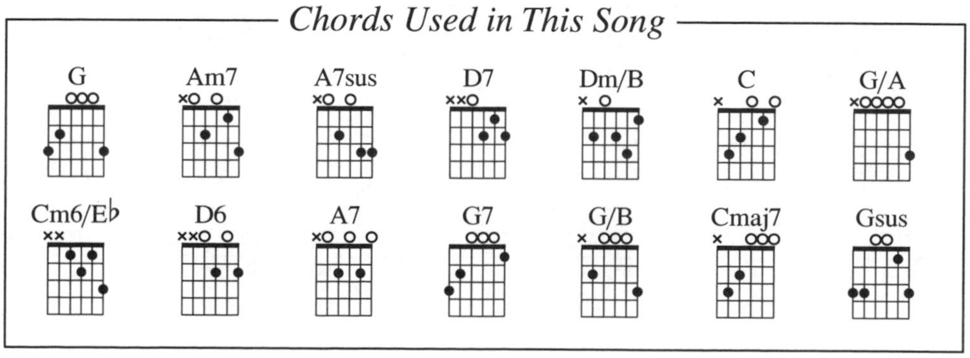
Chords Used in This Song
G Am7 A7sus D7 Dm/B C G/A
Cm6/E♭ D6 A7 G7 G/B Cmaj7 Gsus

Sing to the King

Words and Music by
BILLY JAMES FOOTE
First verse and theme of song come from "Sing We the King"
written by Charles Silvester Horne, 1910

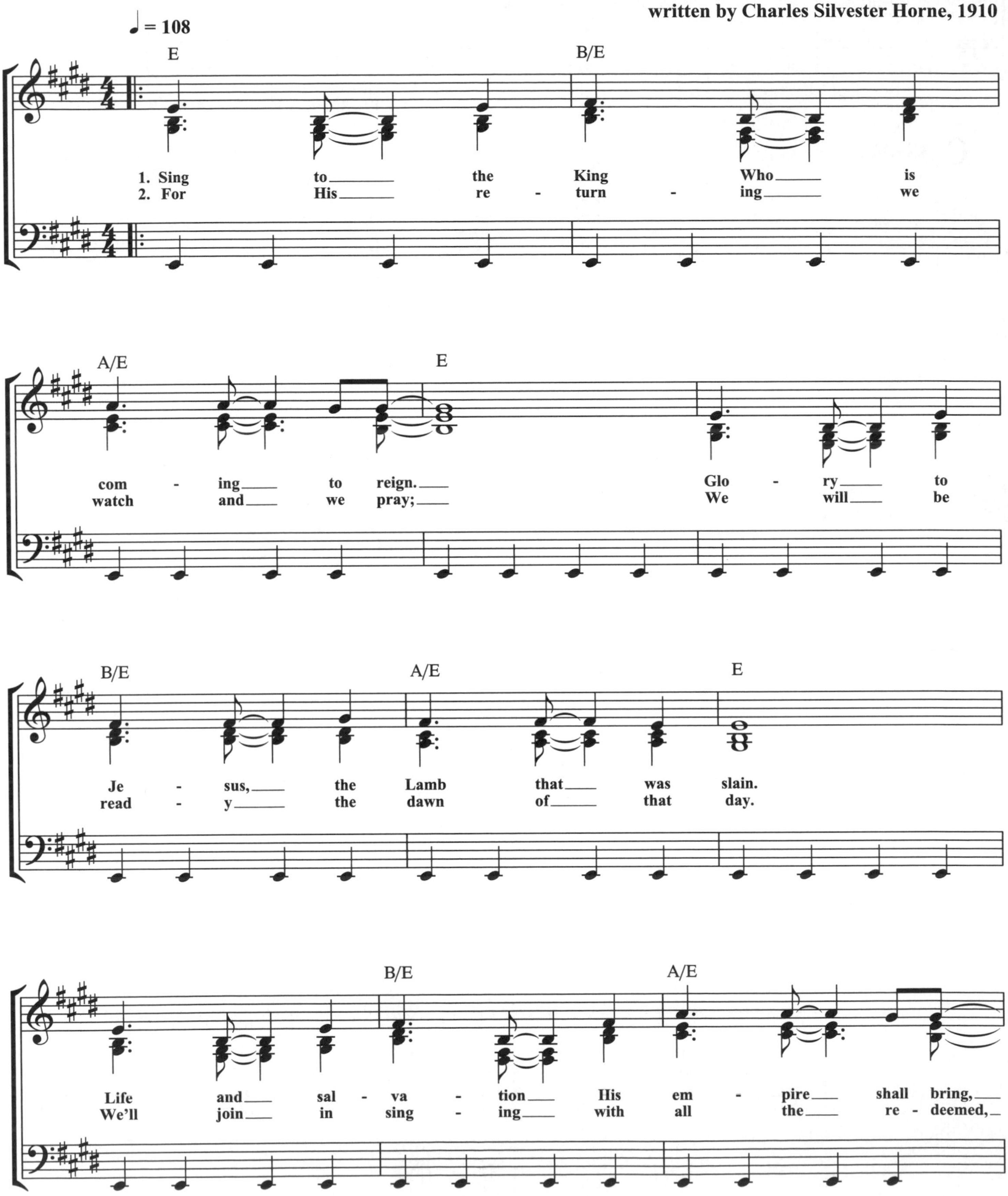
♩ = 108
E
B/E
1. Sing to the King Who is
2. For His re - turn - ing we
A/E
E
com - ing to reign.
watch and we pray;
Glo - ry to
We will be
B/E
A/E
E
Je - sus, the Lamb that was slain.
read - y the dawn of that day.
B/E
A/E
Life and sal - va - tion His em - pire shall bring,
We'll join in sing - ing with all the re - deemed,

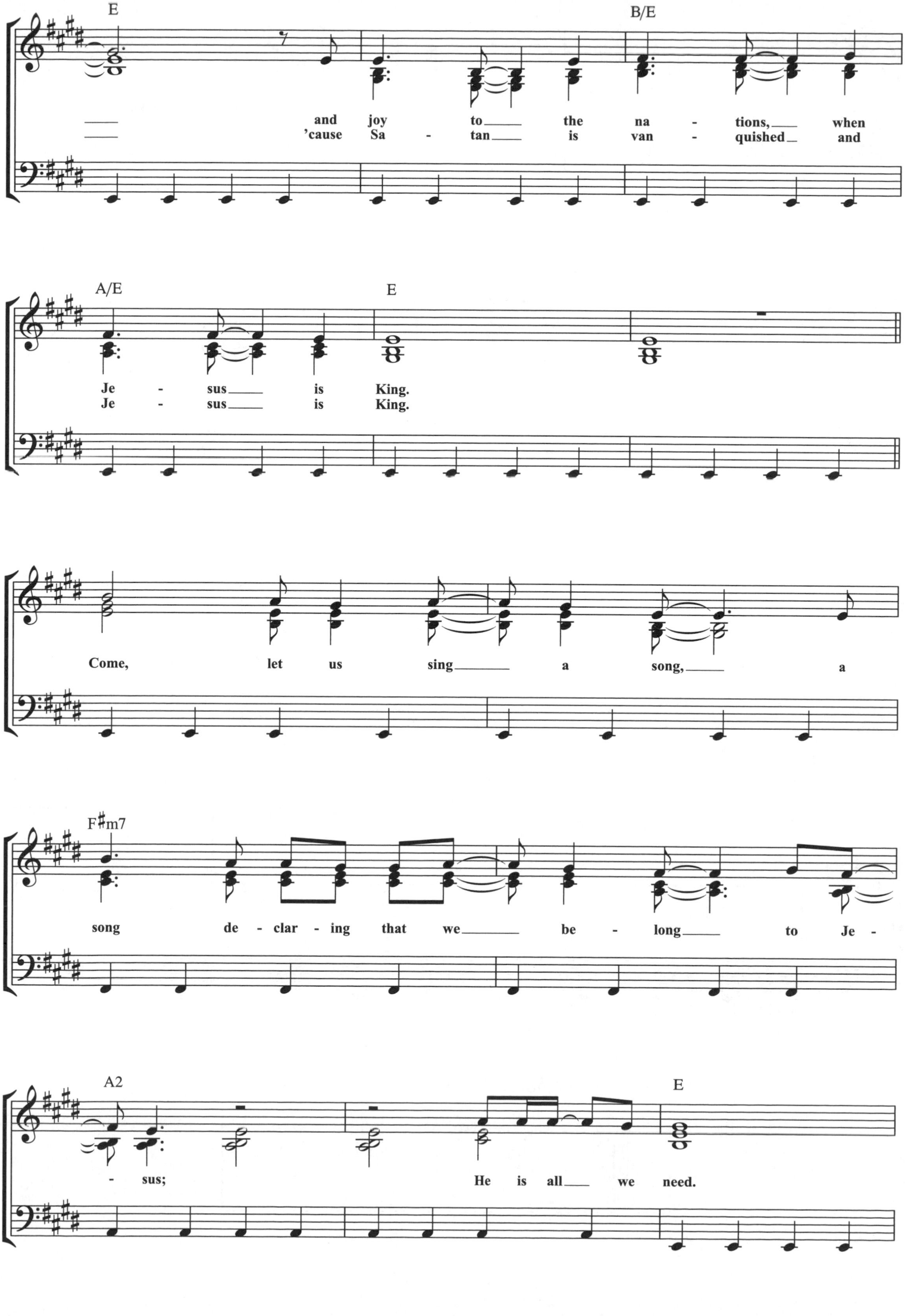
E
B/E
and joy to the na - tions, when
'cause Sa - tan is van - quished and
A/E
E
Je - sus is King.
Je - sus is King.
Come, let us sing a song, a
F♯m7
song de - clar - ing that we be - long to Je -
A2
E
- sus; He is all we need.

D2
E
Lift up a heart of praise.
F♯m7
Sing now with voic - es raised to Je -
A2
- sus;
Sing to the
E
King.
1.
2.

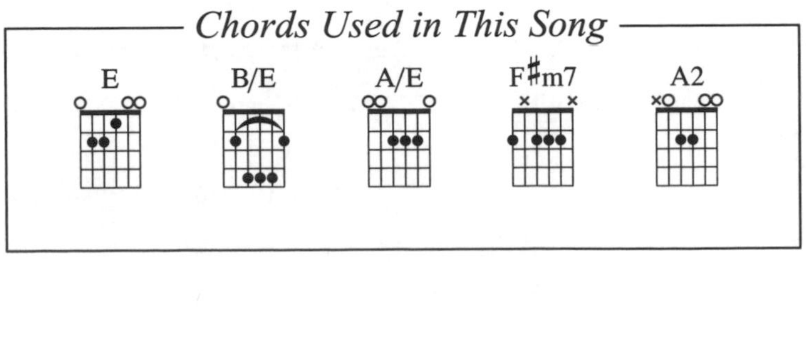
Chords Used in This Song
E
B/E
A/E
F♯m7
A2

Take My Life

Words and Music by
FRANCES HAVERGAL
Arrangement and additional lyrics by
Chris Tomlin and Louie Giglio

♩ = 88
D Asus A Bm
1. Take my life and let it be con -
2. Take my voice and let me sing al -
3. Take my will and make it Thine, it
G2 Em7 Asus D
- se - crat - ed, Lord, to Thee.
- ways, on - ly, for my King.
shall be no long - er mine.
Asus A Bm
Take my mo - ments and my days, let
Take my lips and let them be filled
Take my heart, it is Thine own, it
G2 Em7 Asus D
them flow in cease - less praise.
with mes - sag - es from Thee.
shall be Thy roy - al throne.

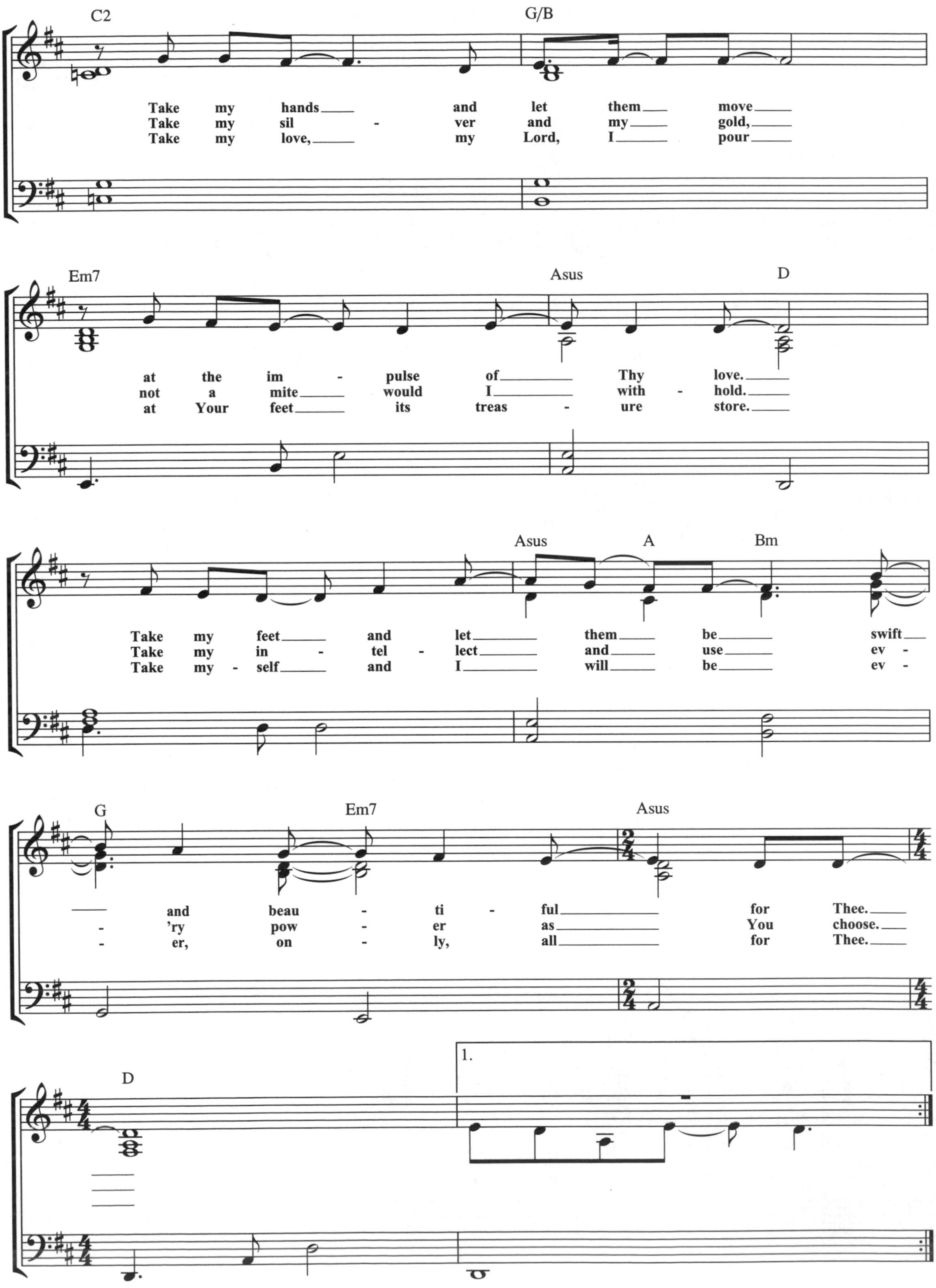
C2
G/B
Take my hands and let them move
Take my sil - ver and my gold,
Take my love, my Lord, I pour
Em7
Asus
D
at the im - pulse of Thy love.
not a mite would I with - hold.
at Your feet its treas - ure store.
Asus
A
Bm
Take my feet and let them be swift
Take my in - tel - lect and use ev -
Take my - self and I will be ev -
G
Em7
Asus
and beau - ti - ful for Thee.
- 'ry pow - er as You choose.
- er, on - ly, all for Thee.
D
1.

2. 3.
Em7
G2
Here am I,
all of me.
Asus
Em7
Take my life,
G2
Asus
it's all for Thee.
1.
D.C.
2.
D

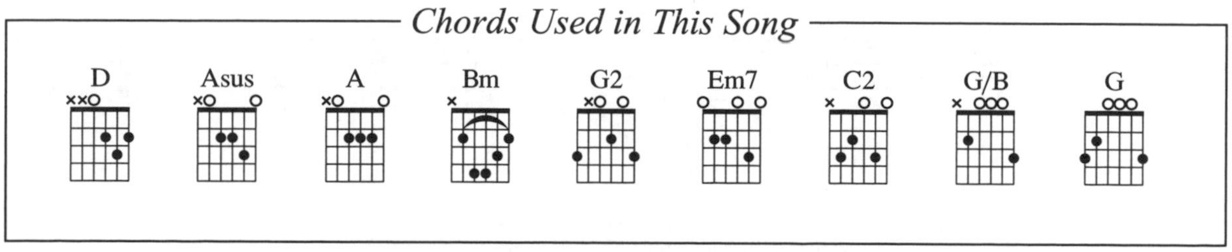
Chords Used in This Song
D
Asus
A
Bm
G2
Em7
C2
G/B
G

Thank You for the Blood

♩ = 116

Words and Music by
MATT REDMAN

C
Em
Am
Thank You, thank You for the blood that You shed,
F
C
Em
F
Stand - ing in its bless - ing, we sing these free - dom songs.
C
Em
Am
Thank You, thank You for the bat - tle You won.
F
C
Em
F
Stand - ing in Your vict - 'ry, we sing sal - va - tion songs, we sing

C Em F G
sal - va - tion's song.
You have
C Em F
o - pened a way to the Fa - ther where be - fore we could nev - er have
C Em
come.
Je - sus, count us as Yours now for - ev - er, as we sing
Am D/F♯ G F
these free - dom songs.
We
C F D/F♯
sing of all You've done,
we sing of all You've done,

G E/G♯ Am G
we sing of all You've done for us, won for us, paid
F C F
for us. We sing of all You've done, we
D/F♯ G E/G♯
sing of all You've done, we sing of all You've done
Am G F C
for us, won for us, paid for us.

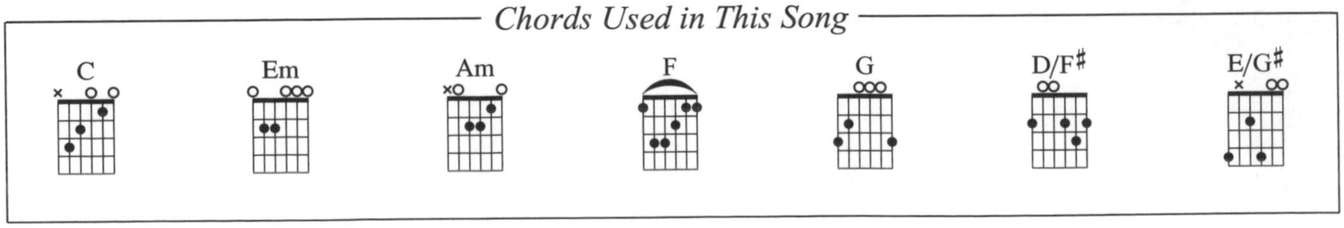
Chords Used in This Song
C Em Am F G D/F♯ E/G♯

The Heart Of Worship
(When The Music Fades)

Words and Music by
MATT REDMAN

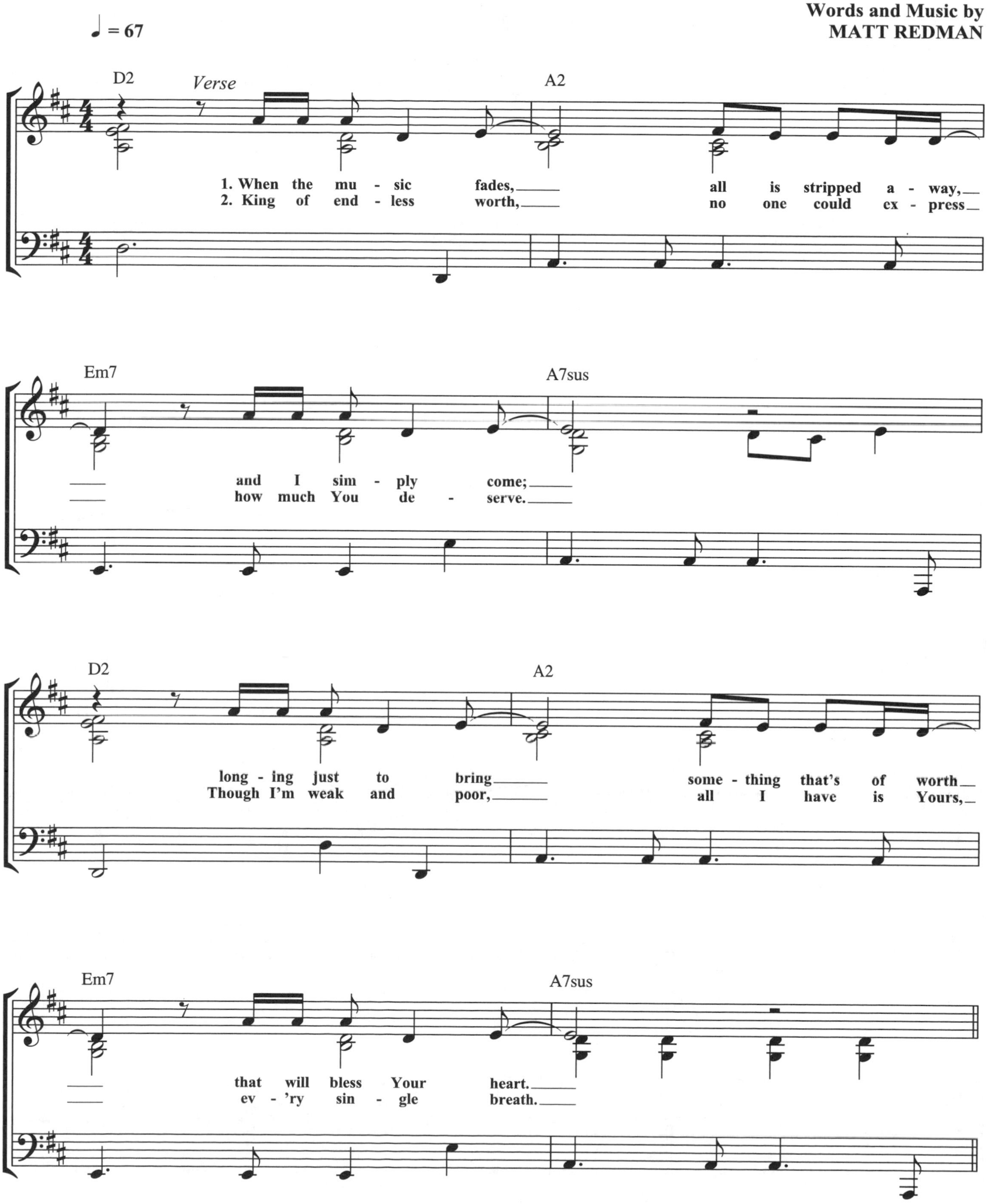
♩ = 67
D2
Verse
A2
1. When the mu - sic fades, all is stripped a - way,
2. King of end - less worth, no one could ex - press
Em7
A7sus
and I sim - ply come;
how much You de - serve.
D2
A2
long - ing just to bring some - thing that's of worth
Though I'm weak and poor, all I have is Yours,
Em7
A7sus
that will bless Your heart.
ev - 'ry sin - gle breath.

Em7 D/F♯ A7sus
I'll bring You more than a song, for a song in it - self
Em7 D/F♯ A7sus
is not what You have re - quired.
Em7 D/F♯ A7sus
You search much deep - er with - in through the way things ap - pear;
Em7 D/F♯ A7sus
You're look - ing in - to my heart.
D2 Chorus A2/C♯
I'm com - ing back to the heart of wor - ship, and it's

Em7
D/F♯
G
A7sus
all a - bout You, all a - bout You, Je - sus.
D2
A2/C♯
I'm sor - ry, Lord, for the thing I've made it, when it's
Em7
D/F♯
G
A7sus
D
all a - bout You, all a - bout You, Je - sus.

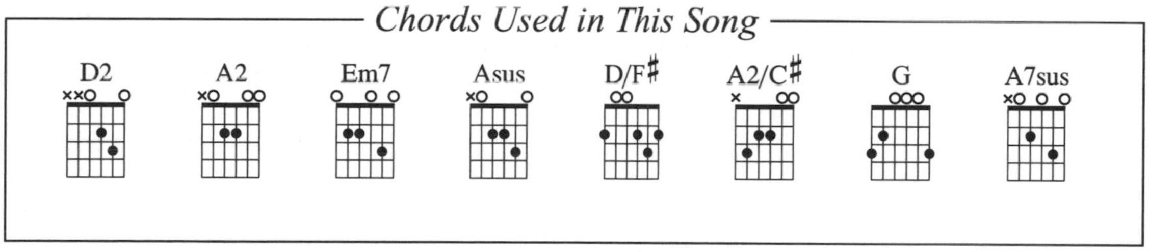
Chords Used in This Song
D2
A2
Em7
Asus
D/F♯
A2/C♯
G
A7sus

The Father's Song

Zephaniah 3:17

Words and Music by
MATT REDMAN

Capo 1 (D) ♩ = 116

Keyboard
(Guitar)
E♭ (D)
E♭/D (D/C♯)
E♭/D♭ (D/C)
I have heard so man - y songs, lis - tened to a
A♭/C (G/B)
Fm9 (Em9)
B♭sus (Asus)
thou - sand tongues, but there is one that sounds a - bove them all:
Cm (Bm)
B♭/D (A/C♯)
A♭ (G)
E♭ (D)
The Fa - ther's song, the
E♭/D (D/C♯)
E♭/D♭ (D/C)
A♭/C (G/B)
Fa - ther's love, You sung it o - ver me, and for e -

Fm9 (Em9) Bbsus (Asus) Eb (D)
ter - ni - ty it's writ - ten on my heart.
A♭/C (G/B) ad lib. on D.S. B♭/D (A/C♯)
Heav en's per - fect mel - o - dy, The Cre - a - tor's
E♭/G (D/F♯) A♭2 (G2) Fm7 (Em7)
sym - pho - ny; You are sing - ing o - ver me
B♭sus (Asus) Cm (Bm) B♭/D (A/C♯) E♭/G (D/F♯)
the Fa - ther's song. Heav en's per - fect
Heav en's per - fect
A♭/C (G/B) B♭/D (A/C♯)
mys - ter - y: the King of Love has
mel - o - dy, The Cre - a - tor's

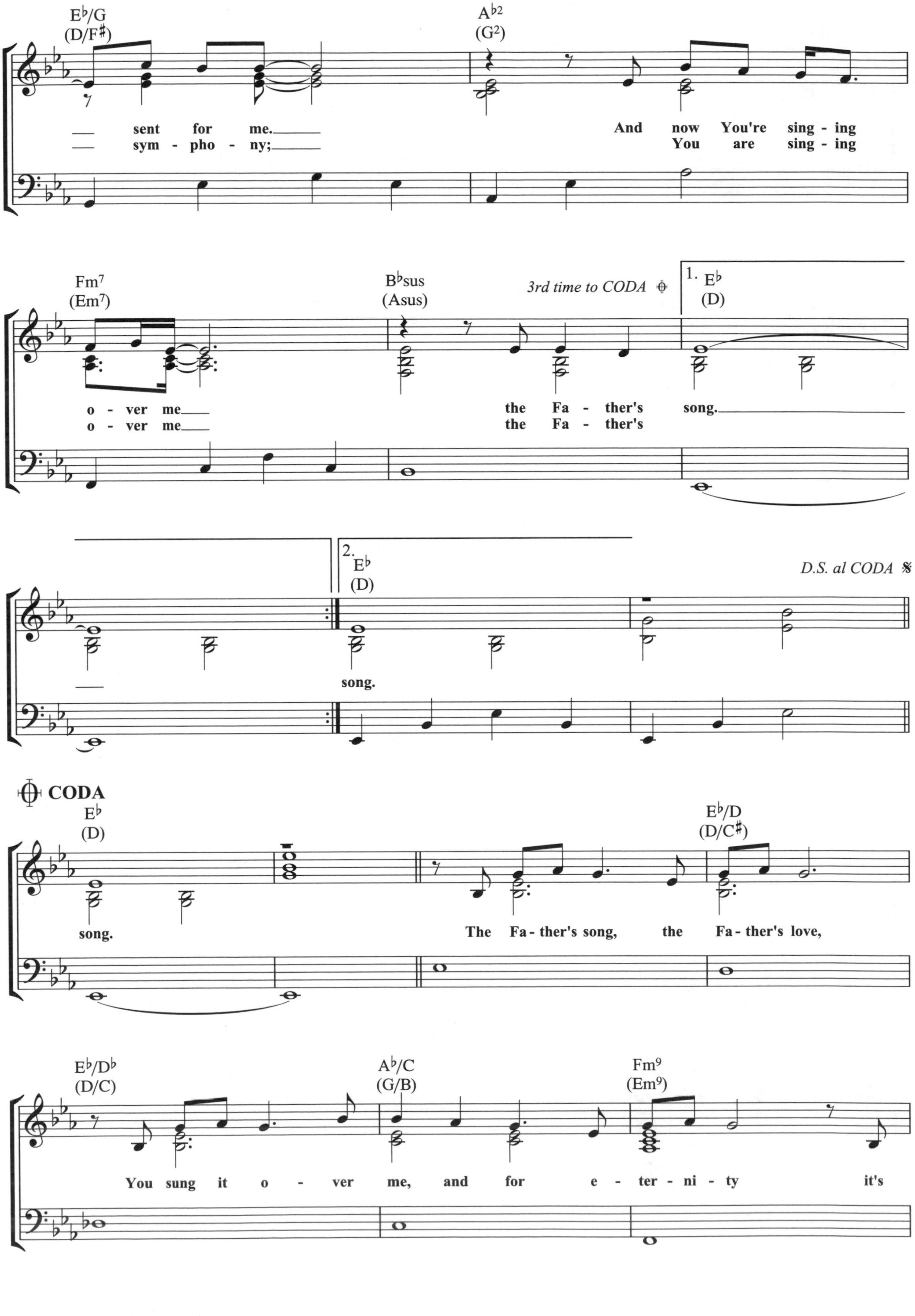
E♭/G
(D/F♯)
A♭2
(G2)
sent for me.
And now You're sing - ing
sym - pho - ny;
You are sing - ing
Fm7
(Em7)
B♭sus
(Asus)
3rd time to CODA
1. E♭
(D)
o - ver me
the Fa - ther's song.
o - ver me
the Fa - ther's
2. E♭
(D)
D.S. al CODA
song.
CODA
E♭
(D)
E♭/D
(D/C♯)
song.
The Fa - ther's song, the Fa - ther's love,
E♭/D♭
(D/C)
A♭/C
(G/B)
Fm9
(Em9)
You sung it o - ver me, and for e - ter - ni - ty it's

B♭sus (Asus)
Cm7 (Bm7)
A♭/C (G/B)
writ - ten on my heart. You've writ - ten it in
Cm7 (Bm7)
A♭/C (G/B)
love. You've writ - ten it in
Cm7 (Bm7)
A♭/C (G/B)
grace, in - to the depths of our
Cm7 (Bm7)
A♭/C (G/B)
E♭ (D)
hearts, Fa - ther.

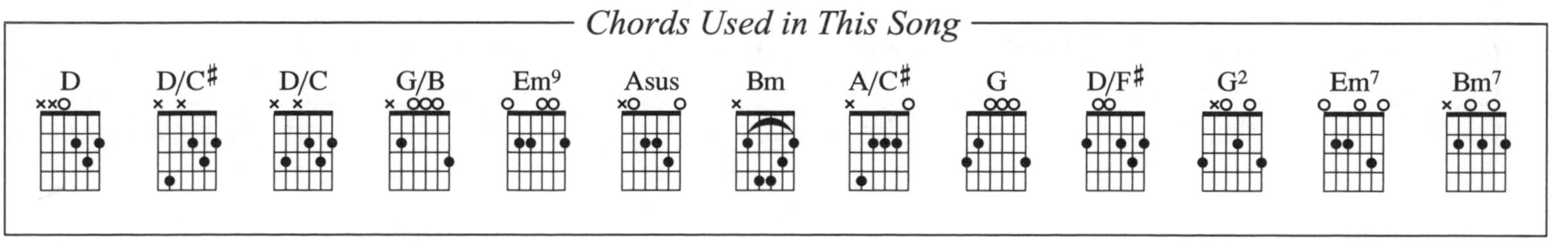
Chords Used in This Song
D
D/C♯
D/C
G/B
Em9
Asus
Bm
A/C♯
G
D/F♯
G2
Em7
Bm7

The Happy Song

Words and Music by
MARTIN SMITH

♩ = 120

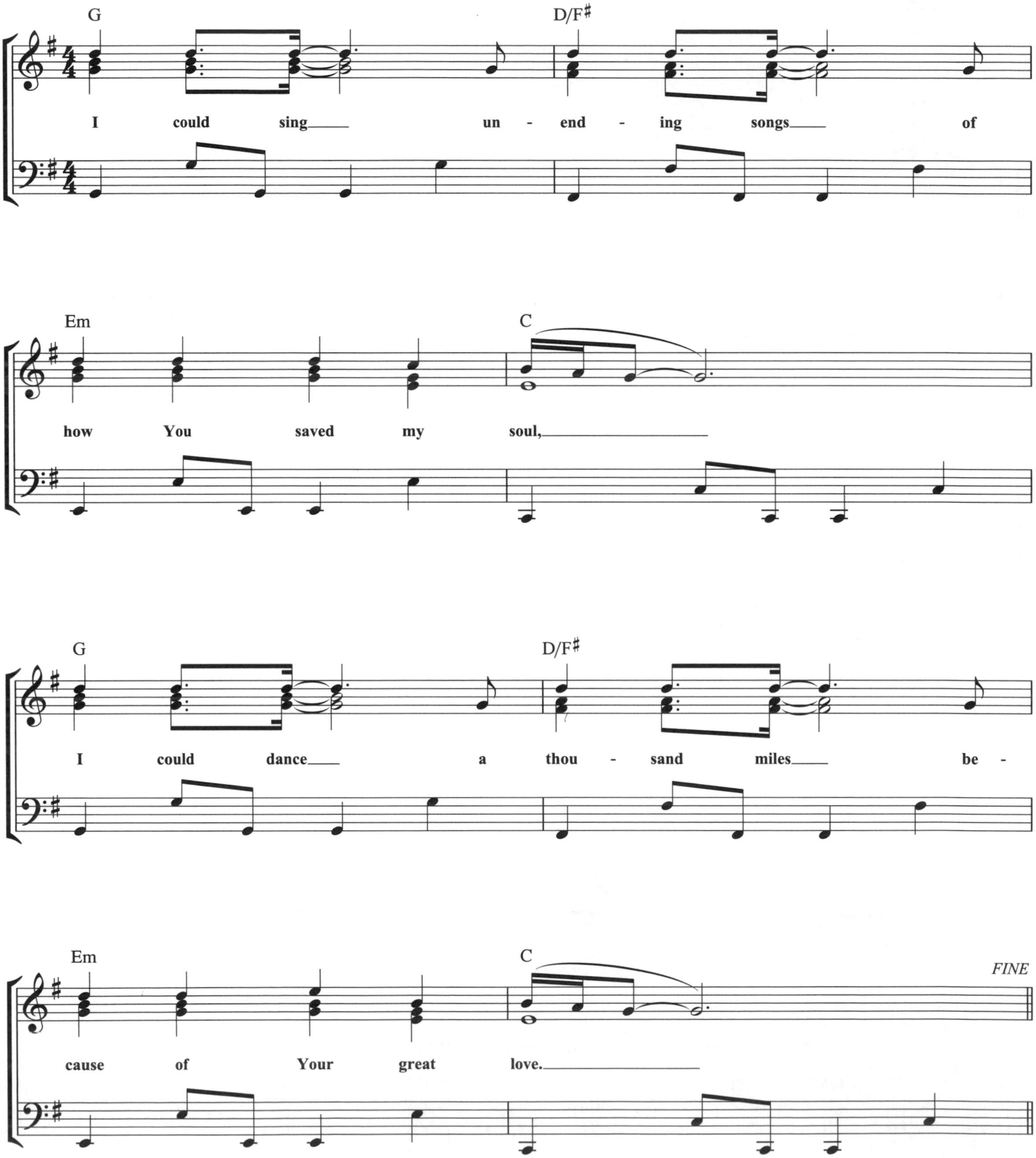
G
D/F♯
I could sing un - end - ing songs of
Em
C
how You saved my soul,
G
D/F♯
I could dance a thou - sand miles be -
Em
C
FINE
cause of Your great love.

G
D
My heart is burst - ing, Lord,
to tell of all You've done,
C
D
of how You changed my life and wiped a - way my past.
G
D
I want to shout it out,
from ev - 'ry roof - top sing,
C
D
for now I know that God is for me not a - gainst me.
Am
Ev - 'ry bod - y's sing - ing now,
'cause we're so

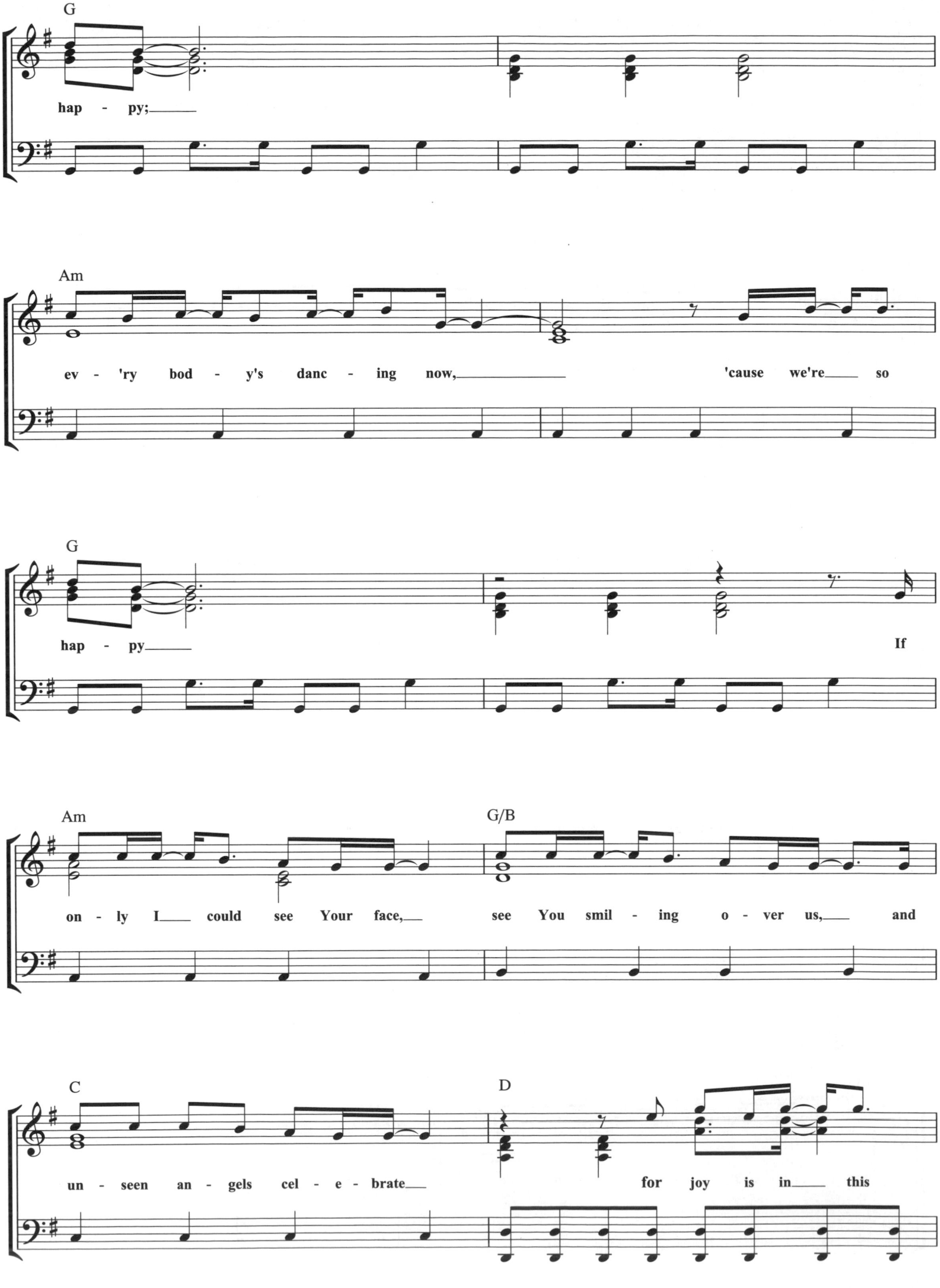
G
hap - py;
Am
ev - 'ry bod - y's danc - ing now, 'cause we're so
G
hap - py If
Am
on - ly I could see Your face,
G/B
see You smil - ing o - ver us, and
C
un - seen an - gels cel - e - brate
D
for joy is in this

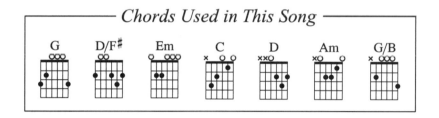

Chords Used in This Song

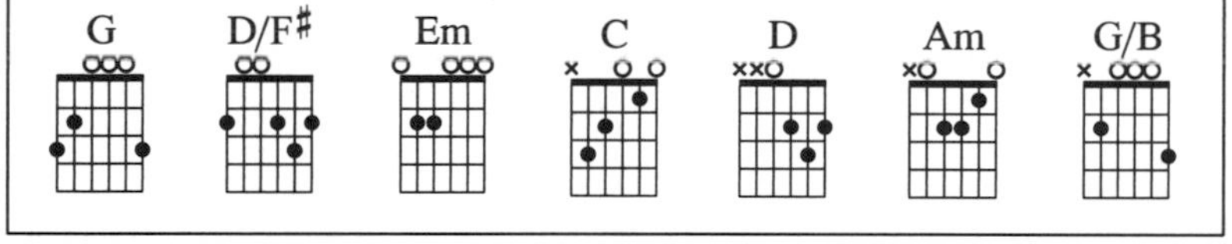

The Power of The Cross

(Oh, to See The Dawn)

Words and Music by
KEITH GETTY and STUART TOWNEND

♩ = 68
D/F♯ E/G♯ A E/B A/C♯
Dmaj7 A/C♯ Bm7 Dmaj7 Esus E
D/F♯ E/G♯ A E7/B A/C♯
1. Oh to see the dawn of the dark - est day.
2. Oh to see the pain writ - ten on Your face,
3. Now the day - light flees, Now the ground be - neath
4. Oh to see my name writ - ten in the wounds,
D A/C♯ Bm7 Dmaj7 Esus E
Christ on the road to cal - va - ry.
bear - ing the awe - some weight of sin.
Quakes as its mak - er bows his head.
For through Your suf - 'fring I am free.

D/F♯ E/G♯ A E7/B A/C♯
Tried by sin - ful men, torn and beat - en then.
Eve - ry bit - ter thought, eve - ry e - vil deed
Cur - tain torn in two, dead are raised to life.
Death is crushed to death, life is mine to live
D A/C♯ Dmaj7 Esus E/D A/C♯
nailed to a cross of wood.
Crown - ing Your blood - stained brow. 1. 2. 3. This the
'Fin - ished!' the vic - to - ry cry. 4. This the
Won through Your self - less love!
D E/G♯ A A/C♯
power of the cross. Christ be -
power of the cross Son of
D E/G♯ A A/C♯
- came sin for us. Took the
God slain for us. What a
D B/D♯ E E/D A/C♯ D
blame, bore the wrath. We stand for - giv - en
life, what a cost. We stand for - giv - en

Chords Used in This Song

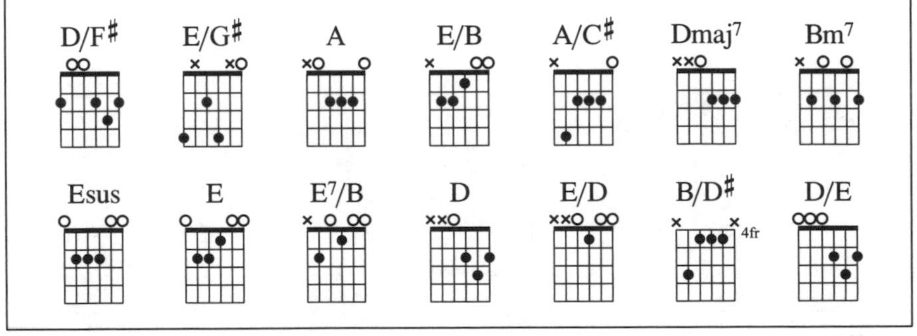
D/F♯
E/G♯
A
E/B
A/C♯
Dmaj7
Bm7
Esus
E
E7/B
D
E/D
B/D♯
4fr
D/E

The Wonderful Cross

Hymn by ISAAC WATTS
Arrangement by Jesse Reeves and Chris Tomlin
Refrain lyrics by Chris Tomlin and J.D. Walt

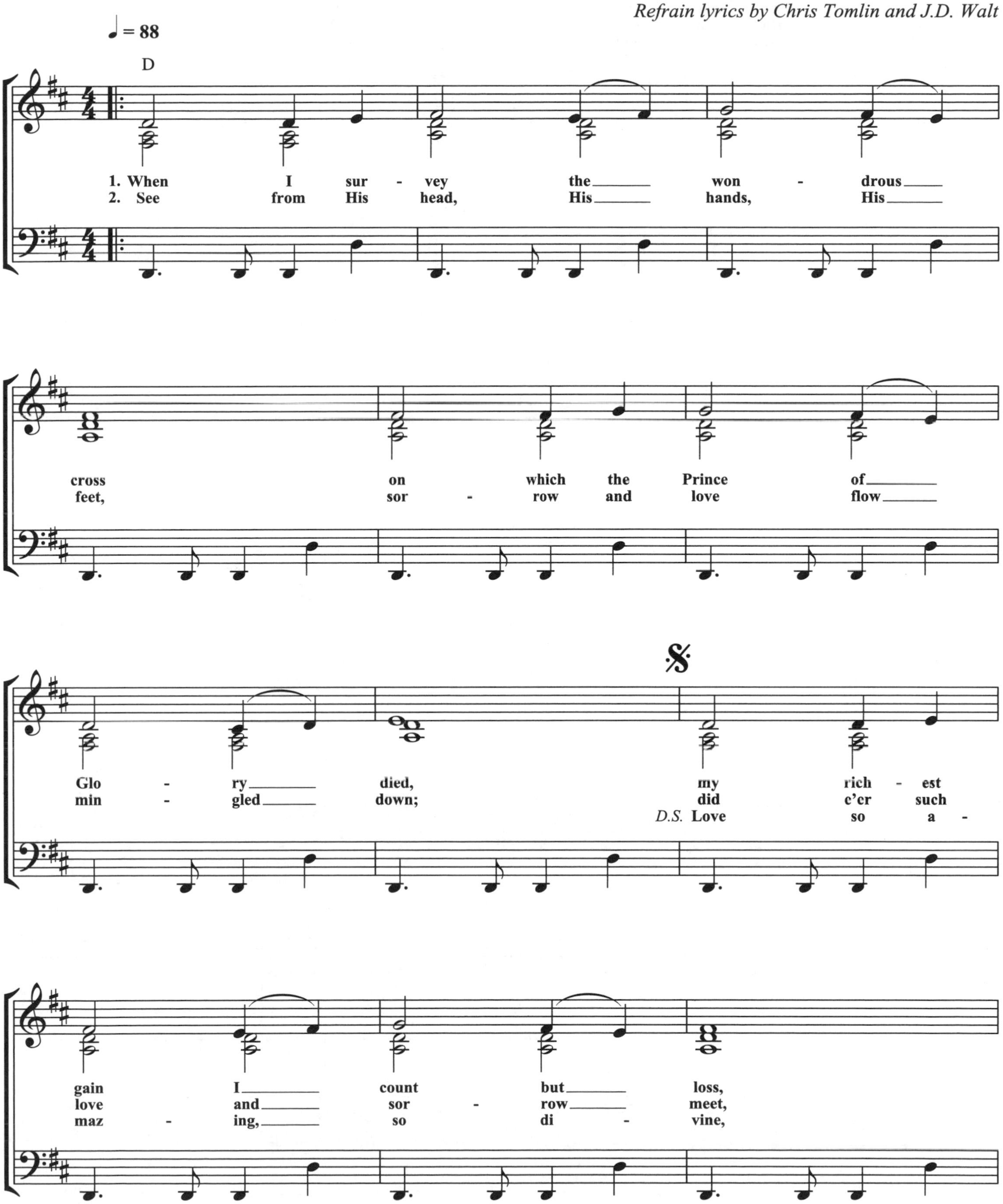
♩ = 88
D
1. When I sur - vey the won - drous
2. See from His head, His hands, His
cross on which the Prince of
feet, sor - row and love flow
Glo - ry died, my rich - est
min - gled down; did e'er such
D.S. Love so a -
gain I count but loss,
love and sor - row meet,
maz - ing, so di - vine,

and pour con - tempt on all my
or thorns com - pose so rich a
de - mands my soul, my life, my
pride.
crown.
all.
G
D/F♯
O the won - der - ful cross, O the
won - der - ful cross bids me come
and die and find that I may tru -
- ly live.
Asus
1.
A
2. 3.
O the

G
D/F♯
won - der - ful cross,
O the
won - der - ful cross;
all who gath -
- er here by grace draw near and bless
Your name.
Asus
1.
A
D.S.
2.
A
D

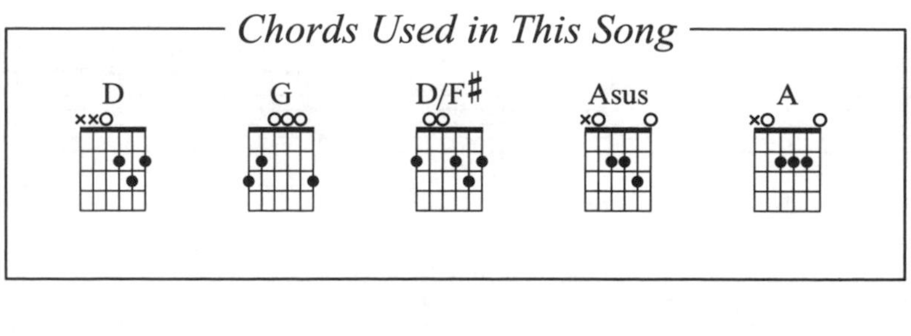
Chords Used in This Song
D
G
D/F♯
Asus
A

There Is A Redeemer

Words and Music by
MELODY GREEN

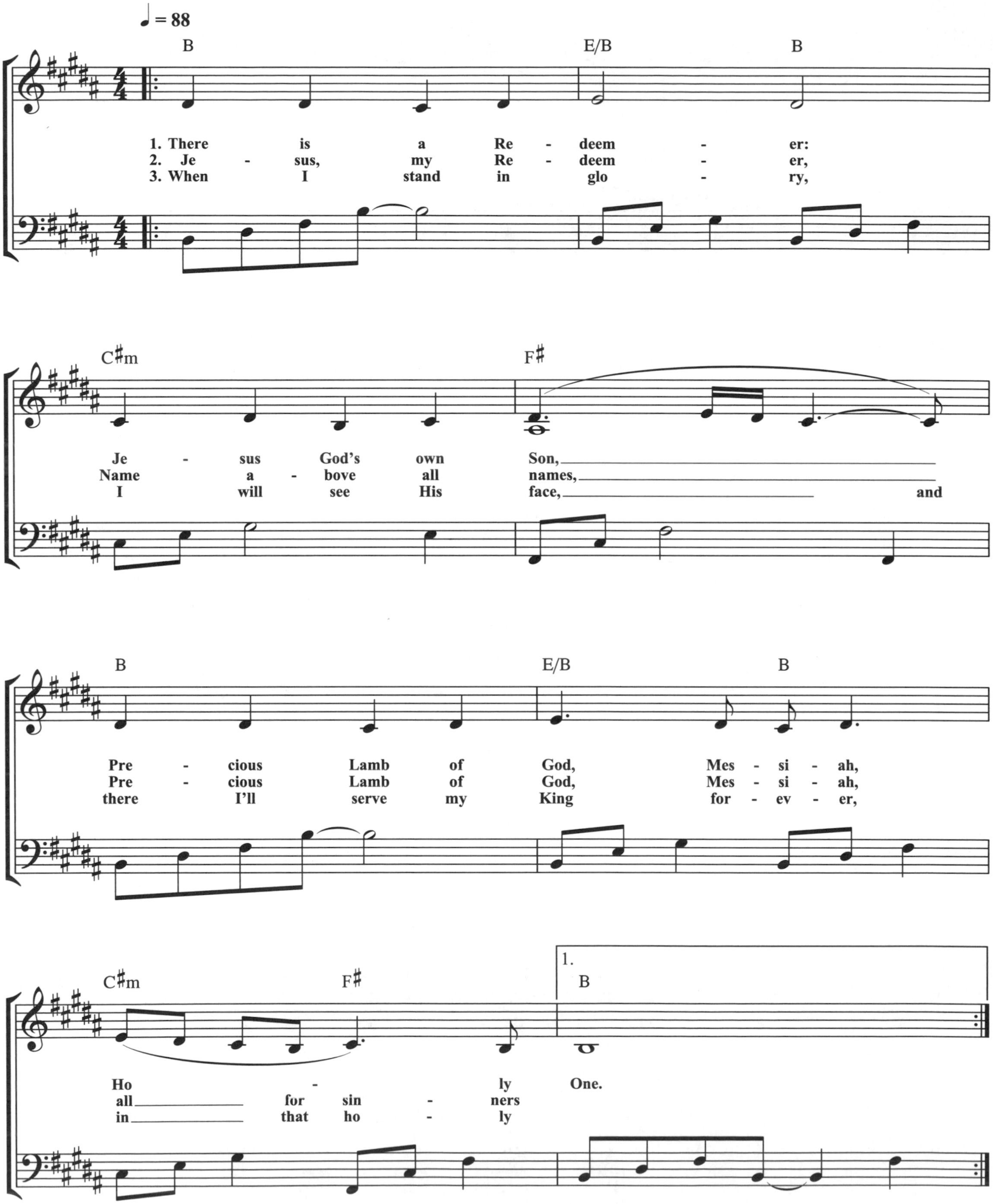
♩ = 88
B E/B B
1. There is a Re - deem - er:
2. Je - sus, my Re - deem - er,
3. When I stand in glo - ry,
C♯m F♯
Je - sus God's own Son,
Name a - bove all names,
I will see His face, and
B E/B B
Pre - cious Lamb of God, Mes - si - ah,
Pre - cious Lamb of God, Mes - si - ah,
there I'll serve my King for - ev - er,
C♯m F♯
1.
B
Ho - ly One.
all for sin - ners
in that ho - ly

2. 3.
B
E
B/D♯
slain.
place.
Thank you, O my Fa - ther, for
C♯m
F♯
B
F♯
giv - ing us Your Son and
B
E
B/D♯
leav - ing Your Spir - it 'til the
C♯m
F♯
1.
B
D.C.
2.
B
work on earth is done.
done.

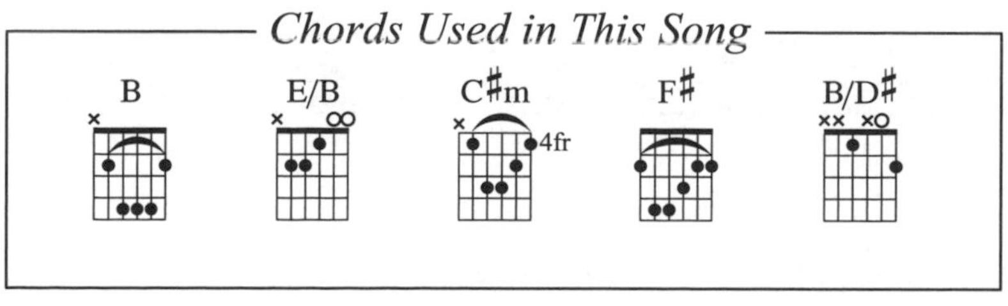
Chords Used in This Song
B
E/B
C♯m
4fr
F♯
B/D♯

Unchanging

Words and Music by
CHRIS TOMLIN

Capo 1 (G)

♩ = 107
Keyboard
(Guitar)
A♭ (G) A♭maj7 (Gmaj7) A♭6 (G6) A♭ (G) A♭maj7 (Gmaj7) A♭6 (G6)
1. Great is Your faith - ful - ness,
2. True are Your prom - is - es,
3. Wide is Your love and grace,
D♭ (C) D(♯4) (C(♯4)) D♭ (C) D(♯4) (C(♯4)) D♭ (C)
great is Your faith - ful - ness.
true are Your prom - is - es.
wide is Your love and grace.
E♭ (D) D♭ (C)
You nev - er change, You nev - er fail, O God.
A♭ (G) A♭maj7 (Gmaj7) A♭6 (G6)
1. A♭ (G) A♭maj7 (Gmaj7) A♭6 (G6)

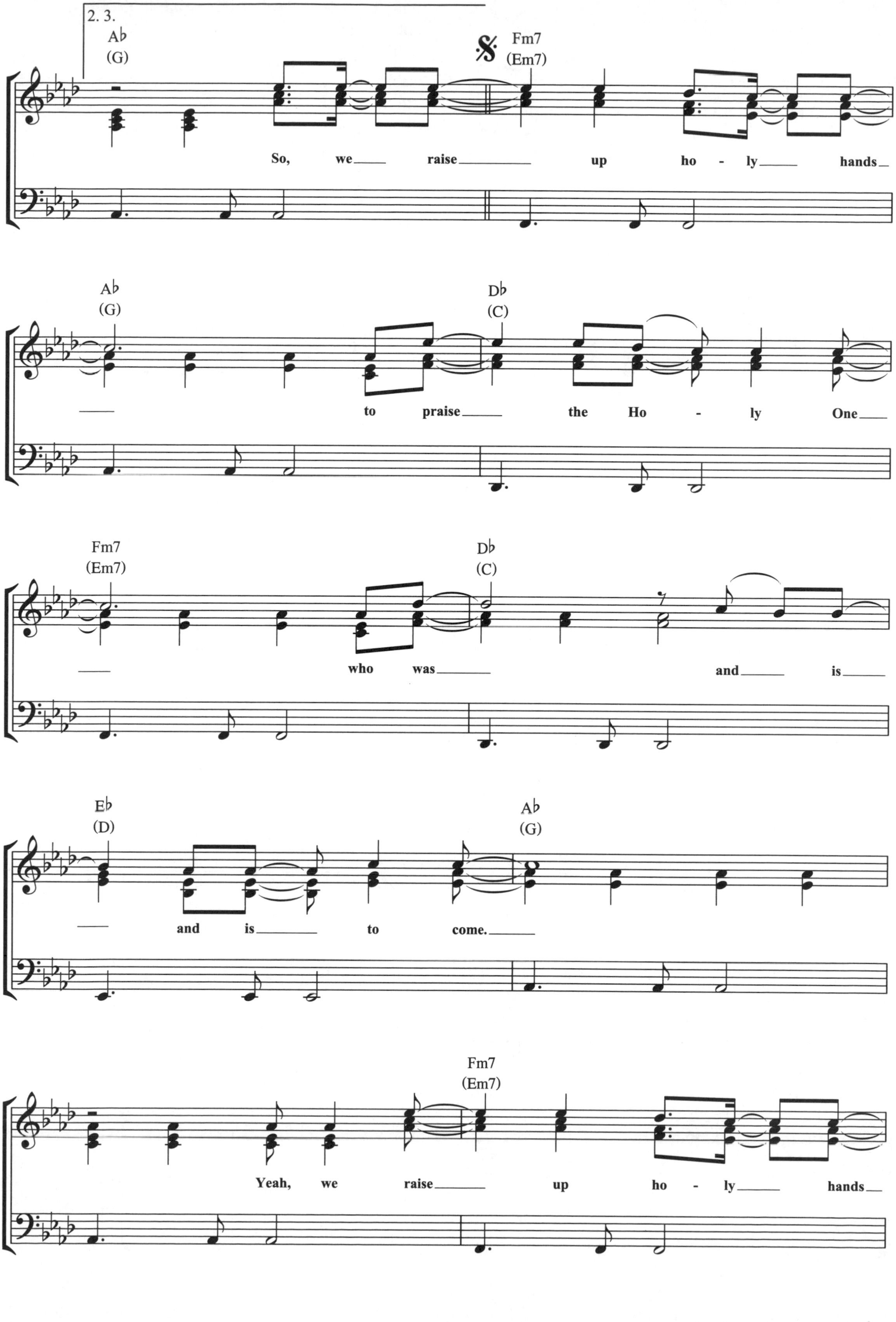
2. 3.
A♭ (G)
Fm7 (Em7)
So, we raise up holy hands
A♭ (G)
D♭ (C)
to praise the Holy One
Fm7 (Em7)
D♭ (C)
who was and is
E♭ (D)
A♭ (G)
and is to come.
Fm7 (Em7)
Yeah, we raise up holy hands

A♭ (G)
D♭ (C)
to praise the Ho - ly One
Fm7 (Em7)
D♭ (C)
E♭ (D)
3rd time to CODA
who was and is and is to come.
A♭ (G)
1.
D.C.
2.
Fm7 (Em7)
D♭ (C)
A♭/C (G/B)
1.
E♭sus (Dsus)
2.
E♭sus (Dsus)
Fm7 (Em7)
You were,

D♭
(C)
A♭/C
(G/B)
You are,
You will al - ways be.
E♭sus
(Dsus)
Fm7
(Em7)
D♭
(C)
You were,
You are,
A♭/C
(G/B)
E♭sus
(Dsus)
D.S. al CODA
You will al - ways be.
So, we raise
CODA
A♭
(G)

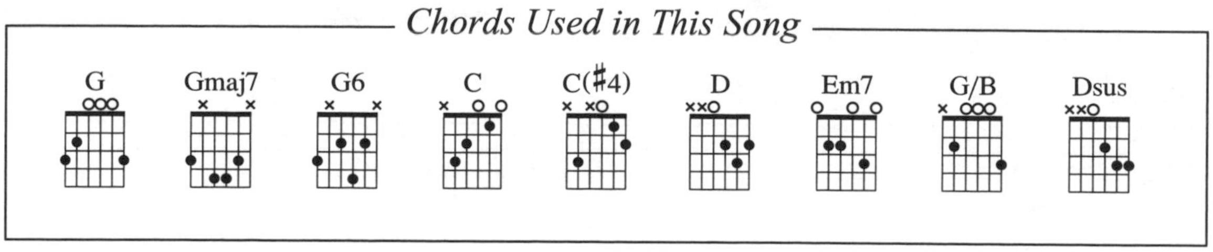
Chords Used in This Song
G
Gmaj7
G6
C
C(♯4)
D
Em7
G/B
Dsus

Unfailing Love

Words and Music by
CHRIS TOMLIN, CARY PIERCE
and ED CASH

Capo 1 (G) ♩ = 68

Keyboard
(Guitar)
A♭ (G)
D♭ (C)
A♭/C (G/B)
1. You have my heart, and I am Yours for - ev - er.
(2. You are my) rock the One I hold on to.
B♭m7 (Am7)
You are my strength, God of grace and power.
You are my song, and I sing for You.
And ev - 'ry-thing You hold in Your hand. Still You make
E♭ (D)
time for me. I can't un - der - stand.
E♭sus (Dsus)

A♭ (G) A♭/G (G/F♯) Fm7 (Em7) A♭/C (G/B)
Praise You, God of earth and sky, how beau - ti - ful is Your un - fail - ing
D♭ (C) E♭sus (Dsus) A♭ (G) A♭/G (G/F♯)
love, un - fail - ing love. And You nev - er change, God, You re-main the
Fm7 (Em7) A♭/C (G/B) D♭ (C)
Ho - ly One and my un - fail - ing love, un - fail - ing
1. E♭sus (Dsus) 2. E♭sus (Dsus) A♭ (G)
love. You are my love.

Chords Used in This Song

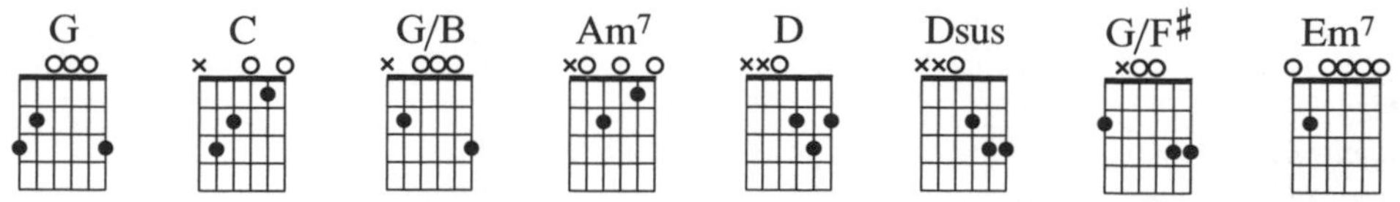
G
C
G/B
Am7
D
Dsus
G/F♯
Em7

We Fall Down

Words and Music by
CHRIS TOMLIN

Capo 2 (D) ♩= 70

Keyboard (Guitar)
E (D) B (A) C♯m7 (Bm7)
We fall down, we lay our crowns at the feet
A (G) F♯m (Em) E (D)
of Je - sus, the great - ness of
B (A) C♯m7 (Bm7) A (G) B (A) E/G♯ (D/F♯)
mer - cy and love at the feet of Je - sus. And we cry
Amaj7 (Gmaj7) E/G♯ (D/F♯) F♯m (Em) E/G♯ (D/F♯)
ho - ly, ho - ly, ho - ly, and we cry

Optional African lyrics:
Re o bama, re I koba naong tsa go Jesu. Lo lorato le legolo naong tsa go Jesu.
O boitshepo, boitshepo, O boitshepo, boitshepo, O boitshepo, boitshepo, O kwana.

Amaj7 (Gmaj7) E/G# (D/F#) F#m (Em) C#m7 (Bm7) B (A) Amaj7 (Gmaj7) E/G# (D/F#)
ho - ly, ho - ly, ho - ly, and we cry ho - ly, ho - ly, ho -
F#m (Em) Bsus (Asus) B (A) E (D) A/E (G/D) E (D) D2 (C2)
ly is the Lamb.
Amaj7 (Gmaj7) E/G# (D/F#) F#m (Em) Bsus (Asus) B (A)
Ho - ly, ho - ly, ho - ly is the Lamb.
E (D) A/E (G/D) E (D) D2 (C2) E (D)

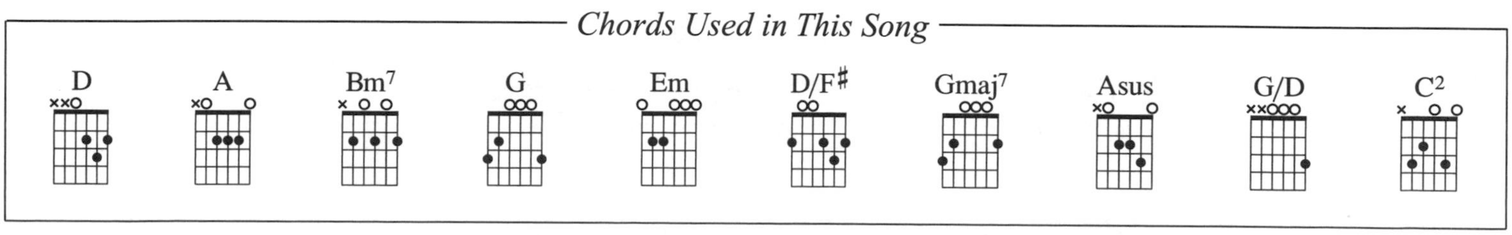
Chords Used in This Song
D
A
Bm7
G
Em
D/F#
Gmaj7
Asus
G/D
C2

When the Tears Fall
(I've Had Questions)

Words and Music by
TIM HUGHES

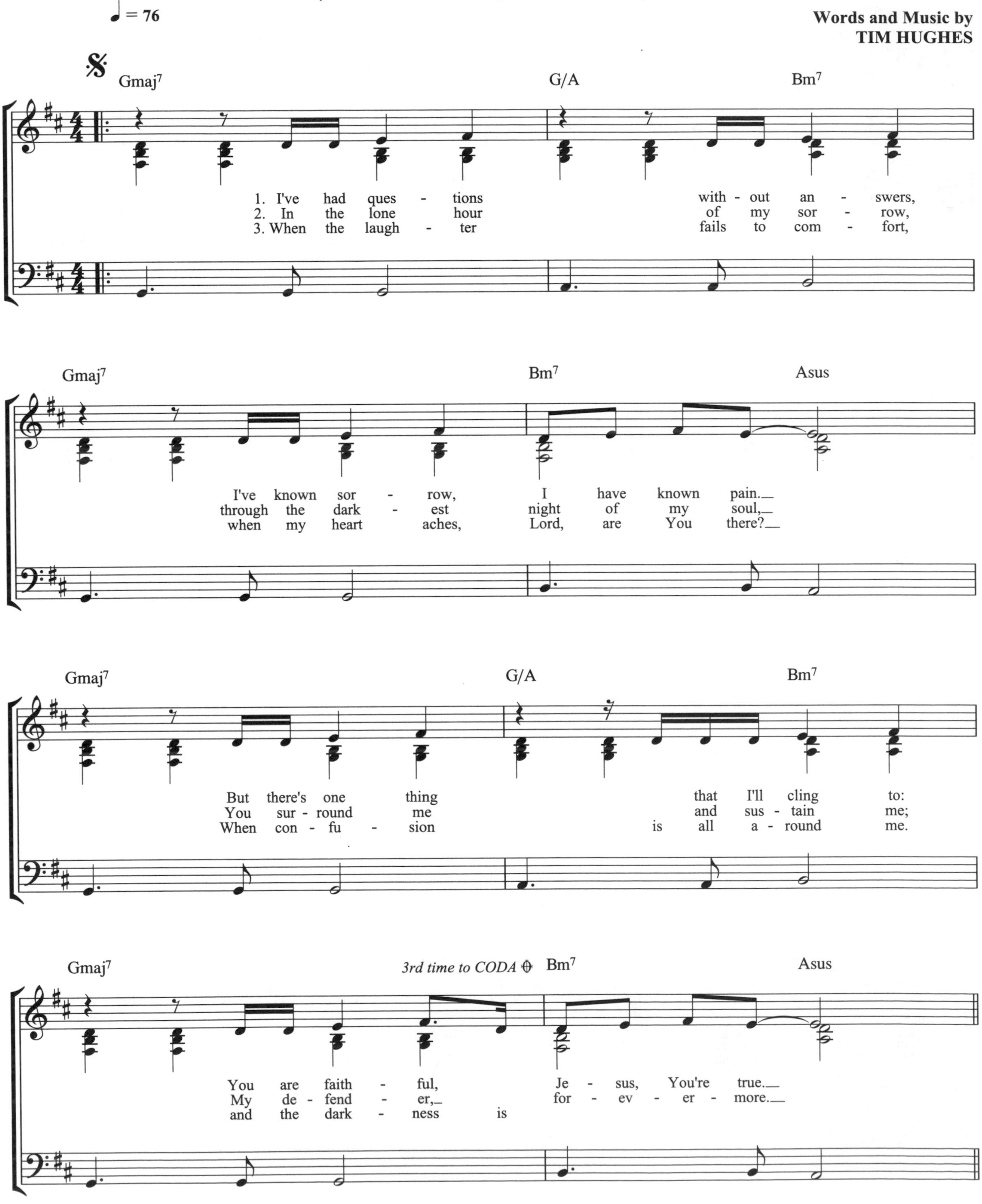
♩ = 76
Gmaj7
G/A
Bm7
1. I've had ques - tions with - out an - swers,
2. In the lone hour of my sor - row,
3. When the laugh - ter fails to com - fort,
Gmaj7
Bm7
Asus
I've known sor - row, I have known pain.
through the dark - est night of my soul,
when my heart aches, Lord, are You there?
Gmaj7
G/A
Bm7
But there's one thing that I'll cling to:
You sur - round me and sus - tain me;
When con - fu - sion is all a - round me.
Gmaj7
3rd time to CODA
Bm7
Asus
You are faith - ful, Je - sus, You're true.
My de - fend - er, for - ev - er - more.
and the dark - ness is

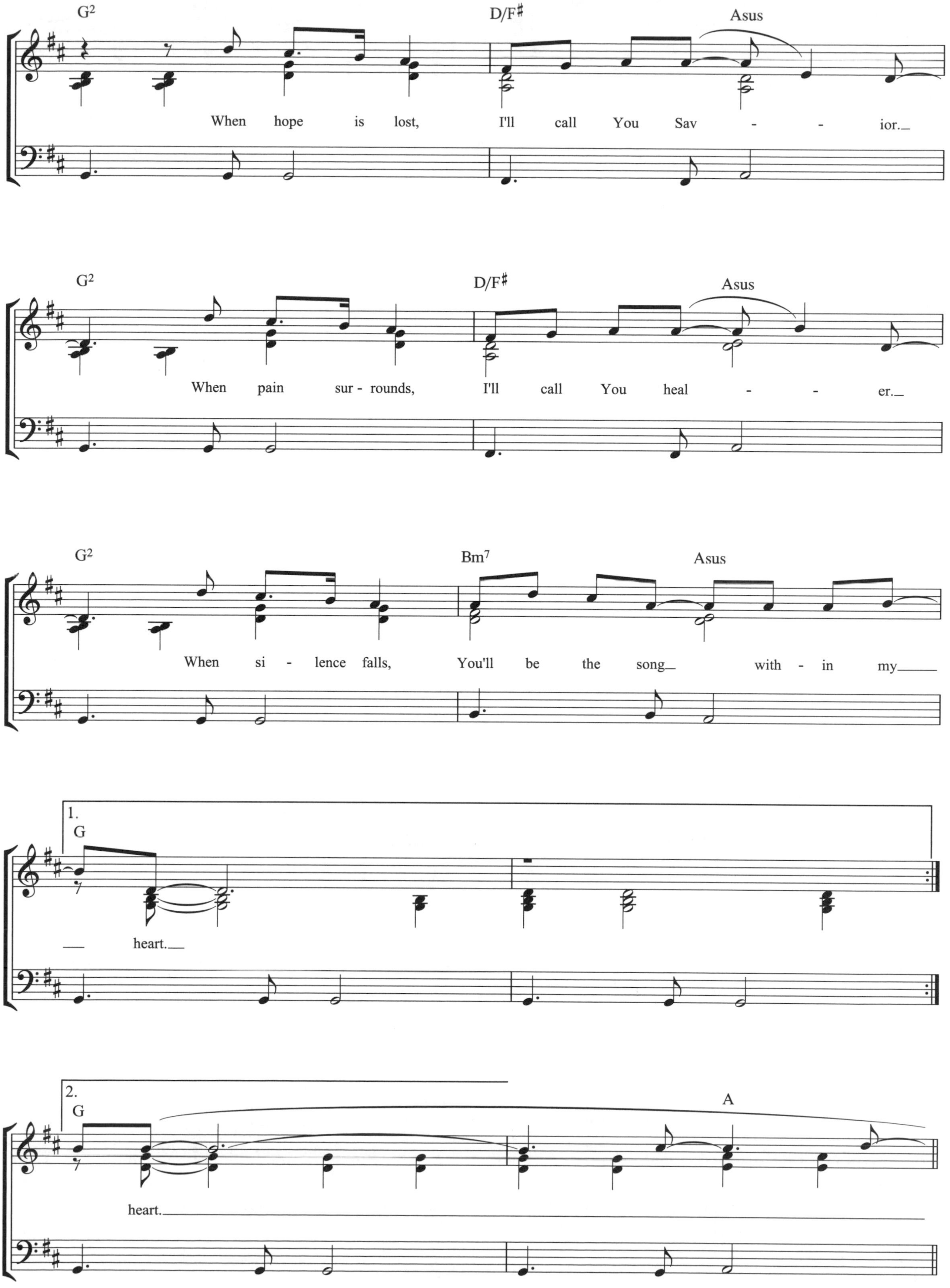
G2
D/F#
Asus
When hope is lost, I'll call You Sav - - ior.
G2
D/F#
Asus
When pain sur - rounds, I'll call You heal - - er.
G2
Bm7
Asus
When si - lence falls, You'll be the song with - in my
1.
G
heart.
2.
G
A
heart.

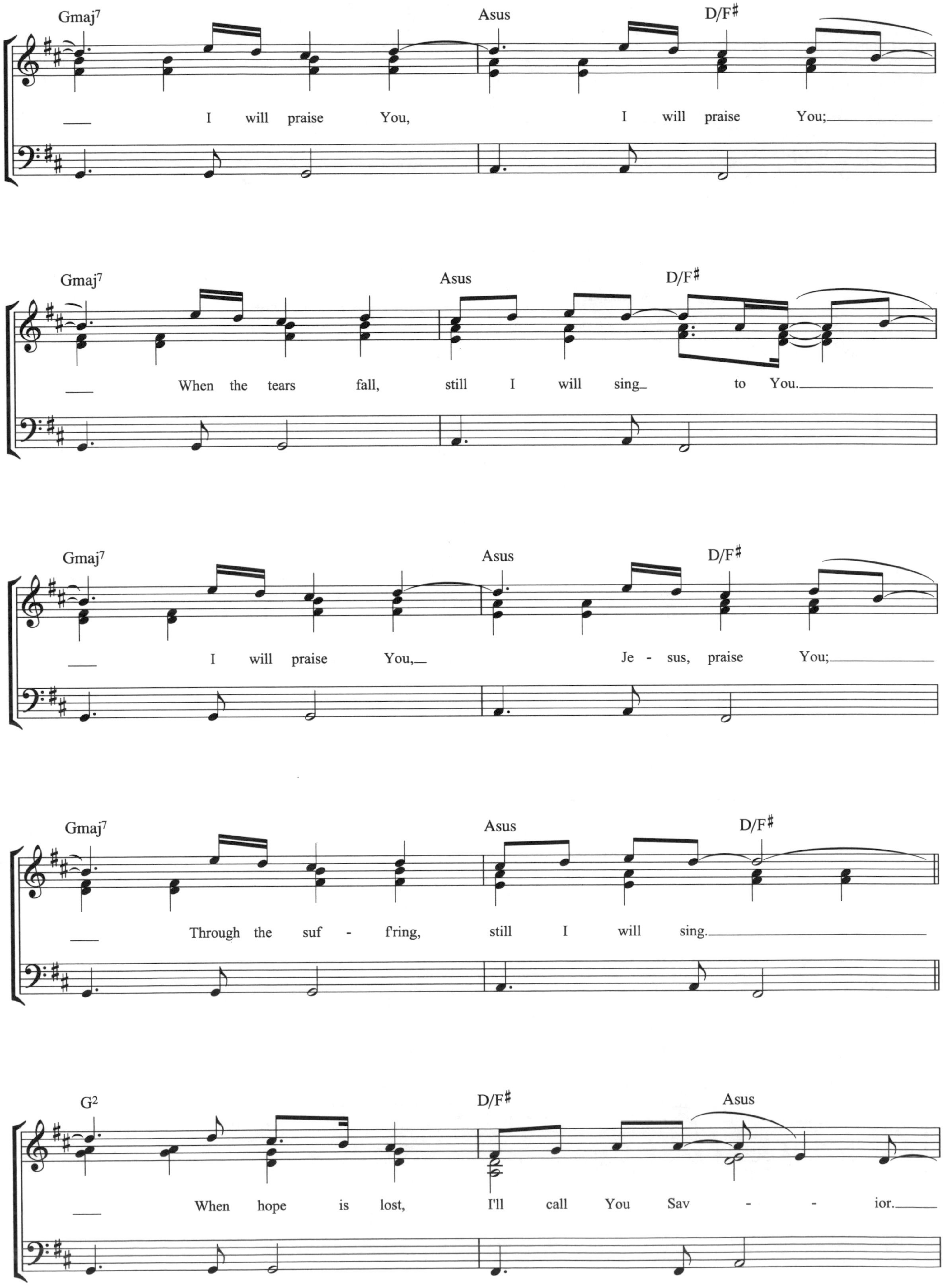
Gmaj7 Asus D/F#
I will praise You, I will praise You;
Gmaj7 Asus D/F#
When the tears fall, still I will sing to You.
Gmaj7 Asus D/F#
I will praise You, Je - sus, praise You;
Gmaj7 Asus D/F#
Through the suf - f'ring, still I will sing.
G2 D/F# Asus
When hope is lost, I'll call You Sav - - ior.

Gmaj7
Em7
When pain sur - rounds, I'll call You heal - - er.
G2
Bm7
Asus
G2
When si - lence falls, You'll be the song with - in my heart.
Repeat as desired
D.S al CODA
Gmaj7
Asus
D/F♯
Gmaj7
Asus
D/F♯
CODA
Bm7
Asus
Gmaj7
E7
my clos - est friend, still I'll praise You; Je - sus, praise You.

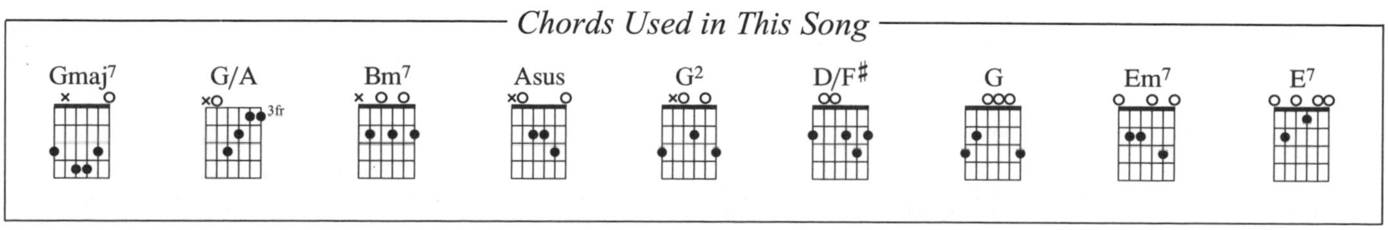
Chords Used in This Song
Gmaj7
G/A
3fr
Bm7
Asus
G2
D/F♯
G
Em7
E7

Undignified
(I Will Dance, I Will Sing)

Words and Music by
MATT REDMAN

Capo 2 (D)

♩ = 133
Keyboard
(Guitar)
E (D)
A2 (G2)
E/G♯ (D/F♯)
B7sus/F♯ (A7sus/E)
I will dance, I will sing, to be mad for my King.
Noth - ing, Lord, is hin - der - ing the pas - sion in my soul.
1. 3.
2. 4.
pas - sion in my soul. And I'll be - come
A (G)
F♯m7 (Em7)
B (A)
e - ven more un - dig - ni - fied than this.

F♯m7 (Em7) B (A) E (D) A (G)
Some would say it's fool - ish - ness, but I'll be - come
F♯m7 (Em7) B (A) E (D) A (G)
e - ven more un - dig - ni - fied than this.
1. 3.
F♯m7 (Em7) B (A)
Leave my pride by my side. And
2. 4.
F♯m7 (Em7) B (A)
Than this.
E (D) F♯m7 (Em7)
La La La La La Hey! La La La La La Hey!
E (D) F♯m7 (Em7)
La La La La La Hey! La La La La La Hey!

E
(D)
F#m7
(Em7)
La La La___ La La Hey! La La La___ La La Hey!
1. E
(D)
F#m7
(Em7)
D.C.
La La La___ La La Hey! La La La___ La La Hey!
2. E
(D)
F#m7
(Em7)
B7sus
(A7sus)
E
(D)
La La La___ La La It's all for You, my Lord!

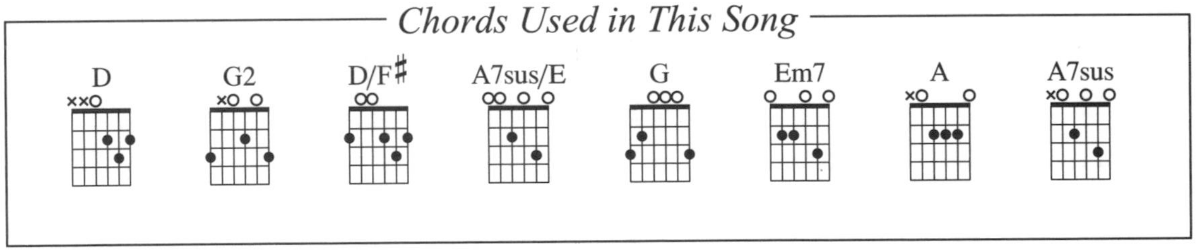
Chords Used in This Song
D
G2
D/F#
A7sus/E
G
Em7
A
A7sus

Whole World in His Hands

♩ = 76

Words and Music by
TIM HUGHES

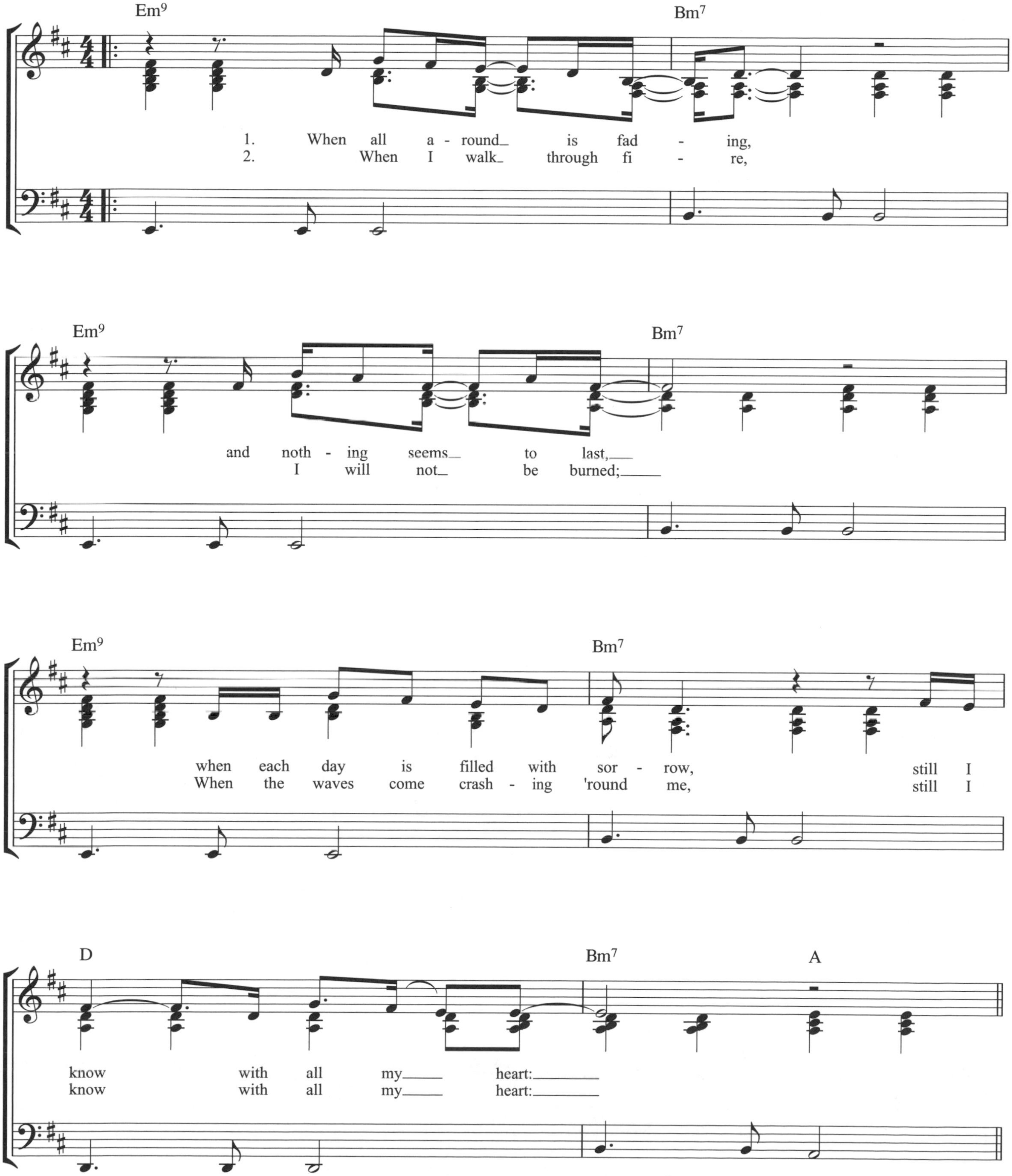
Em9
Bm7
1. When all a - round_ is fad - ing,
2. When I walk_ through fi - re,
Em9
Bm7
and noth - ing seems_ to last,___
I will not_ be burned;_____
Em9
Bm7
when each day is filled with sor - row, still I
When the waves come crash - ing 'round me, still I
D
Bm7
A
know with all my____ heart:_________
know with all my____ heart:_________

D Bm7 Asus A
He's got the whole world in His hands,
D Bm7 Asus A
He's got the whole world in His hands. I'll fear no e-
Bm7 Gmaj7
-vil for You are with me, strong to de-liv-
F♯ Gmaj7
-er, might-y to save.
F♯m 1. A 2. A
He's got the whole world in His hands.

D
Gmaj7
A
He's got the whole world in His hands,
D
Gmaj7
1. A
2. A
He's got the whole world in His hands.
I'll fear no e-
Bm7
Gmaj7
F♯
-vil for You are with me, strong to de-liv-er, might-y to save.
Gmaj7
F♯m
He's got the whole world in His hands.

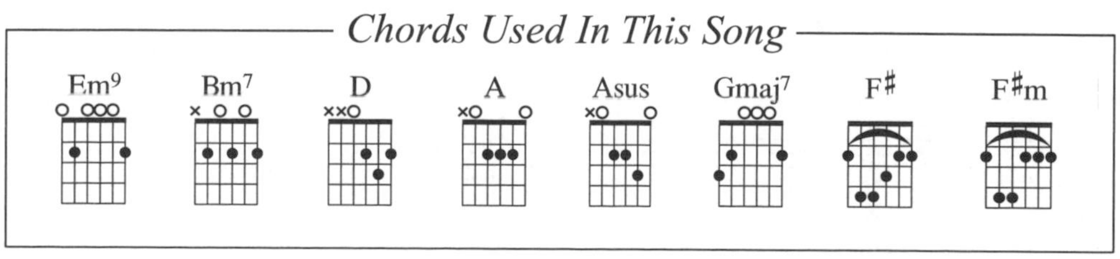
Chords Used In This Song
Em9
Bm7
D
A
Asus
Gmaj7
F♯
F♯m

Wonderful Maker

Words and Music by
MATT REDMAN and CHRIS TOMLIN

Capo 1 (G)

♩ = 77
Keyboard
(Guitar)
D♭2
(C2)
1. You spread out the skies o - ver emp - ty space,
F7sus
(E7sus)
said, "Let there be light;" to a dark and form - less world Your light was
D♭2
(C2)
E♭
(D)
A♭/C
(G/B)
D♭2
(C2)
born.
2. You spread out Your arms
(3.) eye has ful - ly seen how
o - ver emp - ty hearts,
beau - ti - ful the cross, and
Fm7
(Em7)
said, "Let there be light;" to a
we have on - ly heard the

D♭2
(C2)
dark and hope - less world Your Son was born.
faint - est whis - pers of how great You are.
E♭
(D)
B♭m7
(Am7)
A♭/C
(G/B)
D♭2
(C2)
You made the world and saw that it was good. You
B♭m7
(Am7)
A♭/C
(G/B)
D♭2
(C2)
sent Your on - ly Son, for You are good.
E♭/G
(D/F♯)
D♭2
(C2)
What a won - der - ful Mak - er,
Fm7
(Em7)
what a won - der - ful Sav - ior.

Db2
(C2)
How ma - jes - tic Your whis - pers,
Eb/G
(D/F#)
Ab
(G)
and how hum - ble Your love.
With a strength like no oth -
Db2
(C2)
- er,
and the heart of a Fath -
Fm7
(Em7)
Db2
(C2)
- er.
How ma - jes - tic Your whis - pers,
Eb/G
(D/F#)
3rd time to CODA
1.
Absus
(Gsus)
Ab
(G)
what a won - der - ful God

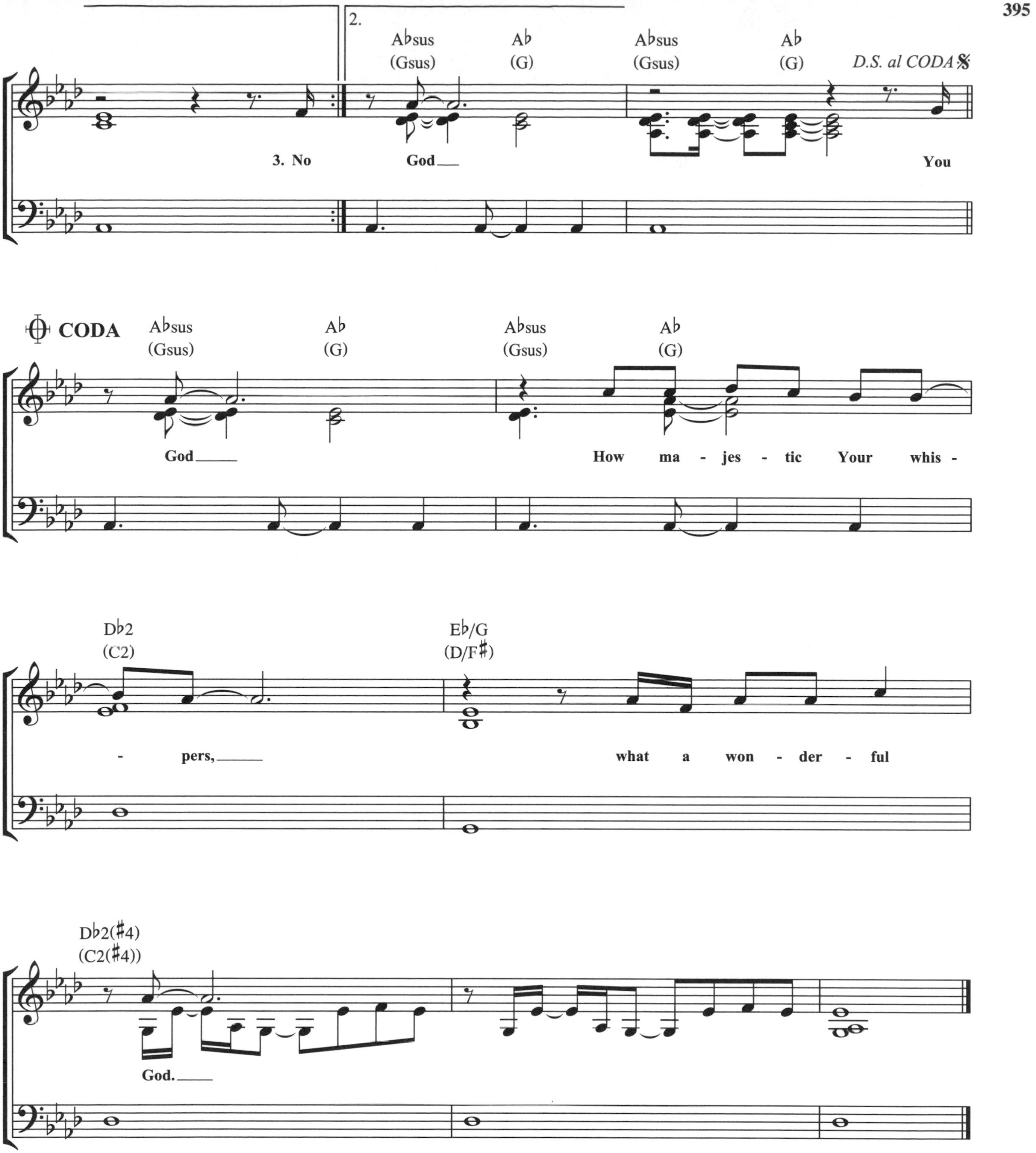

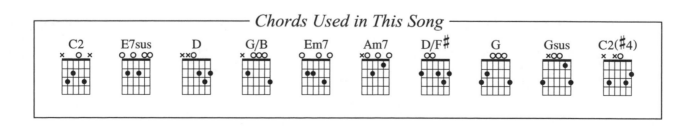

Chords Used in This Song

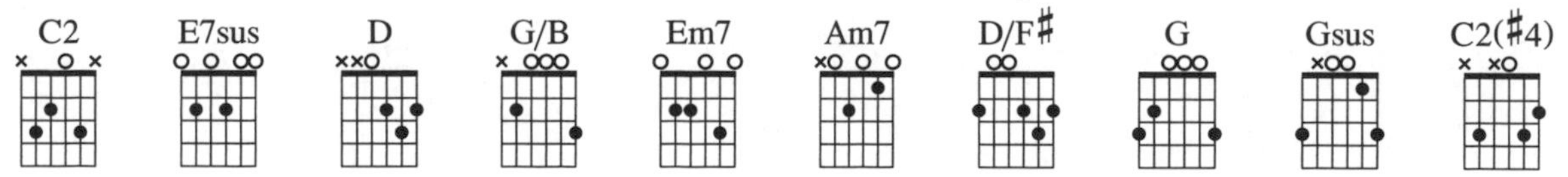

Worth It All

Words and Music by
RITA SPRINGER

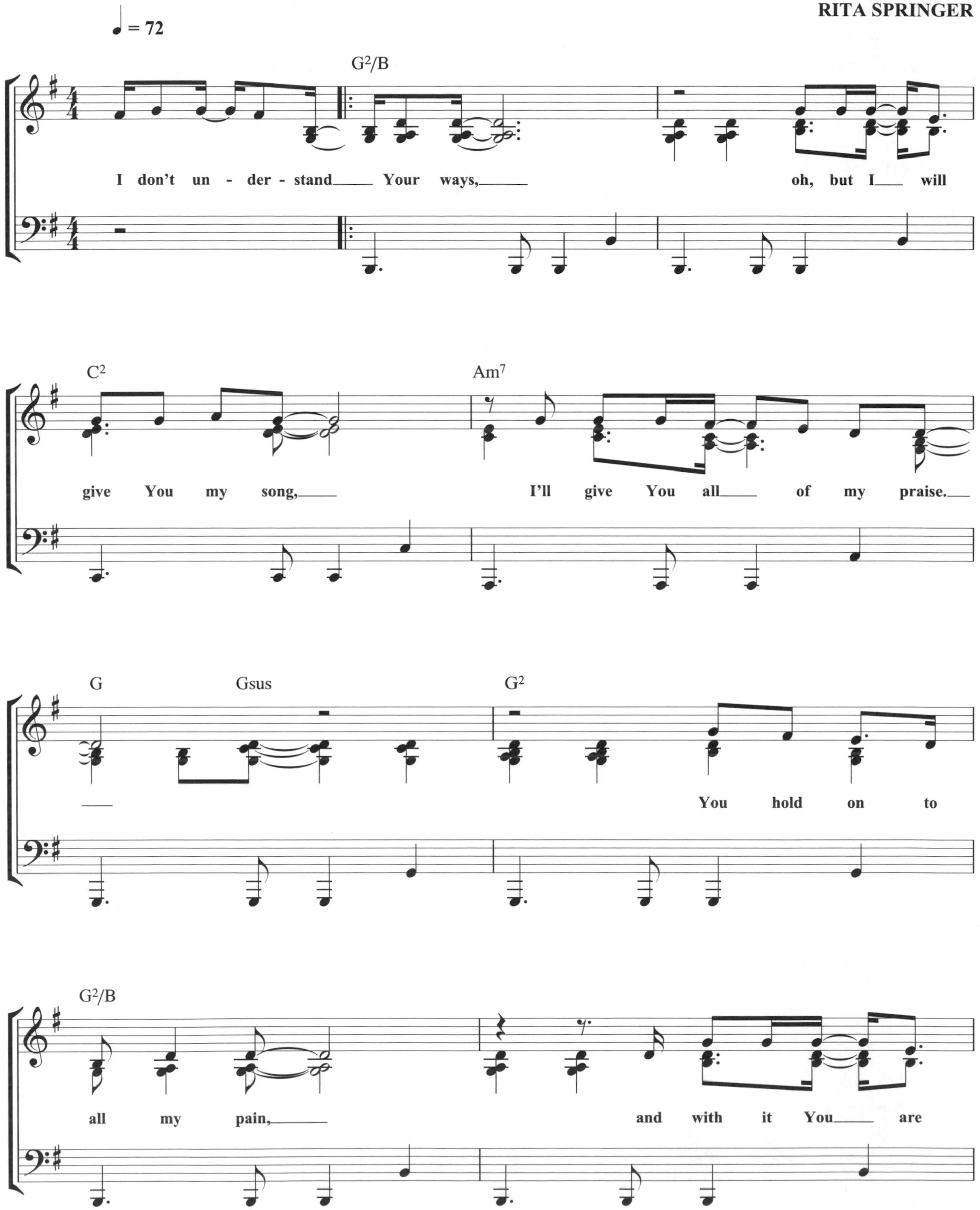
♩ = 72
G2/B
I don't un - der - stand Your ways, oh, but I will
C2
Am7
give You my song, I'll give You all of my praise.
G
Gsus
G2
You hold on to
G2/B
all my pain, and with it You are

C2
Am7
pull - ing me clos - er, and pull - ing me in - to Your ways.
G
Gsus
G
Now a - round ev - 'ry cor -
Em7
Dsus
- ner, and up ev - 'ry moun - tain, I'm not
G
D/F#
Am7
look - ing for crowns or the wa - ter from foun - tains. I'm
Em7
Dsus
des - p'rate in seek - ing, fran - tic, be - liev - ing that the

G
D/F#
Am7
sight of Your face is all that I'm need - ing.
I will say to You:
G
It's gon - na be worth it,
D/F#
it's gon - na be worth it,
Em7
it's gon - na be worth it all.
C2
I be - lieve this:
G
It's gon - na be worth it,
D/F#
it's gon - na be worth it,
Em7
it's gon - na be worth it all.

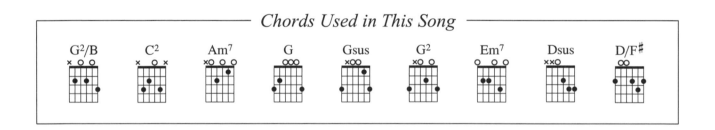

Chords Used in This Song

You Alone

Words and Music by
JACK PARKER
and DAVID CROWDER

Capo 4 (C)
♩ = 130
Keyboard
(Guitar)
E (C) E/G♯ (C/E) A2 (F2)
You are the on - ly one I
You have giv - en me more than
need. I bow all of me at Your
I could ev - er have want - ed, and
feet. I wor - ship You
I want to give You my heart and
lone.
soul.

E (C) E/G♯ (C/E) A (F)
You alone are Father, and You
E (C) E/G♯ (C/E) A (F) B (G)
alone are good;
E (C) E/G♯ (C/E) A (F)
You alone are Savior, and You
Last time to CODA
E (C) E/G♯ (C/E) A (F)
alone are God.
E (C) E/G♯ (C/E) A2 (F2)

E (C) E/G♯ (C/E) A2 (F2)
D.C. al CODA
CODA
A (F) Bsus (Gsus) F♯ (D) F♯/A♯ (D/F♯)
are God. I'm a - live, I'm a - live,
B (G) F♯ (D) F♯/A♯ (D/F♯)
I'm a - live, I'm a - live, I'm a - live, I'm a - live,
1. B (G)
I'm a - live, I'm a - live.
2. B (G) C♯ (A)
F♯ (D) F♯/A♯ (D/F♯) B (G)
You a - lone are Fa - ther, and You

F♯ (D)
F♯/A♯ (D/F♯)
B (G)
C♯ (A)
a - lone are good;
F♯ (D)
F♯/A♯ (D/F♯)
B (G)
You a - lone are Sav - ior, and You
F♯ (D)
F♯/A♯ (D/F♯)
1.
B (G)
B2 (G2)
C♯ (A)
a - lone are God.
2.
B (G)
B2 (G2)
C♯ (A)
are God.

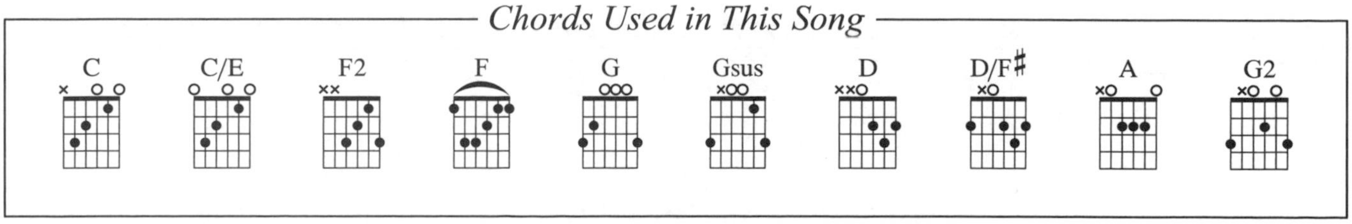
Chords Used in This Song
C
C/E
F2
F
G
Gsus
D
D/F♯
A
G2

You Are My King
(Amazing Love)

Words and Music by
BILLY JAMES FOOTE

♩ = 72
A D Esus
I'm for - giv - en be - cause You were for - sak - en.
A D Esus
I'm ac - cept - ed; You were con - demned.
A D Esus
I'm a - live and well, Your Spir - it is with - in me be -
D Esus A
cause You died and rose a - gain.

D2
A - maz - ing love, how can it be
A
Esus
that You, that my King, should die for me?
A
D2
A - maz - ing love, I know it's true;
A
Esus
it's my joy to hon - or You, in all I
3rd time to CODA
D2
Esus
do, to hon - or

1.
A
You.
2.
A/C♯
You. In all I
D2
Esus
A
do to hon - or You.
You are my King, You are my
1.
2.
D.S. al CODA 𝄋
King. Je - sus, King.

CODA
A
D2
Esus
You. In all I do to hon - or
A/C♯
D2
Esus
A
You. In all I do let me hon - or You.

Chords Used in This Song

A
D
Esus
D2
A/C♯

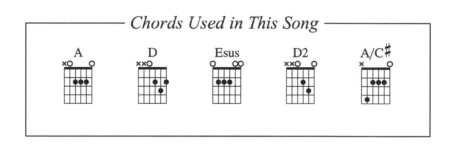

Yesterday, Today and Forever

Capo 3 (D)

♩ = 114

Words and Music by
VICKY BEECHING

Keyboard
(Guitar)
B♭ (G)
Dm7 (Bm7)
1. Ev - er - last - ing God, the
2. Un - cre - at - ed One, You
years go by, but You're un - chang - ing.
have no end and no be - gin - ning,
In this fra - gile world, You
Earth - ly pow - ers fade, but
are the on - ly firm foun - da - tion.
there is no end to Your king - dom.

Gm7
(Em7)
Al - ways lov - ing, al - ways
F/A
(D/F♯)
true,
B♭
(G)
al - ways mer - ci - ful and good,
Dm7
(Bm7)
C
(A)
so good.
F/A
(D/F♯)
F/B♭
(D/G)
Dm
(Bm)
C
(A)
Yes - ter - day, to - day, and for - ev - er,

F/A (D/F♯) B♭ (G) Dm (Bm) C (A)
You are the same, You never change.
F/A (D/F♯) F/B♭ (D/G) Dm (Bm) C (A)
Yes - ter - day, to - day, and for - ev - er,
Gm7 (Em7)
3rd time to CODA
1.
F/B♭ (D/G) C (A)
You are faith - ful, and we will trust in You.
F/A (D/F♯) F/B♭ (D/G) Dm (Bm) C (A)
We will trust in You.
F/A (D/F♯) F/B♭ (D/G) Dm (Bm) C (A)

2.
F/B♭ (D/G)
C (A)
B♭2 (G2)
we will trust in You.
We will trust in You.
F/A (D/F♯)
We will trust in You,
B♭2 (G2)
in You.
F/A (D/F♯)
B♭ (G)
Yah - weh,
F/A (D/F♯)
God un -
chang - ing;
B♭ (G)
Yah - weh,

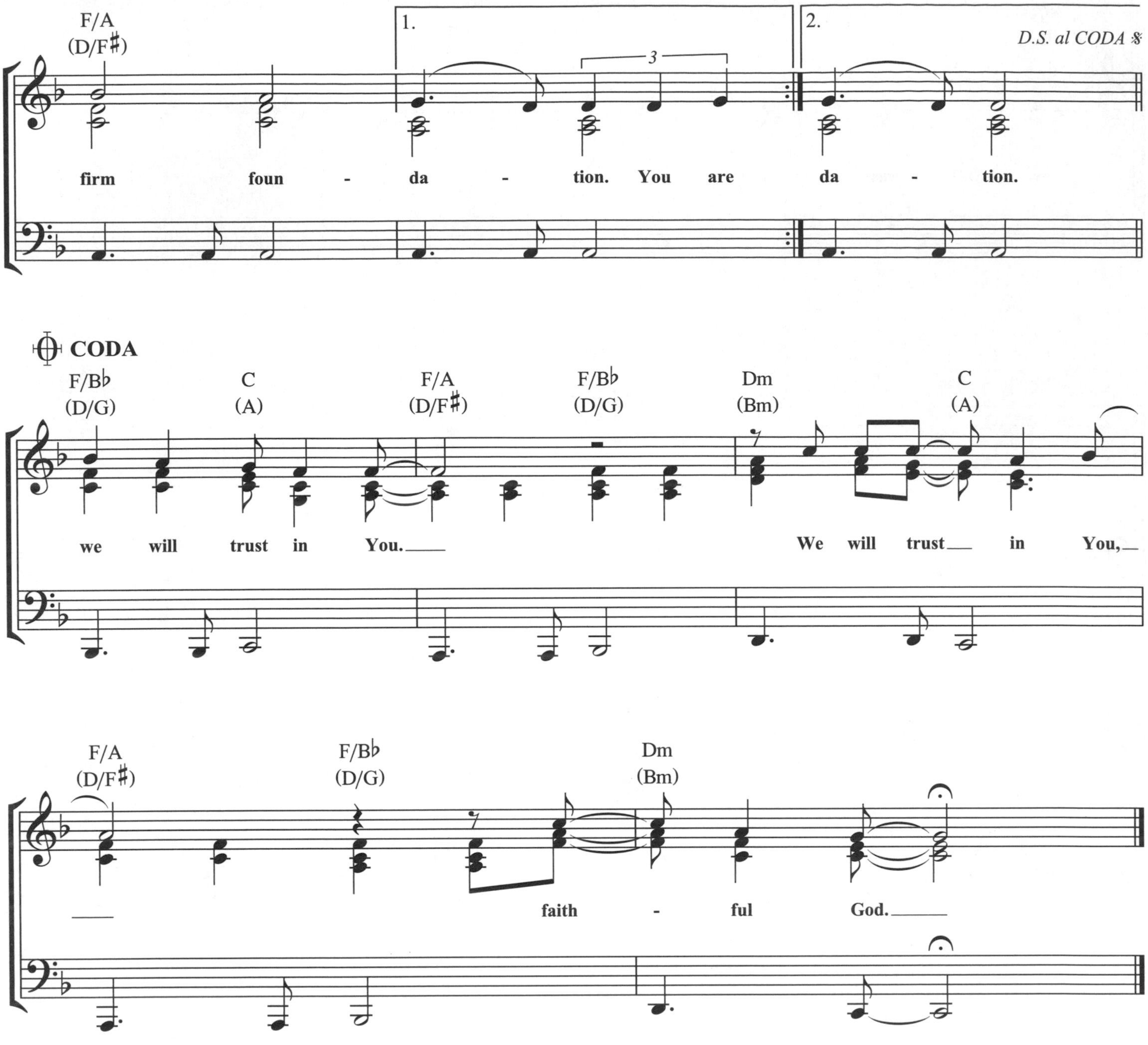
F/A
(D/F♯)
1.
2.
D.S. al CODA 𝄋
3
firm foun - da - tion. You are da - tion.
CODA
F/B♭
(D/G)
C
(A)
F/A
(D/F♯)
F/B♭
(D/G)
Dm
(Bm)
C
(A)
we will trust in You.
We will trust in You,
F/A
(D/F♯)
F/B♭
(D/G)
Dm
(Bm)
faith - ful God.

Chords Used in This Song

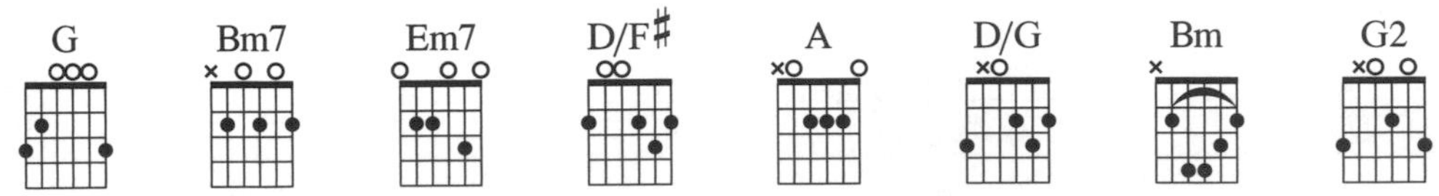

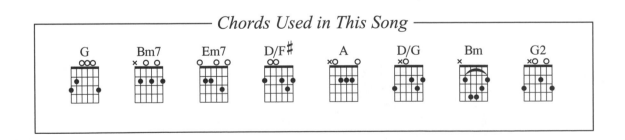

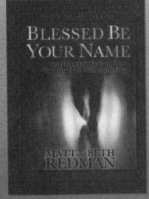

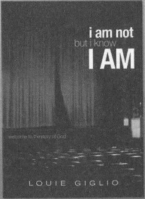

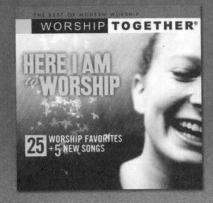

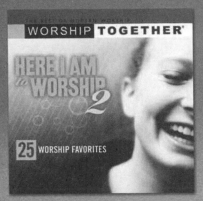

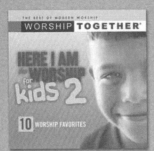

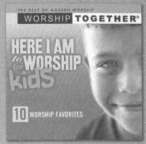

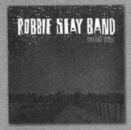

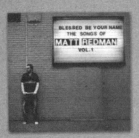

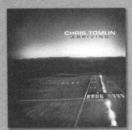

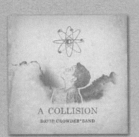

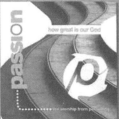

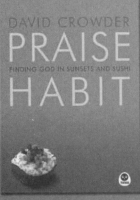